keyboard

PRESENTS

THE EVOLUTION OF ELECTRONIC DANCE MUSIC

keyboard

PRESENTS

THE EVOLUTION OF
ELECTRONIC DANCE MUSIC

EDITED BY PETER KIRN

Backbeat
Books

An Imprint of Hal Leonard Corporation

Portions of this book are adapted from articles that originally appeared in the magazines *Keyboard* and *Remix*.

Published in cooperation with Music Player Network, New Bay Media, LLC, and magazines *Keyboard* and *Remix*. Magazines *Keyboard* and *Remix* are registered trademarks of New Bay Media, LLC.

Published in 2011 by Backbeat Books
An Imprint of Hal Leonard Corporation
7777 West Bluemound Road
Milwaukee, WI 53213

Trade Book Division Editorial Offices
33 Plymouth St., Montclair, NJ 07042

Photo of 1990s rave © Mattia Zoppellaro/Camera Press/Retna Ltd; photo of Frankie Knuckles © Wirelmage/ Getty Images; photo of Richie Hawton © Paule Saviano; photo of Amon Tobin © May Truong; and photo of Flying Lotus © Getty Images. All other photos appear courtesy of *Keyboard* magazine.

Printed in the United State of America

Book design by Damien Castaneda

Library of Congress Cataloging-in-Publication Data is available upon request.

ISBN 978-1-61713-019-9

www.backbeatbooks.com

Contents

Preface   ix

1. KRAFTWERK   **2**
"ELECTRONIC MINSTRELS OF THE GLOBAL VILLAGE"
By Jim Aikin, *Keyboard*, March 1982

**2. DEPECHE MODE, SOFT CELL, THE UNITS,
WALL OF VOODOO, JAPAN, OUR DAUGHTERS WEDDING**   **14**
"NEW SYNTHESIZER ROCK"
By Robert Doerschuk, *Keyboard*, June 1982

"NEW ORDER: ON THE FRINGE OF TECHNO PUNK"
Lee Sherman, *Keyboard*, April 1987

3. THE ETHNOMUSICOLOGY OF DANCE MUSIC   **34**
"DENISE DALPHOND GOES INSIDE EDM CULTURE'S ROOTS"
By Peter Kirn, June 2011

**4. FRANKIE KNUCKLES, JESSE SAUNDERS,
FARLEY "JACKMASTER" FUNK**   **44**
"THE FATHERS OF CHICAGO HOUSE"
By Greg Rule, *Keyboard*, August 1997

5. JUAN ATKINS   **54**
"JUAN ATKINS: TECHNO STARTS HERE"
By Robert Doerschuk, *Keyboard*, July 1995

6. ELECTRONIC BODY MUSIC   **66**
"FRONT 242: THE AGGRESSIVE EDGE OF RHYTHM AND THE
POWER OF RECYCLED CULTURE"
By Robert Doerschuk, *Keyboard*, September 1989

"THE ART OF EXTREME NOISE"
By Francis Preve, *Keyboard*, September 2003

7. RISE OF THE MACHINES   **86**
"ROLAND CR-78, TR-808, AND TR-909: CLASSIC BEAT BOXES"
By Mark Vail, *Keyboard*, May 1994

"AKAI MPC60"
By Freff, *Keyboard*, November 1988

"PROPELLERHEAD: PROPELLING CHANGES"
By Mark Vail, *Keyboard*, April 1999

8 · SAMPLING NATION _____ **104**
"'THEY'RE MAKING SAMPLERS WRONG':
SIX TECHNO SAMPLEHEADS DUMP THE DIGITAL GARBAGE"
By Greg Rule, *Keyboard*, May 1994

9 · CHARLIE CLOUSER ON TECHNO _____ **114**
"TECHNO HOW-TO"
By Charlie Clouser, *Keyboard*, September 1993

10 · THE ORB _____ **124**
"INSIDE THE AMBIENT TECHNO ULTRAWORLD"
By Robert Doerschuk, *Keyboard*, June 1995

11 · ORBITAL, MEAT BEAT MANIFESTO, UNDERWORLD _____ **134**
"PLUGGED!"
By Greg Rule and Caspar Melville, *Keyboard*, October 1996

12 · APHEX TWIN _____ **150**
"STILL HACKING AFTER ALL THESE YEARS"
By Greg Rule, *Keyboard*, April 1997

13 · CHEMICAL BROTHERS _____ **154**
"WATER INTO ACID: THE CHEMICAL BROTHERS BLOW UP"
By Greg Rule, *Keyboard*, June 1997

14 · DAFT PUNK _____ **166**
"ROBOPOP: PART MAN, PART MACHINE, ALL DAFT PUNK"
By Chris Gill, *Remix*, May 2001

15 · RICHIE HAWTIN AND JOHN ACQUAVIVA _____ **176**
"THE SOUNDS OF SCIENCE:
RICHIE HAWTIN PUTS THE TECH IN TECHNO"
By Chris Gill, *Keyboard*, December 2001

16 · BT _____ **186**
"THE MIND OF BT"
By Stephen Fortner, *Keyboard*, December 2005

17 · AMON TOBIN _____ **194**
"THE BIG SCORE"
By Bill Murphy, *Remix*, April 2007

18 · FLYING LOTUS   202
"FLYING LOTUS: DARKNESS AND LIGHT"
By Noah Levine, *Remix*, August 2008

"FLYING LOTUS: ON SPLICING BEBOP AND HIP-HOP DNA"
By Drew Hinshaw, *Keyboard*, July 2010

19 · AUTECHRE   208
"AUTECHRE: EASY TO BE HARD"
By Ken Micallef, *Remix*, April 2008

"5 QUESTIONS WITH ROB BROWN OF AUTECHRE"
By Greg Rule, *Keyboard*, June 1996

20 · CRYSTAL METHOD   216
"CRYSTAL METHOD: UNITED BY SYNTHS, DIVIDED BY NIGHT"
By Peter Kirn, *Keyboard*, November 2009

21 · ROBERT HENKE (MONOLAKE)   224
"THE COMPOSER, ARTIST, AND ABLETON LIVE IMAGINEER
LOOKS TO THE FUTURE"
By Peter Kirn, June 2011

Preface

Do drum machines dream of electric sheep?

Maybe, despite claims otherwise, drum machines can have soul. Listen to the stories of the artists operating the computers and electronics, and you hear a struggle for human expressive liberation. It's one necessitated by the very devices that make those expressions possible. The same machines that tie us to desks by day, that revel in the impersonal and virtual, can also set us free, make us get personal, make us sweat. They make us sedentary, then musicians make them groove; they attack musicianship, then musicians adapt them to new musical techniques and skills.

Alongside jazz, the blues, and rock and roll, you can count electronic dance music as one of the great cultural–musical hybrids of the past century, one that crosses boundaries racial, cultural, and geographic. And here, culled from the pages of *Keyboard* and *Remix* magazines, you can read about that history as it happens. The stories are written about artists, by artists, so the conversations have the quality of one musician talking to another—because that's what they are. As a result, sometimes the contents tend to the philosophical, and sometimes they recount the day-to-day process of making electronic music, warts and all. Musicians curse hardware and dream of the next tool that will solve their problems. (In some cases, those dreams turn out to predict what's coming, and it isn't as impossible as we imagine.)

Because of *Keyboard*'s "geeky as we wanna be" attitude, that includes gory details of every bit of gear, every knob tweak. Oddly, this is sometimes more meaningful in hindsight than it seemed at the time. Forgotten techniques come to light, exposing the workings of now widely recognized sounds. The arc of musical history follows the arc of technological evolution, from MIDI to sampling to software.

There are numerous revelations: Kraftwerk on why Germans don't mind techno-fetishization in the way Americans do, Aphex Twin and Daft Punk removing their masks to talk about what they do, Juan Atkins on the sources of techno, Richie Hawtin finding digital vinyl for the first time, the creators of the MPC and 808 talking engineering and art. Various artists talk about why dancing is a necessary societal and personal adaptation, as pioneers in Detroit and Chicago who spin futuristic, funk-inspired beats imagine a more hopeful planet that contrasts with harsh realities on the streets. Everyone complains about boring gear, buggy gear, boring music. Everyone here does something about it.

Behind the romance of the dance floor, the process of making beats with technology is messy and painstaking. It's filled with accidents, DIY solutions, hacks. Even these legendary artists see resistance from audiences, labels, and the press.

But, like you, they are no less passionate about the music.

For its part, some of *Keyboard*'s own biases are telling. Tuned in to the rock scene, distant from disco, *Keyboard* is slow to see the coming of house and techno. Some of the reporting is ahead of its time; other stories are retrospective. Looking back to the attitude in the early '80s, the American audience the magazine describes is, if the writers here are to be believed, sometimes deeply divided on issues like race and culture, technology and experimentation. And in the magazine's rush to list impressive gear rigs, it sometimes seems out of touch with, for instance, young Detroit techno artists buying cheap gear and starting a musical revolution.

But dutifully, insightfully, a roster of great writers digs passionately into the worlds of music and music making, as journalists like Jim Aikin, Bob Doershuck, Greg Rule, Francis Preve, and Steve Fortner, among others, cover musicians from a musician's perspective. We've left their words mostly untouched, because the stories they left behind are like a time machine, and in the fast-moving world of digital music technology, even 2001 can turn out to seem oddly distant. We also add two previously unpublished articles into the mix; ethnomusicologist Denise Dalphond shares her perspective from Detroit, and Robert Henke talks music, technology, and the future.

This collection is in no way encyclopedic. If you think you see artists left out, artists who deserved to be here, whose omission is a crime against music history, you're right. With the explosive diversity of output in the field, there's simply no way to fit it all in. Instead, you'll find a selection of scenes, windows into musical change, and choices that I found represented the best writing and most personal artistic moments. I'm indebted in that quest to the help of Stephen Fortner and, in particular, heroic efforts by Lori Kennedy at *Keyboard* to dig through years upon years of archives in paper form. To anyone who would claim that the value of the printed periodical is fleeting, you need only discover the pleasure of unearthing these articles, articles that allow us to cover 30 years of history in the present tense. Reading them makes me want to retreat to a studio—or bedroom—and make music. I hope you'll feel the same way.

Perhaps the most promising reflection in these pages comes in the rapid evolution of tools in the final sections. Suddenly, there's hope—ironically, voiced by Robert Henke, a man best known for his association with a piece of software—that tools can ultimately fall away and become invisible.

And maybe, armed with the collected artistic words of the past decades, that will finally help us discover the ghost in the machine.

Peter Kirn
New York
June 2011

keyboard

PRESENTS

THE EVOLUTION OF ELECTRONIC DANCE MUSIC

Kaftwerk.

Kraftwerk

ELECTRONIC MINSTRELS OF
THE GLOBAL VILLAGE

By Jim Aikin || *Keyboard*, March 1982

lectronic dance music could start almost anywhere, but Kraftwerk is a fitting on-ramp. What seemed at first pastiche proved prophetic: Kraftwerk's quirky journeys along the Autobahn and experiments with pocket calculators proved to hold in them the seed for a new direction of music. The band's musical idiom and technological devices presaged electronic dance musics to come, while being rooted in rock. But more than that, Kraftwerk pointed to a new musical futurism, one that re-imagined the musical relationship to new technologies. Keyboard's Jim Aikin, himself a published science-fiction writer, is a fitting voice to lead us into that world. Kraftwerk's techno-futurism laid the groundwork for techno, for Juan Atkins, for designing sounds on the PC. But Keyboard visits them here before any of those influences had come to fruition, as the German artists are synthesizing just that new futurist approach. —PK

Once upon a time, "the future" was something that hadn't happened yet. It lay up ahead of us somewhere in the distance, filled with an unknown potential whose features and even outlines were unguessable. But during the 20th century, an extremely odd thing has happened. In the 1920s, science-fiction writers began developing detailed scenarios of what the future would be like, and since World War II the technology for making those scenarios come true has been expanding at an unprecedented rate. By now, our sense of history as a linear progression into the future has collapsed. We're living in the future today; there's no way to escape from it.

> "America is very shy when it comes to electronics. It's still a highly schizophrenic situation. People have all the latest state-of-the-art technology, and yet they put wood panels on the front to make them feel comfortable."
>
> —RALF HUTTER (KRAFTWERK)

Most of us have ambivalent feelings about the future. On the one hand, we're happy to take advantage of the products and processes it offers. We get instant cash from automatic bank teller machines, play with computer and video games, use articles made of plastic and other synthetic materials dozens of times a day, talk to our relatives long-distance via satellite relay, and hop on jets that take us to Europe in six hours. But on the other hand, the future makes us uneasy—sometimes very uneasy. We're not happy about having computerized dossiers on our private lives hidden in secret government memory banks. We're disturbed by the way eight-lane freeways (to say nothing of strip mines) deface the landscape. We yearn for simple answers to the bewilderingly complex social problems that erupt at every turn. We want to feel that we're important and unique as individuals, not just faceless, interchangeable units in a giant machine.

Kraftwerk is a group of four musicians who play their own unusual brand of electronic rock, using synthesizers and related hardware. But that's not the whole story. More important, Kraftwerk is a visionary stance, a philosophical alternative, a suggestion that we might develop an entirely different attitude about living in the future. This accounts for the extreme, almost obsessive nature of their music—and perhaps it also explains why they haven't been more widely accepted in the United States. We may not be ready for their message yet.

The message is that we can develop a friendly, relaxed, accepting attitude toward working and living with machines. Most of us still feel obscurely threatened by machines—*depersonalized* and *mechanical* are dirty words. According to Kraftwerk spokesman Ralf Hutter, "America is very shy when it comes to electronics. It's still a highly schizophrenic situation. People have all the latest state-of-the-art technology, and yet they put wood panels on the front to make them feel comfortable. Or they develop new plastics and try to imitate the appearance of wood. They use modern technology to try to re-create the Middle Ages. This is stupid." In contrast, Kraftwerk's custom-built musical equipment looks like what it is. "We go more for the minimalist or direct approach," Hutter explains. "Technology as an art—technology as it is. We have nothing to hide."

This attitude has obvious roots in the Bauhaus school of functionalist architecture that flourished in the '20s, in which pips, wiring, and girders were frequently exposed rather than hidden behind walls. But Kraftwerk's preoccupation with technology stems more directly from the predominantly industrial environment of Dusseldorf in the '50s and '60s, where Hutter and co-founder Florian Schneider grew up. Although their music today seems to be firmly based in rock, they both studied traditional classical music at the Dusseldorf Conservatory, Hutter studying piano and Schneider flute, and then moved on to performing improvised avant-garde music. "At that time," Hutter recalls, "the only places we could find to play were at universities and art museums. Musical clubs wouldn't book us. The music world is very reactionary, isn't it? It's all about ticket sales.

"The first problem we faced," he goes on, "was to find the type of music we wanted to play. So we started out with pure sound. Florian had an amplified flute, and I had some contact microphones which I put on metal plates. Also, we used to put contact mics on my clothing so that the sounds I made by moving were part of the music." Even at this early stage, they were breaking down the barriers between performer and instrument, between man and machine. One of the reasons they stopped using conventional instruments (an early incarnation of Kraftwerk, prior to 1974, actually had a guitarist) was that these instruments imply conventional relationships between the performer and the instrument and thus produce a conventional sort of music with which the listener then has a conventional relationship. In place of this, Hutter and Schneider have experimented with using such unusual interfaces as beams of light that could be interrupted, like electric-eye door openers, to trigger musical effects with the body, The ultimate, they feel, would be an instrument that "instantly produces whatever sound you can think of" by a direct link with the mind. This would imply a complete symbiosis of organism and technology.

In 1970 Hutter and Schneider established their own recording studio, which they called Kling Klang, a German word that means just what you think it means. Hutter owned a Farfisa organ, and in 1971 they acquired their first synthesizers. A Minimoog, we asked? An ARP 2600? Hutter was vague. "Yeah, mostly those," he replied. "We had all the small models from all the different major brands. We had an English one [probably an EMS Synthi]. Sometimes they were very nice. But they don't make them anymore. Today they are already antiques. By now we have sold them or given them to other people." Most of their equipment today is custom-built.

During the next few years they released several albums that were distributed only in Europe. But popular acceptance was slow. "Germany is a cultural vacuum," Hutter explains. "All the music on the radio was Anglo-American when we started. We had a German name and we sang in German, so they wouldn't play us on the radio. People were very upset, because nobody was supposed to do this kind of thing. We didn't have a living of music of our own in Germany. It has only been in the last ten years that there has been a cultural awakening. Now there is a lot of German electronic music."

Another difficulty they faced initially was working with drummers. "Our music was always very energetic rhythmically," Hutter says. "We include the body, not just the mind." But drums posed problems in concert. "We always had problems with drummers because they were always banging, and they didn't want to turn electronic. We were working with feedback and tape loops and things, and they didn't understand that. Also, ordinary drums are very loud onstage, but past the tenth row you can't hear them. A loudspeaker, on the other hand, you can place anywhere in the room." The solution was to build percussion synthesizers that gave them complete control over the drum sound, and to find musicians who could play these new instruments in a new way—"without a lot of sweating and jumping around." Today, two of the four musicians in Kraftwerk are primarily percussionists. Karl Bartos and Wolfgang Flur strike percussion pads with metal sticks, as well as activating and changing the programming on automatic percussion devices. "We built our own drum machines," Hutter points out, "because we were really not pleased with the drum boxes you buy. Some of them are nice, but mostly they sound very Latin. We wanted more machine-like sounds, because that is more what we are about. Our electronic drums are not great inventions or great innovations," he goes on, "but having them has made a strong psychological impact on our performance."

Kraftwerk (which means "power station" in German) first came to the attention of American audiences in 1975, with the release of the *Autobahn* album [Mercury, SRM-1-3704]. The 22-minute title track, with lyrics about riding down the freeway, got some radio airplay in a shortened version. This was the first time they had included vocals in their music. "For nine years," Hutter recalls, "we were afraid to put our voices on tape. We're still paranoid about this, but by now we can handle it." Perhaps partly because of this paranoia, Kraftwerk was one of the first groups to experiment with the vocoder, a device that imprints the pattern of a voice on some other sound and thereby removes the vocalist himself from the finished sounds while leaving the words intact. "When we read that Herbie Hancock was the first to use a vocoder, we laughed, because in Germany we had been doing that for seven or eight years." Of course, the vocoder is also a way of making synthesizers and other mechanical sounds sing words, which further blurs the distinction between people and machines.

The success of *Autobahn* led to a series of LPs for Capitol Records, which released *Radio-Activity* [ST-11457] in 1976, *Trans-Europe Express* [SW-11603] in 1977, and *The Man Machine* [SW-11728] in 1978. But while these albums received favorable notice from critics and helped build a cult following for the group, none of them became the kind of runaway sellers that record companies dream about. Following *The Man Machine*, Kraftwerk vanished from the scene for three years before reemerging last year on the Warner Bros. label with *Computer World* [HS-3549], an album whose theme is the links between people and computers. From a group that had already given us songs with titles like "The Robots," "Spacelab," and "Neon Lights," what could be more natural?

"We are not musicians. We're musical workers."

−RALF HUTTER (KRAFTWERK)

It's an open question how far they can take this image of themselves as robotic, or how serious they are about it. On *Radio-Activity* they sang, "I'm the transmitter, I give information, you're the antenna, catching vibration." On *Trans-Europe Express* the message was, "We are showroom dummies." By the time *Man Machine* came around, this had become, "We are the robots." So it should come as no surprise that the photos of Kraftwerk on the jacket of *Computer World* aren't actually of the musicians themselves, but rather of a set of life-size mannequins with the musicians' faces. This probably qualifies as self-parody—the technique of consciously overdoing what people who are familiar with your image would expect you to do. But there's a point behind it. As early as 1977 Hutter was speculating, "We are thinking of playing in two cities at the same time. We send some computers to concert halls in different cities . . ." All they have to do now is animate the mannequins and let *them* play the show.

Which raises an interesting possibility. Five years from now, if you see Kraftwerk in concert, how will you be able to know for certain whether you're seeing them, or their robots? Hutter would argue, we suspect, that it doesn't matter. "We are not musicians," he explains. "We're musical workers." On another occasion he puts it this way: "We consider ourselves not so much entertainers as scientists. We work in our studio laboratory, and when we discover something that is true, we put it on a tape." In other words, they conceive of themselves as functional parts of a music-making machine. The functions currently fulfilled by human beings are not necessarily functions that can be filled *only* by human beings. Computer programs for composing music are still in a very primitive stage of development, but there is no reason why future pieces of music, ostensibly by Kraftwerk or by other popular artists, might not be assembled by a computer operating according to parameters programmed into it—or according to parameters it develops on its own.

During the three-year hiatus between *Man Machine* and *Computer World*, Kraftwerk rebuilt all their equipment, with the help of technicians Joachim Dehmann and Günter Spachtholz, so it could be taken on the road. In fact, what audiences saw during their 1981 tour was the Kling Klang studio itself onstage. "We play studio," Hutter explains, "so we had to take the studio with us. We don't have duplicates of any of our equipment; we have only what we are always working with. It's all in units that break down and go into different cases, and the various components fit together. Some of the components we have are standard things like echo machines, but more than half of the equipment is custom-built, built by us or with our regular engineers because we couldn't play the music we wanted on regular instruments. We have a couple of standard electronic keyboards, and a small mixing board, and we have digital storage for relatively short-term information, up to six seconds. With this, we can store sounds and have them played back rhythmically. Then we have our special electronic percussion systems, which can be programmed for different electronic sounds. We have made up a couple of percussion sounds ourselves, with special circuits. And then we have our singing computer, our synthetic speech machines."

Singing computer? Right. It turns out that some of the mechanical-sounding vocal parts on *Computer World* weren't vocoder at all. The technology already exists for generating computer speech from scratch, and Kraftwerk utilized it in the tune "Numbers" to create a track in which the computer provides the rhythm by counting "one, two, three, four," in various languages. On another tune, a pocket language translator was used. This is a gadget that lets you type in a word and speaks the word back to you in several languages. (For those of you have the album, the translator is what says, "Business, numbers, money, people," in the title track.) At other times they operate standard EMS vocoders and a customized Sennheiser vocoder, "which Mr. Sennheiser built specially for us in the early '70s."

Because the group is so heavily into technology, it's not surprising that they manage to get hold of prototypes of gadgets that aren't being marketed yet. "We call up companies," Hutter says, "and find out about things like special computers that are being used only for office types of things—sales figures, accounting, data storage on people, passport control. We feel that the computers should be used more creatively. And when we hear [about] things, we step in and try to get them. We have been quite lucky, because the creative people in these companies, the inventors, find great pleasure in talking to other people besides just businesspeople. The inventors have almost a boyish or playful attitude, and they're more open when you call them. Normally, within the big companies, the creative people are always having the marketing people tell them that this will never make it, so they're open to exchanging ideas with creative people from outside."

The 1981 tour also incorporated some small handheld keyboard instruments made by—you guessed it—Casio, the calculator company. The whole band stepped out from behind their consoles to perform at the edge of the stage using these instruments. "This is very liberating for us," Hutter declares. "In the past we have been accused of being boring, because we were always behind the control boards. I don't think the criticism was entirely justified, but certainly there was something to it. But now that we have some things we can walk around with, I think we have broken the barrier of just controlling machines." In addition to the musicians, the Kraftwerk show involves extensive visuals that are put together by Emil Schult, who also gets songwriting credits on some Kraftwerk tunes. The musicians themselves are intensely involved in video, and many of the tunes are conceived of as having both sound and visual elements.

Since most of the better-known electronic music—by Wendy Carlos, Larry Fast, and Tomita, for example—is recorded track by track in a laborious process where a single composition may take weeks or even months to complete, it comes as a surprise to find that Kraftwerk records most of their music fairly quickly. "We don't do that many overdubs," Hutter reports, "because our machines are working, and we set everything up simultaneously. Then when we feel that a piece is together, we record it. We go for the total sound at one time. We might add some vocals here or there, but because we work every day in the studio, everything is set up for us—it's like our living room. So once we have the special sound we want, we record it very quickly, because to create it from individual tracks . . . we find that most of the music that is done on individual tracks is very boring. It's like when you have a collection of insects and they're walking all over your garden, and then you pick them up individually and sterilize them and stick them to the wall. I think people do that all the time. They break the music apart and record it on 24 or 32 different tracks, and really all the tracks contain nothing. Most of the time we use only ten tracks. Sometimes only two or four tracks." The vocals are recorded on tracks by themselves, however.

"We always record the albums in German and then make synchronized versions in English, and some in French, or even Japanese and Italian."

Even in the English versions heard in the United States, however, there will be phrases in other languages. In "The Robots," for example, a voice pronounces a phrase in Russian that Hutter translates as, "'I'm your servant, I'm your worker.' The word 'robot' actually means 'worker,'" he explains. Along with their message about the unification of man and machine, it seems, Kraftwerk is suggesting that we are all citizens of the same global community. "This is because we live in Dusseldorf," Hutter points out. "It's in Germany, but it's only 20 minutes from Holland and a little more than half an hour from Belgium, not even two hours from France. It's a very mixed area."

The tunes "Europe Endless" and "Trans-Europe Express" also express this idea. "We travel a lot in Europe," Hutter reports. "And it's not like in America, where you travel a thousand miles and you're still in America. Here we have to adapt to different situations more. And electronic music, I find, is by nature an international medium. Radio waves go around the world, and this music can be understood and can communicate with people all around the world." This is especially true of Dusseldorf, because the town was the center of German industry before World War II and consequently was bombed and completely destroyed. The entire city today is newly built. "All our traditions were cut off," Hutter says. "It left a vacuum. We are the first postwar generation, and so we are the beginning of something new."

Because Dusseldorf is still heavily industrial, the sounds of industry have themselves had a direct impact on Kraftwerk's music. "Our first album was recorded in a studio that was right in the middle of an oil refinery," Hutter recalls. "When we came out the door we could hear the sound of those big flames burning off the fumes—all kinds of industrial noises. Even engines are a kind of music. You can hear the harmonics in their tones. When you walk down the street you have a concert—the cars play symphonies. And we use this fact in our music. In 'Autobahn' the cars hum a melody. In 'Trans-Europe Express' the train itself is singing."

But in spite of this emphasis on sound effects, much of Kraftwerk's music has straightforward tonality and simple, easy-to-understand melodic lines. Entire sections of a tune or even whole tunes may be played on a single chord. The music is invariably in 4/4 time and virtually always falls into precise, regular four-bar phrases. Which certainly doesn't sound progressive when you describe it that way. The effect on the listener, however, is another story. The regularity of the phrasing and the highly repetitive melodies produce a hypnotic effect. The music always fulfills our most basic subconscious expectations about how a phrase will round out; instead of being jarred by unexpected shifts, we are lulled into a receptive state. This regularity obviously reflects the uniform structure of life in the machine age, but it also calls to mind a pronouncement of Steve Reich, a classical composer who articulated his turn away from the arcane complexities of serial writing toward a simpler, more accessible style by saying, "I don't know any secrets of composition that you can't hear." In other words, like the pipes and girders in a Bauhaus-inspired building, everything in a Kraftwerk tune is out in the open.

The effect of this compositional simplicity is to direct the listener's attention toward the sounds in any given texture—the synthetic percussion, the shimmering background chords, the rich melodic tone colors, and the synthesizer effects. And it is in these sounds themselves and their interlocking rhythmic relationships that Kraftwerk shines. Every tune is a pulsating kaleidoscope of electronic sound. The pulse and phrasing sometimes bring to mind both disco and new wave, but there is a bounciness, and also a kind of restraint or economy, that is a vital element of their style. Generally all the instruments in a mix are clearly audible, and each contributes something specific to the whole. There is no superfluous decoration, any more than there is in an engineer's drawing.

Currently the world of popular music seems to be divided into two camps—those who like electronic sounds, and those who feel that the high-gloss tone of a synthesizer is sterile and lifeless. Even musicians who do use synthesizers sometimes try to disguise the fact. Brian Eno, for example, says that he prefers to subvert the sound of an oscillator by introducing some slight distortion and unevenness, so the result will sound more like an acoustic instrument. But for Kraftwerk, clearly, the synthetic sound is exactly what they want. "Except for our voices," Hutter says, "there is no member of the group producing direct acoustic sounds. We create loudspeaker music." It would be a mistake, though, to assume that their music is entirely devoid of expressive nuance. Their instruments are built to produce warm, rich tones, and there are constant small alterations in timing and tone color that keep the impression from becoming static.

The idea of "creating loudspeaker music" again reflects the pragmatic Bauhaus approach. As somebody else once remarked, "What's this fuss about electronic music? When you listen to a recording of Toscanini conducting Beethoven, you're listening to electronic music." Pretending that you're really hearing Toscanini, and not an amplified electrical signal, is an exercise in self-delusion, an attempt to flee from the reality of living in the future.

In a 1977 interview in *Sounds*, Hutter and Schneider put it this way: "We must move on from the hippie mystical religious stance of the 1960s. The hippies were fugitives from technology. They didn't face the problems, they just ran away. But this is stupid. Wherever you run in the world today, a microphone can pick you up. In the past people said that God could hear everything. Today it is the tape recorder that can hear everything. The tape recorder is the new God."

Certainly this is an extreme view, but it's probably more realistic than most of us would like to admit. Our relationship with our world *has* been changed forever by technology. The changes in music alone have been immense, and Kraftwerk has documented the changes both in music and in the world at large in a way that few other artists have. The major criticism that might be leveled at them is that at times (as in "Neon Lights" and "Pocket Calculator") they seem to be seduced by the glamour of technology rather than examining its deeper implications. They seem to be paying more attention to surface appearances than to underlying substance. But then, that's a sin of which just about everybody in this technological culture is guilty. Maybe, after all, it isn't themselves that Kraftwerk are parodying. Maybe they're parodying us.

Depeche Mode.

2

Depeche Mode, Soft Cell, the Units, Wall of Voodoo, Japan, Our Daughters Wedding

NEW SYNTHESIZER ROCK

By Robert Doerschuk || *Keyboard*, June 1982

From their use of machine rhythm to their approach to timbre and technology, the scene Keyboard dubbed "neo wave" was not a throwback to rock past, but the seed of something new. Whether received as direct influence or absorbed through musical zeitgeist, the musical idioms being developed by the rockers on this panel would come to shape electronic dance music to come. As they wrestle with challenges technological and cultural, they connect with issues no less relevant decades later. —PK

The new wave has crested. About five years ago it began surging across the then-watery musical landscape, stinging audiences that had been lulled by MOR and disco with its sharp, cold spray. Suddenly the established stars of rock looked a little older, prematurely graying in their late 20s before the onslaught of groups like Blondie, Devo, Talking Heads, and Elvis Costello.

Hard to believe it all happened half a decade back. For keyboard-playing fans of progressive rock, still scuffling for bits of news about Keith Emerson and re-programming nostalgic orchestral synthesizer effects, the following news may be even more unsettling: New wave is dead. Already. Elvis Costello is singing duets with George Jones, Blondie is dabbling in seven conceptual albums, and in their footsteps new, younger players are experimenting, exploring, grabbing for a place at the cutting edge of modern rock.

In a way, it's all predictable. Rock is a constantly regenerating phenomenon. When one generation of artists gets a little too flabby, or starts straying a bit too far from the basics of the music, it gets elbowed aside by impatient newcomers, eager to get back to the sound, beat, and stance of rock at its simplest. A mellow Elvis Presley, tamed by the army, led to the Beatles, whose successive cuteness and artsiness stimulated the psychedelic movement, in whose burned-out ashes the anti-romantic seeds of punk and new wave were sown.

But while styles change, while the cycle spins on, the tools stay roughly the same. Rock means guitars, drums, and, thankfully, keyboards of one sort or another. The current revival of essential rock involves, if anything, a greater use of keyboards than any similar return to rock roots. But in almost every other respect, a refugee from the '60s or even the mid-'70s would find huge differences between the rock of those days and what is happening now. This means, in turn, that the use and function of keyboards, especially synthesizers, has undergone some breathtaking changes in the journey from Tomita to Deutsch-Amerikanische Freundschaft.

What many post–new wave bands have in common with earlier stripped-down rock groups is an interest in playing more for dancers than for listeners. Where older acts as diverse as the Who and Styx tend to appear before sedentary, some-times demurely seated crowds in stadiums and vast concert halls, performances by Orchestral Manoeuvres in the Dark, Depeche Mode, and their brethren usually work best in the more traditional rock setting—hot, sticky clubs jammed wall to wall with bodies leaping about to an irresistible 4/4 rhythm.

These new bands pursue a familiar formula—heavy on the second and fourth beats, with compelling counter-rhythms from the bass and as little adornment as possible. In short, the tried-and-true rock and roll blueprint. In fact, their subservi-ence to the beat is more complete than was the case with Little Richard, Creedence Clearwater, and other oldies, because of the disco influence. Most disco records center around the drums, in some cases almost exclusively the bass drum, with orchestras, guitars, and everything else except vocals mixed down to nearly a subconscious level. Although the ideology of the music hasn't much relevance to the young synth rockers, they are children of a radio era that has saturated the airwaves, street corners, and brain cells with disco's merciless pulse.

Inevitably, this has had its impact; even the dreariest, most nihilistic lyrics shout out in post–new wave ensembles over a bedrock beat that should set the most danced-out feet tapping. But though the lyrical focus differs, with disco composers seldom searching beyond sex and neo-wavers often dipping into anger and alienation for inspiration, the impact on dancers is nearly identical. Both Donna Summers and Soft Cell's Marc Almond have an ability to project a kind of detached desperation through their vocals, but much of that projection is due to the hypnotic power of the unsyncopated repetitive electronic riffs over which they sing.

To further this effect, many new bands have turned from live drummers to rhythm machines, which allow for unvarying sequences of identical percussion sounds and eliminate any possibilities of trance-breaking irregularities in the less dependable hands of human drummers. Some groups, like Orchestral Manoeuvres, do use drummers onstage, though even then the impact of electronic rhythm units can be heard in the steady beat the drummers are assigned. But more frequently, in the work of Soft Cell, the Human League, Throbbing Gristle, Tuxedomoon, and the now-defunct Suicide, digital boxes have replaced trap sets.

Sound familiar? This is the approach pioneered by the German techno-rockers Kraftwerk. Their straightforward beat, minimalist textures, and use of pointy razor-edged synthesizer sounds awakened many young keyboardists to the fact that keyboard electronics did not necessarily have to follow the color-washed soft-focus footsteps of Tomita or Jean-Michel Jarre. Any consideration of the new style must acknowledge Kraftwerk, especially in their fusion of disco and techno, as the movement's musical godfathers.

Of course there are other branches in the music's family tree. Spiritually, the lineage stretches back to the early '50s. In its pure state, rock and roll has always been iconoclastic, with certain inseparable and generally anti-establishment connotations. Little Richard's manic antics were beyond the comprehension of the adult word in the Eisenhower era; the fact that white kids listened to black music, let alone music played by a black man wearing mascara and suggestively writhing all over a piano keyboard, caused perhaps more dinner-table anxiety than the prospect of nuclear war.

As society loosened up in the liberal '60s, rock performers had to probe further into the dark corners of parental fear for equivalent effect. The faint hint of androgyny in the Beatles, the delinquent scruffiness of the Rolling Stones, the flamboyant communism of the Haight-Ashbury bands, all measured this escalating assault on grown-up standards. But when the heavy artillery rolled out in groups like the Doors, the Fogs, the Velvet Underground, the New York Dolls, and the MC5—groups that cultivated vaguely occult, sleazy, arrogant, anarchistic, and/or sexually bizarre facades—anti-establishment posturing began to become a fine art. The music had finally hit America's funny bone. Shock rock was born.

Image-wise, the ramifications are still being felt today. In traditional showbiz, performers smile, laugh, and dance for audiences. Because of the shock-rock ethic, these entertainment techniques are frequently abandoned by bands who get their energy by mobilizing their audience's instincts for rebellion. The problem is that it can be difficult to draw the line between image and reality; no doubt many old-time vaudevillians were genuinely happy people, and as the Sid Vicious and Joy Division legacies demonstrate, many shock rockers seem to be genuinely strange, as well.

But it would be a mistake to dismiss the new bands as pure shock rockers. A close listen to the best of their work reveals a growing musical sensibility, a feeling for orchestration and linear composition, and an overall discipline frequently absent in the best of some highly regarded progressive-rock artists. The singers may appear to wrestle with the ideas of pitch and melody, but this is a stylistic issue; just as early jazz singers dismayed oldsters with their neo-African melisma, so might today's Barry Manilow fans be distressed by the emotional yowls of Jim Morrison's and Johnny Rotten's vocal progeny.

More to the point for us is the keyboard work. One characteristic of many new bands is how they build tension between the singing and the synthesis. Like Morrison in "The End," Soft Cell's Marc Almond conjures chilling images in a tortured, wailing delivery, but where the Doors supported Morrison's excursions with their two improvisations, David Ball lays down meticulous patterns designed to highlight through contrast, rather than to complement, the singer.

A similar approach underscores the more anarchic efforts of Throbbing Gristle and New Order: the distance between cathartic vocals and restrained, even rigid, electronic accompaniment can create a powerful effect.

It follows, then, that technical virtuosity is not an especially relevant attribute in this style. Since much of the impact of neo wave synthesis stems from machine-like repetition—a technique also employed by the equivalent anti-romantics in classical music, the minimalists—the keyboard flourishes of the Keith Emerson school would be definitely out of place in this context. Solos in the traditional sense, improvisations realized on the keyboard, are a rarity; at most you might find occasional four-bar single-line passages, more fills than solos, such as at the end of the Units' "Bugboy."

Instead, the focus shifts to the arrangement. The droning organ sounds and underplayed fills of Ray Manzarek in the Doors and John Cale in the Velvet Underground's

"Heroin" are the real rock antecedents of the new synthesists. Like Manzarek and Cale—both technically adept keyboardists—they are more interested in integrating into the whole than in standing out front. This attitude is also reflected in the early work of Jimmie Destrie with Blondie and Steve Naive with Elvis Costello's Attractions, the most prominent figures in the new wave revival of Farfisa and Vox organ sounds. But from a few adherents here and there, among them Joe "King" Carrasco, the Insect Surfers, and Tex-Mex nostalgists like Augie Meyer of the Sir Douglas Quintet, most new keyboardists who want old-timey electric organ effects find it easier to store them into their synthesizers as one of an array of possible programs.

The fact is that the neo-wavers are just as concerned as Tony Banks or Patrick Moraz with orchestrated sound, but they tend to work from the background. Even when Wakeman is only laying down synthesized strings, he does so with such panache that there is no mistaking his identity. His younger counterparts prefer sublimating themselves to the beat, inserting short rills or patterns of subtly contrasting colors. Case in point: the tiny tonal variations in the riff that constitutes DAF's "Liebe auf den Ersten Blick," from *Gold und Liebe*. If you want to listen, you must listen carefully to appreciate synthesist Robert Görl's meticulous touch.

But if you want to dance instead, you can do that, too. And so the cycle is once again completed. For listeners who are used to sitting and letting orchestral synthesized chords or a string of lightning-bolt licks wash over them, new wave synthesis may he an acquired taste. But once again something different is happening in rock, as the first swing back to basics in the synthesizer era, there is as much in it for the head as there is for the feet.

Partly because of the relatively low-key roles they lean toward, there are no superstars, no Hendrixes or Emersons, among the young synthesists. Their bands have followings, but sometimes the most devoted fans have trouble remembering the names of the players whose records they consume. This is true especially in the States, since many pioneering neo wave groups are English, and some of the most important of these have never played any American engagements.

For this reason, *Keyboard* indulged itself in a series of trans-Atlantic phone interviews with some of the leading lights in this still-fresh movement. We also talked to the keyboardists in three American bands whose work ties in with that of the European pioneers. While no two of the artists in the following assembled interviews should be considered clones of one another or anyone else, they all share at least one thing in common: an interest in using the synthesizer in rock as it's never been used before, in part to get back to where the music in its essence belongs.

Some of the people we spoke with—Martin Gore of Depeche Mode, Layne Rico and Scott Simon of Our Daughters Wedding—are close to the mainstream of pop music, using rhythm machines and sequencers to pound out a disco-derived dance beat. Others—Scott Ryser and Rachel Webber of the Units, David Ball of Soft Cell—also adhere to a steady rhythm, but with darker overtones more clearly reminiscent of punk and new wave, while Richard Barbieri of English group Japan, Chas Gray and Stan Ridgway of Wall of Voodoo, and Peter Principle of Tuxedomoon all shy from the tyranny of the sequencer and pursue freer forms in their own ways.

What it goes to show is that even at this early stage of its development, the new rock synthesizer vanguard is branching beyond stereotypes and finding room to create in ways unforeseen by the trendsetters of a decade ago.

Let's begin by finding out about your musical backgrounds. Did you take a lot of piano lessons, for example, or were you mainly self-taught?

Richard Barbieri (Japan): I was self-taught, really. I was never taught how to play by anyone, and I didn't start off on the piano. I've never felt comfortable with acoustic piano. It was really only when I started using synthesizers that I felt I could be useful and do something interesting, or put over what I wanted to do.

Had you had any electronic music experience before you got into synthesizers?

Barbieri: Not really, no. It was a very naive kind of thing. I just started, and carried on from there. I was just lucky that I had the right people around me from whom I could gain influences and whom I could influence in turn, and that's really how Japan came about. I joined probably six months after the band was formed. We're all self-taught. I'd say there's probably only one real musician in the band—Steve Jansen, the drummer.

Scott Ryser (the Units): We got together about three years ago. Rachel and I met at a Tuxedomoon concert at the Mab [Mabuhay Gardens, a San Francisco club]. We were both hauling some equipment for them, and we just got to talking. It turned out that Rachel was doing an experimental performance in the windows at the abandoned J. C. Penney building downtown. We wound up collaborating. Rachel painted the windows black from the inside, and as I played some synthesizer music while films were being shown, she'd gradually scrape the stuff off the windows so people could start peeping in.

Were you both visual artists before getting into music?

Rachel Webber (the Units): I was, but Scott has more of a background in synthesizer. He bought the first synthesizer to come into San Francisco. I started singing with Scott, then I ended up playing synthesizer, too, because it was more gratifying to help write music.

Layne Rico (Our Daughters Wedding): We also started off as friends in the San Francisco Bay area. About two years ago we had a band that was similar to the Cars, a rock-style guitar band. We had no synthesizers at the time, but finally we incorporated a couple of keyboard players—Scott [Simon] and someone else. Then we got tired of that guitar-drum lineup, so we all moved to New York. I traded my drum kit for the new percussion synthesizers, and Keith [Silva], the lead vocalist, dropped his guitars and learned to play keyboards. We thought that would be more interesting, because most of the music we were listening to at the time was more or less electronic, European things that American bands weren't playing.

Martin Gore (Depeche Mode): When we got rid of our guitar players, it was mainly because we didn't have any transport at the time. We had to get one of our friends to take us everywhere in a van, and it was very difficult to get in touch with him all the time. It was far easier for us to just play synths, because they are very portable.

Everywhere we played we just showed up with our synths in suitcases, then hired a PA and played through it.

But wasn't there also a musical reason for scrapping the guitars?

Gore: The guitars were getting rather boring. They've got just one sound all the time, and though you can flange it and do things like that, it's still basically the same sound.

David Ball (Soft Cell): I originally started with guitar, too, but I got bored because there really wasn't much you could do with it. I was interested in different types of sound, so I got rid of the guitar and got a synthesizer.

Was Soft Cell always a duo, as it is today?

Ball: We did start out as a duo. Marc [Almond, singer] and I started working together in 1979, when we were both in college at Leeds. Marc was in a performance that was more like cabaret, and I was doing soundtracks with him. Then we decided to do something more commercial. We came up with about ten songs and played our first gig in the autumn of 1979.

Chas Gray (Wall of Voodoo): We also started out doing soundtracks. Stan, our guitar player, and I rented an office off Hollywood Boulevard, in late '77, specifically to do film soundtracks. We had a couple of two-track tape recorders, a file cabinet, a desk, and a light—no typewriter, and we were kind of low on clients, too. But we made a lot of tapes.

Stan Ridgway (Wall of Voodoo): Eventually the company turned into a band.

Were the instruments you used on the soundtracks similar to what you later used onstage?

Ridgway: Not really. Onstage there's so much you have to do, but when you have the freedom of tape you can do a lot of manipulation with acoustic or electric sounds. We used to specialize in slowed-down or sped-up tapes sandwiched in between real-time stuff, because we couldn't really play fast enough on the keyboards to get the speed we needed. We used to play it at a comfortable tempo, then get it faster on another track, and it sounded pretty good.

Do you feel that your experience with soundtracks gave you any insights with synthesizers that you might otherwise have lacked?

Ridgway: Well, we always felt that music was for generating moods, and trying to play fast in a virtuoso type of thing wasn't something we were interested in. We were more interested in a feel that had nothing to do with musicianship.

Do you feel that keyboard virtuosity is not as important to new styles of synthesizer playing as it was in the past?

Ridgway: Yeah, and I think I understand why. When the synthesizer first came out, it was looked upon pretty much as a crazy organ. You had players like Chick Corea and Jan Hammer trying to make it sound like a guitar. But in formal music, people had been using the instrument for a long time before that, and it just took some time for the two ideas to catch up with one another.

Barbieri: I think people tend to use synthesizers in a more subtle way now.

Ball: The technical skill now lies in actually programming the synthesizer, rather than in playing the keyboard. I don't think of synthesizer players as keyboardists, actually. There are keyboard players who play piano and organ, and there are synthesizer players who are more like technicians. Of course there are really good piano players who can do great things on synthesizers, too.

Ryser: It's more a matter of good taste now, or just generally being creative. I don't think it's as necessary as it used to be to have lots of impressive licks. Some of these new synthesizers, like the Sequential Circuits Pro-One, will play arpeggios for you. My sequencer is Sequential Circuits, too, and I can program it at a snail's pace, then just speed it up to whatever tempo I want.

In that sense, you really differ from the bands of the '60s, with their extended solos.

Ryser: Yeah. It's more important to me to contribute to the sound of the band than to play a solo. When any of us does solo, it's more to create a dialog between the instruments, as opposed to just sticking one player out in front.

Simon: Exactly. Solos should be pertinent to the vocal line and the message you're trying to get across. When you have singing involved, belaboring an instrumental section just takes away from the song. And the kids get a little bored: Even if someone is excellent on an instrument, all the licks start to sound the same if it goes on and on.

Ryser: In the '60s people got outside of the structure more, and now it's a thing of getting back into the structure, making the players in the group work really well together.

Simon: As soon as synthesizers came along, everyone said, "Oh, wow, outer space!" and that type of thing. That lasted until the players matured, and then synths started to take on a different meaning: horn lines, guitar lines, background noise, or what have you, rather than the Keith Emerson "Lucky Man" standard glide.

What are your thoughts now about people like Emerson and Rick Wakeman?

Simon: They were very good keyboard players, that stands by itself.

Ryser: For my part, I think my style is a reaction against guys like Emerson and Wakeman. When they first came out, I really liked them, but after a while it got too pretentious.

Ball: I really used to hate the kind of things they were doing, because it was like just impressing people by how fast they could play a riff. To me, that doesn't mean anything. There's no feeling there; it's just technical brilliance.

Is having that kind of technical skill in any way a liability in your music?

Principle: No, not at all. I couldn't imagine anything that would be a liability if it comes from talent. It's not what you have, but the way you use what you have, that makes good art.

Ridgway: But in a lot of ways I think having a knowledge of music has helped us out a lot more than just having a knowledge of the keyboard. It's interesting to be talking to a keyboard magazine, because we've never really considered ourselves keyboardists at all.

Yet there is a lot of synthesizer on your albums.

Ridgway: I know, but it's still funny. We've played them, but our area of expertise is different. The idea of a monophonic synthesizer, where one note is played at a time, opened up a whole different approach to the keyboard. For centuries being a keyboardist was a two-handed thing. You worked in an orchestral sense. Then when a keyboard came along that was just a trigger to generate sounds out of a synthesizer, that completely changed things.

Gore: When you use a lot of sequencers and things like that, you don't really need much technical playing ability. But you still need some sort of know-how, some sort of musical knowledge to know what sounds right. When a note sounds wrong, you should know how to change it accordingly. When people talk about just leaving a sequencer running to finish a song, it's not that simple.

Ball: Groups that are dominated by sequencers I find a little boring, actually. I think a lot of people are possessed with the idea that because machines can do that kind of thing, you've got to let them steal the limelight. Those people seem to be into the idea that the medium is the message. Kraftwerk is a perfect example.

Principle: We started out as a drone group, but we've never really used the sequencer trip, maybe because it's sort of a familiar sound.

A lot of sequencer music really makes me angry. We've never had one. If somebody gave one to us, maybe we'd do something intelligent with it.

Ryser: The sequencer does take a lot of the fun away from playing. Now that our percussionist, Jonathan Parker, plays keyboard, he'll play some of the old sequencer parts. It's just more fun to not use it in a live situation, and it creates more interplay. You feel there's more energy happening. For composing it's great to use rhythm machines and sequencers, but onstage I think it's just a little more exciting to do the live thing. It's more like an orchestra when you see all these different people playing different parts, as opposed to just having a machine do them.

On the Digital Cowboy record, Scott, you included a note reading, "No Sequencers Used." Why?

Simon: I think a bit of the humanity is lost. And we're trying to get the fact across in our music that we are human beings. We're not machines playing machines. Also we're trying to state that we are different from a lot of other bands that do use sequencers. Take that bass pattern on "No One's Watching" [from *Digital Cowboy*]. That's a traditional sequencer pattern, but I played the whole part through with my fingers. When I do it live, sometimes I make a mistake, but I can also make it sound more energetic without the sequencer. I can accent different notes and change the feeling in a way the sequencer can't.

Still, you must hear the similarity between the patterns you play and the sequencer lines of Kraftwerk.

Simon: Oh, sure. They're great. I've been listening to them since 1976 or '77, when I first met Keith and Layne in California. But they are a bit different from us. We are a band that plays on electronic instruments, whereas they are an electronic band. We're not just using tape loops and feedback and stuff; we're striving to write music on electronic instruments because they are more interesting than conventional guitars and drums.

Ball: Kraftwerk had my favorite sound in electronic music: That's what first attracted me to synthesizers.

Was Kraftwerk an influence on Japan, as well?

Barbieri: I suppose we were inspired by them in a way, because we work with sequencers, but only to that extent.

And your sequencer work is much less a factor in your music than in theirs.

Barbieri: We use it for a much sparser kind of rhythm than they do. We play it against the drums, as well, as opposed to adhering to a strict four-bar thing. It plays between the intervals of the drum pattern, rather than having the drums following the sequencer pattern. We tend to split them up into two separate things so that they play against each other and create different rhythms.

Webber: Kraftwerk is obviously someone we get compared to a lot, because they've been around for a while. But when we started, one of the slogans 415 Records hyped us with was, "Humans playing synthesizers." The whole thing was that we were human, we weren't machines. Now it seems like there's a definite trend away from synthesizers as machine-oriented noise creators. If anything, it's turned in the other direction, with bands like Orchestral Manoeuvres and Soft Cell.

Ryser: I think the whole machine thing is still a big area to explore. I'm not against it, because it is a big part of what you hear every day outside your house.

But still, I find it hard to listen to people like Klaus Schulze or Tangerine Dream because it is so emotionless. When I got into synthesizer, it was more because of people like Wendy Carlos. I felt with her stuff, especially in *A Clockwork Orange*, that there was a lot more feeling to it.

How much of a challenge is it to get past the electronic framework of your music, especially given the influence of Kraftwerk, and make it seem more emotional, if that's what you're trying to do?

Core: I don't think we've had that problem. There are a lot of bands around who do play synthesizers very coldly. But I think we've gotten away from that.

Principle: That's why we're interesting to a lot of people. We use electronics for a lot of what we do; we use saxophone and violins, too, but a lot of times it's a heavily treated electric violin, and even so we still manage to cut it and the emotions somehow come through. This is one of the enigmas of Tuxedomoon as compared to our peers. I'm pro-emotion. I'm pro-everything that's human. I don't think the way of the future is to close off certain circuits in your nervous system, by drugs, willpower, religion, or whatever. We have to open them all by these same means!

> "When we started, one of the slogans 415 Records hyped us with was, 'Humans playing synthesizers.' The whole thing was that we were human, we weren't machines."
>
> —RACHEL WEBBER (THE UNITS)

Much of the immediate emotion in Soft Cell seems to come from the singer's style.

Ball: But I don't think my particular playing sounds cold, either. It doesn't have that mechanical, repetitive sound, because I play manually, rather than relying on really precise machines that lose that human sort of feel. But even bands that don't rely on sequencers often show their influence in how they use cyclic repetitions of notes. The fact that they're played by hand may escape the notice of the listener, who just hears something that obviously was inspired by machine-like sequencer patterns.

Ball: But Brian Eno once said, "Repetition is a form of change."

Webber: I know that my bass lines are usually pretty repetitive, but I think it's kind of nice and a little more free to have something like that going on with a percussionist doing things on top.

Ryser: In fact, we're always thinking we're not repetitive enough. Repetition is nice for dancing, and since we like to dance ourselves, that's one way we get into a good groove and stay on it.

So is dancing an important element in your music?

Webber: Yeah, definitely. I like the audience to inspire me as much as we inspire them, and when they're just sitting there looking like they're watching TV, it isn't very inspiring. The music has to be able to get them up.

Ryser: It's fun to play that kind of music, too, because you can jump around a little bit more easily. I feel like I take myself too seriously all day; I don't want to do it when I play music, too.

Simon: But you know, I think dancing is less important now. I have a feeling that people want to listen a little bit more to what's going on. They want to be able to move their bodies a little bit, but it's not necessary to go out and go crazy on every song. If there's a message there, people want to hear it. Rock in the middle and late '70s didn't have much of a message, the way there was in the '60s. There is a need for that now.

Principle: I don't argue against dance-oriented music with lyrics like that, because one of the blessings of rock and roll is the fact that it describes your problem and also gives you the solution, which is to dance away into a dervish delirium. A lot of the world is in that mood right now.

And you feel the new synthesizer rock addresses that need?

Ball: Sure. It's hypnotic as dance music. That's the whole essence of it. People are so limited and restricted, crammed into offices and trains. They can't move around, so they just want to shake and go wild. Dancing is what they do rather than hitting or killing somebody.

> "People are so limited and restricted, crammed into offices and trains. They can't move around, so they just want to shake and go wild. Dancing is what they do rather than hitting or killing somebody."
>
> —DAVID BALL
> (SOFT CELL)

Principle: There is a lot of soulful, fiery dance-oriented music in New York, but I think that kind of inspiration has drifted away from English music. When I was a kid, English music was very interesting, but now it's very flat.

Webber: The English bands really go for an extremely simple drum sound, just four to the bar, if they have a drummer. In a way that's what separates us from all the synthesizer music that's happening right now in England, especially with our percussionist and drummer. We try to remain simple in what we do, but it's still a little more creative than that.

Gore: Well, I'm a bit biased, but I think a bit more thought goes into our rhythm than us laying down a disco track. Most disco records sound very much the same to me. We do use a powerful bass drum and snare sound, and they are mixed up loud, but we don't start by saying, "Let's make this a dance record," although most of them are.

Doesn't it seem like the use of drum machines by many new bands contradicts claims that they're trying to go closer to human feeling?

Ball: Well, we use drum machines because they're convenient. I couldn't play a drum kit, but with the Roland TR-808 or the Linn you can program as you go along; it's like live playing. You don't just type out a rhythm part and let it play; you can actually put in fills as you go along, and that enables me to play drums using a keyboard or switches rather than drumsticks.

Do you try to approximate a drum sound as closely as possible?

Ball: Yes. I always thought the snare sound on drum machines was a little thin, so when we record the drum machine, with each drum sound on a separate channel, we take the electronic snare signal and feed it into a small speaker which is placed on top of a real snare, then we record that. So the drum machine is triggering a real snare drum!

Principle: But the whole idea of using electronics for rhythms instead of a drummer is to get something that sounds different from real drums! That's one thing I don't like about rhythm machines! They have imitation drum sounds on them. Look at the Roland: You can treat it with a fuzz box or flanger or echo, but you never get away from that drum sound.

On the other hand, it sounds like the Depeche Mode bass drum sound is not even remotely an attempt at imitating the tone of a real bass drum.

Gore: Since we've started making records, we've always used an ARP 2600 for the bass drum because we've never found a drum machine with a powerful enough bass drum sound. We run it through the sequencer. We like the snare sound on our Roland TR-008. Our Korg KR-55 also has quite a good snare. We chose them both mainly to get a good snare drum.

The snare sounds on Soft Cell's "Sex Dwarf" and on "Talking Drum" by Japan seem to be cut off at certain points. Did you use a noise gate on it?

Barbieri: That's exactly what we used. It took quite a long time, because there's a lot involved with the special type of delay you want, but on "Talking Drum" we used the noise gate on the snare and on the toms.

Ball: We had some sort of limiting amplifier that clipped the sound so that it died very abruptly, leaving a kind of ringing reverberation.

Layne, why did you move from regular drums to electronic percussion with Our Daughters Wedding?

Rico: I like the drums, but I couldn't get some of the sounds I wanted from them, because all you can do is hit a stick against the skin. So I used my knowledge of drumming and syncopation and changed it all over to playing keyboards. My drumming was where I got all my rhythm-machine ability.

Barbieri: We use a lot of electronic percussion, too, always manually played by our drummer, so it's a matter of myself programming the appropriate sounds, usually drum sounds on a synth, then having Steve play them.

You also do mix rhythm machines in with your electronic drums, don't you?

Rico: That's exactly right. We like the sound of a rhythm machine, but they can get too repetitious, just going *click clack click clack* all night.

Ridgway: If something comes up that only a machine can do, and it does it a lot better than the drummer, than Joe [Nanini, Wall of Voodoo's drummer] isn't averse to playing on top of it. But it is a machine, not a drummer, after all. We would never want to replace the drummer with a rhythm machine: that's not the idea.

Ryser: We definitely made a decision to have drummers as opposed to just electronic drums, but we'd like to start using electronic drums to augment the percussion.

What do you like about them?

Ryser: The textures, the tones. They'd be nice to intersperse with real drums. When we record we use a vibraphone, but our percussionist now plays keyboard instead because the vibes we so hard to mike onstage. I really like the slight tonal variation between the keyboard and a percussive instrument like vibes. It's the same with electronic and real drums. To have the two textures together would be nice.

Ridgway: Our drummer is into experimenting with textures, too. He devised this set of frying pans attached to a practice pad that he plays along with the sequencer at the end of "Back in Flesh" [from *Dark Continent*]. You can't tell which is which!

Martin, what do you get in Depeche Mode from playing with a rhythm machine that you don't get from a live drummer?

Gore: That's a difficult one for us to answer, because we've never used a drummer. Even when we first started, with a guitarist and bass guitarist, we used a small drum machine. We've never felt limited by it, though.

Principle: When we bought our Roland rhythm machine, we used it mainly to trigger us into inspirational moods. We write a lot of music in improvisational situations, recording onto cassette and later extracting various interesting passages. But we've kind of moved away from that, because the Roland is so stupid. It only plays in 4/4; you can't do different tempos, and it doesn't understand unevenness. We just recorded a 12" 45, three songs with heavy electric guitar and not one drumbeat on the whole record. I'm really proud of that. [*Laughs.*]

There's a cut on the American Japan album, titled "Ghosts," that has no drum track, either.

Barbieri: It is very difficult to play without a drum track because there is no real timing. The only timing we could follow was the bass synthesizer, which kind of denoted the chord changes. I think it came over quite well. That's probably one of the best examples of my keyboard work. The arrangement is what's interesting about the track. It's a very straight vocal line, but we decided to make the arrangement a bit strange.

Do you feel that different kinds of synthesized sounds are popular these days than were popular in the progressive-rock era?

Gray: I think so. When they were used on a more traditional level, people tried to approximate the sound of a real instrument with a synthesizer, so they didn't come up with as many jolting sounds.

Like the one you used on "Back in Flesh."

Gray: That was an Oberheim mini-sequencer plugged into two holes in the back of the Minimoog that it wasn't supposed to be plugged into, according to the manufacturer, but it's also run through this little gizmo box I built at home.

Ridgway: Then you turn all the filters off on the Moog, fiddle with the box, and the sounds come out.

Ball: In the early days, most synthesizers sounded the same. The Moog sound seemed the most popular. It's developed now to the point that you can use a synthesizer and people won't realize that's what it is, which I really like. It's not that you're trying to deceive anyone; it's just that you can get the feel that you've dreamed about. People can't say the synthesizer is just a gimmick that makes silly little sounds, because it isn't doing that anymore.

Ryser: In the '70s they were going for more of a guitar sound. It was more of a Jan Hammer thing. Now I'd say synths are used either percussively or with longer melodic tones.

Webber: And new possibilities will come along as time goes on. Kids who play video games hear a lot of weird sounds, and when they go hear a synthesizer band they'll be able to relate to it on that level.

Simon: To me it goes back to the desire to have a raw edge in music. People who are playing string synthesizers now prefer to hit chords and pull off rather than keep it down, because it's so convenient an instrument that players I know instinctively back off from it.

That is a major change from the way progressive-rock synthesists used string lines in the past.

Simon: That's the fun thing about it. The beat is very important. You have to define it first. Once that's done, then you have all the room in the world to color a song.

Gore: We don't make conscious attempts to imitate the sounds of real instruments, but a lot of times the sounds we're looking for come very close to conventional instruments. They might not be exact replicas, but they sound very much like the originals.

Barbieri: We try to make almost every single sound as acoustic as possible. If we knew how to play those acoustic instruments well enough, we'd drop synthesizers altogether. I much prefer the sound of traditional instruments. We're merely using synthesizers to create that.

Ridgway: But to me, there really isn't any point to that. I like the way synthetic strings sound. If I wanted to have a real-sounding violin on a record, I would get someone to come in and play one.

Principle: We only use machines to give us more possibilities to make mistakes.

Do you feel like you're involved in a significant trend that's changing the direction of rock and roll?

Ryser: I think so. We're doing it in a reactionary way. It's like, there's been enough of this other stuff: How about something different?

Simon: Yeah. Sometimes we'll be sitting around talking, and someone will say, "God, it feels good that something we just happened to be doing is working, and besides that it's new and important." Bands like Human League, OMD, and the Units are all in a new thing, and as it matures, us artists who are presenting the music grow up, and kids who are fifteen now will start using these instruments to play something different, too.

Principle: Well, I don't want to paint the picture either way, because it's too romantic. I don't expect to be the mainstay of a new evolution. I'm not on that much of an ego trip.

> "New possibilities will come along as time goes on. Kids who play video games hear a lot of weird sounds, and when they go hear a synthesizer band they'll be able to relate to it on that level."
>
> —RACHEL WEBBER (THE UNITS)

Do you have any apprehension that synthesizers may simply fall into a new kind of clichéd use?

Principle: I think they already have.

What can you do to avoid that in your own music?

Principle: I don't worry about it.

Barbieri: It does sound to me like something new is happening, but everybody does seem to be doing the same thing. It's all going into another style again.

Ridgway: I would only say that it sounds as if a lot of musicians have figured out that less is more.

Ball: That's what I hated about a lot of the '70s rock bands that had synthesizers. They overcomplicated things. The return to simplicity is good.

Gray: That seems to be what a lot of other people are doing right now, and as a result everyone has sort of stumbled onto a certain basic style of using the synthesizer.

Webber: There are a lot of similarities among synthesizer bands. You really have to be original and creative with what you do with a machine, because it's really easy to get into a quirky little synthesizer sound. It doesn't take much to come with that kind of a thing.

Barbieri: It's just a matter of choosing your influence, and if you choose the current music scene as your influence, then I don't really hold much hope. If you tend to pick your influences from something more diverse, whether it's Erik Satie or Frank Sinatra or traditional Chinese music, then you could come up with something original.

One last question. If you had to explain what's happening now in music to a rock fan who had somehow fallen asleep in the late '60s and slept through the '70s, what would you say?

Simon: I'd ask him to go back to the '50s and listen to the kind of steady keyboards that Fats Domino played in "Blueberry Hill."

Webber: I'd tell him not to go shopping, not to take out any loans, and to try to survive.

NEW ORDER: ON THE FRINGE OF THE TECHNO-PUNK

By Lee Sherman || *Keyboard*, April 1987

Most bands strive to be understood, but New Order feeds on contradictions. Until recently, their philosophy was: Don't put your pictures on the album sleeves, don't do interviews, let your records speak for themselves. New Order's music is insular, self-absorbed, and yet the quartet is best known for upbeat dance tunes like "Blue Monday" and the Arthur Baker–produced "Confusion." Punk purists who have followed it since its days as the angst-ridden Joy Division see its embrace of keyboard technology as a sellout, while more traditionally trained musicians might consider its primitivism pure heresy.

"Electronic music is the next stage on from punk," insists lead vocalist/guitarist/keyboard player Bernard Sumner. "Music is not technique. It's soul, the spirit you put into something. I hate people who say synthesizers are crap, we're all going to play guitars. I don't like that kind of snobbery. It's like people's attitudes were to the electric guitar in the '50s. To me, keyboards are just another instrument that can play different frequencies and provide different textures. I don't differentiate between them and other instruments. I'm open to anything that's new."

Punk's do-it-yourself approach was still on the agenda when Sumner, bass player Peter Hook, and drummer/keyboard player Steve Morris formed New Order after Joy Division vocalist Ian Curtis committed suicide in May 1980. After adding keyboardist Gillian Gilbert, they began relying more heavily on keyboards. "I think electronics are good because you don't have to practice for a month to be able to get a song across," says Sumner. "You can just write it and get it across the next day."

The kinetic sequencer patterns employed in "Blue Monday" found the band its first mainstream success when the record became a dance-floor favorite in June 1983. But New Order hasn't exactly embraced success. Though the band now records for the Warner Bros. subsidiary Qwest, Sumner insists that their musical ideals haven't changed since the early days on the independent Rough Trade label and points out that keyboards have had a place in New Order from the start. "As Joy Division was evolving, synthesizers were evolving," he recalls. "Those were the days of punk, but Ian used to give us records by Kraftwerk. Before we went onstage we would play *Trans-Europe Express*."

Compared to the state-of-the-art setup employed by the band today, the approach then was positively low-tech. "When we started using keyboards, I used to build the synthesizers and sequencers myself from electronic components, kits that cost $150 each to make. I used to have a friend that was a computer engineer who designed them for us."

The gear then included an ARP Omni II and a homemade monophonic synth called a Transcendent 2000. "Our producer, Martin Hannett, read an article by Robert Moog which suggested breaking a synthesizer up into twenty bands on a graphic equalizer. So he put it through a graphic and put it through a Marshall time modulator, which is how we ended up with the keyboard sound on *Closer* [by Joy Division, 1980, out of print]. There are no sequencers. We played it all by hand because at that point you couldn't get sequencers."

Now the band relies heavily on MIDI to achieve its multi-textured yet direct sound, enabling it to perform parts it might not otherwise have the facility to play. The members of New Order admit to their limited technique, adding that they are more concerned with the end result then with achieving recognition as virtuosos. "Our intention is a complete dismissal of technique, because I believe our music is something that anyone can feel," says Sumner. "If we ever learn to play, I'd like to stop doing what we do for a while. The important lesson to be learned from punk, which everyone gets wrong, is that it doesn't matter how you play, it matters what you play."

And, keyboard-wise, what does the band play? Currently, its setup includes three Octave-Plateau Voyetras, one for manual playing, one used as a sequencer, and one set aside as a spare. It also employs a pair of Yamaha QX1 sequencers and an E-mu Emulator II. All of these are MIDIed to a Yamaha TX416 rack. According to keyboard technician Andy Robinson, one of the most important elements in New Order's rack-mounted arrangement is the use of spares, so that if anything goes wrong he can quickly switch over to another synth or drum machine through two

Sycologic M16 MIDI matrix switchers. Electronic drum parts are played by three of the band's four members on a Yamaha RX11 drum machine and Simmons SDS-7s. The band's interest in unusual sounds is emphasized by its use of the Hohner Melodica, which Curtis began using, after he had heard it on records by reggae musicians, for the string sounds on the song "Atmosphere," and Sumner's use of the Melodica live is a high point in New Order concerts.

Clearly, Sumner is concerned about having his records become too dependent on trendy keyboard sounds. To avoid this, New Order tries to maintain a balance between acoustic and electronic instrumentation. He also has an idea for a new source for digital sampling. "I've thought about sampling some old 78 rpm records, using old music to write new music with," he says.

Off the road, Sumner's listening selection tends toward Beethoven, Wagner, and "anything that doesn't have drums in it." Symphonic strains have found their way into the music of New Order in the past, most notably on "Elegia," an instrumental from last year's *Low-Life* [Qwest, 1-25289] that would suggest the band has a future in film scoring. Indeed, the movie *Pretty in Pink* features three songs by New Order, but it wasn't until recently that the group had the opportunity to compose music specifically for a film. "Personally, I find it quite interesting because I think in pictures," says Sumner of his work on *Salvation*, a film by underground director Beth B. about a Hell's Angel and a television evangelist. The soundtrack features four New Order songs. Two were outtakes from *Power, Corruption, & Lies* [Qwest, 1-25308], while the other two were newly written for the film.

For Sumner, writing music is extremely time-consuming, though he claims it helps to compose at night. "You don't have medium-wave radio over here, but in England we do, and at night you get much better reception because of the ionosphere. Also, when people have gone to sleep, I think there's less interference with your own brain. You can think much clearer at that time of night than you can during the day when everyone else is awake. Or it could just be that it's quieter."

Whether writing for film or for the next New Order album, Sumner believes that the time has come for him to move beyond the old morose preoccupations of Joy Division. "With Joy Division we explored the dark side of life, and we explored it to the full," he says.

"Now it's time to move on and explore the other side." But what about those musicians who still believe that you have to be depressing to be serious?

"I think," Sumner muses, "they should see a doctor."

> "Electronic music is the next stage on from punk. Music is not technique. It's soul, the spirit you put into something."
>
> —BERNARD SUMNER (NEW ORDER)

Rave, circa mid-'90s.

3

The Ethnomusicology of Dance Music

DENISE DALPHOND GOES INSIDE EDM CULTURE'S ROOTS

By Peter Kirn ‖ June 2011

E thnomusicologist and writer Denise Dalphond, completing research into dance music at Indiana University and author of the respected blog Schoolcraft Wax, has taken research into the field. Working in Detroit and at Indiana, she's gotten to know some of dance music's most legendary names, compiling over a hundred hours of interviews and, she says, challenging her notions about how the music evolved across race and geography. She shares with us some of the big picture of electronic dance music's emergence.

How would you say electronic dance music drew from synth rock, from bands like Kraftwerk and New Order? How does it relate to essentially lyric-driven rock, and how did this exchange take place between countries, as with the scenes in the U.S. and U.K.?

Synth rock, and synthesizer music in general, was extremely influential to the development of electronic dance music, particularly in Detroit. Bands like Kraftwerk, New Order, Yellow Magic Orchestra, Neu!, Can, Faust, and other new wave and no wave artists from the U.K. and the U.S. inspired a lot of electronic music produced by Detroiters. Electro-funk is also a major part of the legacy of electronic dance music. George Clinton, Parliament, Parliament Funkadelic, Sylvester, Sly and the Family Stone, all could be heard on Detroit radio alongside synth rock, classical music, classic rock, '80s pop music, and early hip-hop. Developing at around the same time from similar influences, hip hop shares a reciprocal relationship with techno, house, and electro. Egyptian Lover, Mantronix, Newcleus, and Man Parrish are frequently listed as influential by electronic music producers from Detroit and Chicago. Also influential was electronic art music by musicians like Steve Reich and Phillip Glass, as well as disco and later, garage, from New York City. There was also a great deal of mutual influence between Detroit and Chicago in the 1980s. Derrick May regularly visited Chicago to see Ron Hardy, Larry Heard, and Frankie Knuckles DJ, returning to Detroit with a trunk filled with house records from Chicago DJs and record stores.

There is a vast catalog of songs that Chicago and Detroit DJs play as a way of educating listeners. I can speak to Detroit's specific heritage because that is where my expertise lies. This catalog of songs is made up of cuts that Charles "Electrifying Mojo" Johnson would play on Detroit radio, or that Ken Collier would play in a club. Both Mojo and Collier are cornerstones of Detroit's music history. Mojo began his career as a radio disc jockey in 1977 on AM radio in Ann Arbor. Shortly after that, he began playing on Detroit radio programs, inspiring thousands of listeners all over southeast Michigan with his multi-genre approach to sharing music, as well as his theatrical approach to radio. One segment of his program was called the "Midnight Funk Association," in which he would sonically land the mothership over the airwaves, telling listeners to flash their headlights, flicker their front porch lights, or dance on their backs. Mojo would play everything that I listed above, and more. He broke Prince to Detroit listeners and interviewed him on the radio, initiating a lengthy and mutual love affair between Prince and Detroit. Mojo also debuted music by Detroit's techno pioneers, such as A Number of Names, Cybotron, Model 500, Rhythim Is Rhythim, and Inner City. Ken Collier was a DJ in Detroit most known for his nights at a club called Heaven in the 1970s, 1980s, and early 1990s. He was an integral member of Detroit's black gay house and disco scene. He mentored many young DJs and producers in Detroit and encouraged them in the 1970s and early 1980s to travel to New York City and Chicago to experience the music and intense energy of clubs like the Paradise Garage in New York, and the Musicbox and the Warehouse in Chicago. Detroiters who benefited from his mentoring include Delano Smith, John Collins, Kelli Hand, Felton Howard, Alan Ester, Stacey "Hotwaxx" Hale, and Duane "In the Mix" Bradley.

I would say that the gap between vocal music and electronic instrumental music is much smaller than at first glance. Much of Detroit's early electronic music included vocal lines, like A Number of Names' "Sharevari," much of the Cybotron and Model 500 catalogs, and Inner City. Even though techno is, at first glance, purely instrumental music, the use of lyrics in primarily robotic ways continued among Detroit producers in the 1990s with groups like Underground Resistance, Drexciya, and Dopplereffekt, in particular. The geographical gap between Europe and the U.S. is also much smaller than at first glance. Sound bridges that gap. Detroit and Chicago were fortunate to have people like radio disc jockeys and club DJs who had access to a wide range of music, had the resources to share it on a massively public scale, and who were dedicated to sharing all kinds of music from around the world to listeners.

How did early techno and house relate to disco, particularly given America's somewhat mixed feelings about disco (and perhaps discomfort with the culture that created it)?

There is a direct lineage from disco to techno and house music. Many techno and house-music producers grew up in the 1970s listening to disco alongside funk and rhythm & blues. Unfortunately, there is a lasting and powerful discomfort with disco in mainstream American culture, culminating at the famed Disco Demolition Night at Comiskey Park in Chicago on July 12, 1979. The discomfort with and active dislike of disco stems from homophobia and racism. People in attendance at the disco record burning describe the collection of records being destroyed that night as simply black records, funk, blues, rhythm & blues, as well as disco. The disco-sucks backlash was not simply about sound; it was a backlash about people, sexuality, and skin color as much as, if not more than, what was actually on those records. Detroit had an anti-disco group known as D.R.E.A.D., Detroit Rockers Engaged in the Abolition of Disco. They refer to themselves as "Detroit's non-violent anti-disco league." The D.R.E.A.D. membership card coupled with the Electrifying Mojo's Midnight Funk Association membership card makes for a humorous pairing.

Ken Collier played plenty of disco alongside funk, electro, italo, and other electronic dance music. Detroiters called all of this music progressive in the '70s and early '80s. It was also called garage, underground, and house in places like Chicago and New York City. After the national backlash against disco, people continued to love and listen to the music. They just did it in a much less visible way. It went underground again in clubs and morphed into other genres like techno and house.

What cultural climate helped give birth to this music in America?

I think there was a widespread willingness to hear something new. Major social and political change of the '60s and '70s was tapering off by the late 1970s and early 1980s. The social activism and optimism of the '60s, and violent rage and disappointment paralleled by continued activism in the 1970s, with respect to race, politics, war, affected people and communities around the United States and around the world in profound and lasting ways. Music continued through all of this change, progress, and struggle to inspire people and bring them together. In Detroit, after Berry Gordy and Motown left for Los Angeles in 1972, it seemed like there would be a cultural void. Certainly nothing like Motown ever took its place, but there are thriving pockets of culture and community in Detroit today; and sound, on a much smaller scale, inspires and brings people together in this hard city.

Simultaneously, analog electronic instruments and equipment were becoming more widely available around the United States throughout the 1980s. Young men and women in Detroit could go to music stores like Grinnell's in Detroit (Juan Atkins's grandmother would take him there when she needed new sheet music for church) and play around with synthesizers, sequencers, and drum machines. These instruments were affordable enough that some kids could ask their parents or grandparents to purchase them. Terrence Parker, an influential house music producer, DJ, and skilled turntablist from Detroit, asked his father to buy him turntables. His dad came home from the store with one, and Terrence graciously explained to his father that he indeed needed two; it was not a slip of the tongue, his father did not hear him wrong. Casio SK-1 synthesizers cost $100. Four-track tape decks were available and easier to acquire than two turntables. Plenty of youth in Chicago and Detroit figured out how to make music using a four-track cassette mixer, layering their own voice, singing or speaking, over multiple tracks of pre-recorded music.

As electronic dance music was in its infancy, people all over the United States were taking cues from new sounds that fed them in ways that nothing else could. In Detroit, there was a sizable African American middle class. Being middle class afforded them greater freedom to explore sounds and fashions from other parts of the world, Italy in particular. Some young entrepreneurs formed party promotion clubs, giving them names like Giavante and Charivari, and would host parties in nightclubs and halls around Detroit. In Chicago, gay clubs in which all people were welcome and the atmosphere was one of love, acceptance, and fun, as well as sex, fostered a musically and culturally innovative scene that continued to draw in musically inclined youth from around the city, gay and straight. New York City offered the same thing, although in much greater numbers. In all these urban scenes, musical creativity, openness, and innovation were a driving force that continues to influence people today, although in very different ways.

Artists like Juan Atkins also appear as futurists, a thread that with varying degrees of optimism seems to weave in and out of EDM. How has the conceptualization of the future related to the music's evolution? And what does that mean for a body of music whose principal aim, by definition, is dancing?

Futurism, looking ahead, outward, beyond whatever one's current reality is, has been a continuous tenet of electronic dance music. This music is definitely for dancing, but it is simultaneously intellectual in stunning ways. Electronic musicians are expressing themselves in primarily nonverbal ways through sound using highly technological equipment. In places like Chicago and Detroit, where life was often a struggle, violence, gangs, drugs, racism, homophobia, all of these things impacted young people of color in serious ways in the 1980s. For many, music was an escape. For musicians like Maurice Herd (Pirahnahead) and Marcellus Pittman, it was the only alternative they saw to trouble and danger in the streets.

> "Futurism, looking ahead, outward, beyond whatever one's current reality is, has been a continuous tenet of electronic dance music. For musicians like Maurice Herd (Pirahnahead) and Marcellus Pittman, it was the only alternative they saw to trouble and danger in the streets."
>
> —DENISE DELPHOND

Drexciya, a Detroit electro group formed by Gerald Donald and James Stinson in the early 1990s, was formed upon an extensive mythology. Drexciya was an underwater world, much like Atlantis, populated by descendants of pregnant enslaved African women thrown from slave ships. Themes behind Drexciyan songs often include water torture of white people. I can hear the water in their music—it's just beautiful. The violence and torture undertones are a bit harder to hear, but just as fascinating and strange.

If you had to characterize the different epochs of dance music, the major scenes, how would you do so? It seems starting in the '90s, there is an explosion of the microgenre unequaled today even despite greater access to online distribution.

I have a tendency to try to avoid using genre categories and quickly tire of microgenre divisions, sometimes to a fault! If I must characterize epochs, I would do it geographically and socially, more than sonically. Electronic dance music began in the United States in urban communities of color in the late 1970s and early 1980s, much of it without any kind of name at that point. It was relatively small, locally specific, and offered people an expression, a place to go, and a freedom that was unavailable in any other context. In the late 1980s, record collector Neil Rushton came to the U.S. in search of house music. Through Chicago, he was led to Detroit and in 1988 released *Techno! The New Dance Sound of Detroit*, which was a compilation featuring Juan Atkins, Derrick May, Kevin Saunderson, Anthony "Shake" Shakir, Blake Baxter, Eddie "Flashin'" Fowlkes, and Mike Banks. It was on this compilation that Juan Atkins decided at the last minute to call his track "Techno Music." That is the first public mention of the term *techno* in relation to electronic music from Detroit. The release of house and techno music in Europe initiated an explosion in the late 1980s of acid house and other forms of electronic music in clubs, at festivals, and at raves around Europe. Parties grew to enormous sizes, with thousands in attendance, and electronic dance music quickly became synonymous with drug use. Drugs were a part of electronic dance music cultures in Chicago, Detroit, and New York City during the 1970s and 1980s, but not in such widespread and extreme ways as in European, and soon American, rave culture. Young white suburban middle-class kids in the U.S. quickly picked up on the large-scale parties that were becoming popular in Europe and began throwing big old parties themselves. In the late 1980s and early 1990s, regional rave scenes developed around the United States. Many similarities existed between these regional scenes, but there were differences in terms of dress and musical taste. The Pacific Northwest, the Midwest, and New England/East Coast all had regionally specific ways of throwing raves. The Midwest rave culture of the 1990s often featured Detroit and Chicago DJs, who were influential techno and house producers. Richie Hawtin initiated Detroit with large-scale parties in the 1990s. Many local promoters and DJs began throwing these kinds of parties in and around Detroit in clubs, warehouses, and lofts. Groups like Voom, consisting of Eric Lynch, Alan Bogl, Mark Bitsche, and Steven Reaume, became major party promoters in Detroit during the 1990s. Similar types of parties occurred in Chicago. The primarily African American house and techno scenes in Chicago and Detroit of the 1980s were not replaced by raves. It all continued to exist, sometimes overlapping and intermingling, and occasionally mutually exclusive. There were parties held in warehouses in Detroit in the mid-'90s attended by mostly white middle-class kids from outside of the boundaries of Detroit proper at which the door entry was 25–35 dollars. Young African American kids living in the neighborhood where the party was being held could not afford to get into the party, or were sometimes denied access in the expressed interest of "safety." Detroit's 1990s party culture was not built on tenets of racism and exclusionary politics. Many of the events were filled with people from different ethnic backgrounds. However, because Detroit has a history with violence, gangs, drugs, and widespread poverty—and because its population consists mostly of people of color—race, ethnicity, and class prejudices cannot be ignored. The year 2000 marked gradual dying out of raves in Detroit, and the first year of the Detroit Electronic Music Festival. Carl Craig led the first two years of the festival as the artistic director. Derrick May and Kevin Saunderson each took a turn at running the festival. Since 2006, local event production company Paxahau has successfully organized the festival with increasing success in terms of attendance and production values.

It seems easy to name early pioneers in the music, harder, as in any history or musicology, to determine the likely impact of artists with more recency, robbed of foresight. But which artists would you say continue to make a dent in the larger culture in recent years? Which do younger artists appear to be following?

Seminal electronic musicians of the 2000s, in my opinion, would include the following people:

Todd Osborn (Osborne, Soundmurderer, Superstructure): Multigenre producer who makes funky house, jungle, and really exciting electronic beats as Superstructure. He also has a few piano-composition releases under his own name. He made and records with his own talkbox. He is a lecturer for Red Bull Music Academy.

Mike Huckaby: House music producer from Detroit. He was the primary dance-music buyer at Record Time in Detroit for fourteen years and often heralded by local producers and DJs as an incredible mentor. He teaches music production courses at a youth organization called Youthville Detroit.

Theo Parrish: Originally from Chicago, now calls Detroit home. He composes music as a sound sculptor, making very brain- and booty-stimulating music that I would be remiss to assign to a genre category! He is a very exciting DJ, pairing jazz with disco, hip hop, R&B, techno, house, and his own lengthy James Brown edits and other edits of rare funk and soul songs.

Marcellus Pittman: Still coming into his own as a producer, but only because he hasn't released much. His releases thus far have been inspiring and coveted, particularly *Unirhythm Green*. He DJs and produces mostly dark and deep house and electro. He is a member of the 3 Chairs with Kenny Dixon Jr., Theo Parrish, and Rick Wilhite.

Ectomorph (Erika Sherman and Brendan M. Gillen): Electro group from Detroit. Originally started by Brendan and Gerald Donald of Drexciya and Dopplereffekt. They use primarily analog gear: drum machines, sequencers, synthesizers. According to Brendan, Erika brings a unique approach to rhythm and tones in their compositions. She has an ear for non-Western scales and uses various "tunings" and scales in her productions. They perform live PA sets with Erika on synths and drum machines and Brendan using Ableton.

Flying Lotus: Young experimental and multigenre producer. In 2007 he joined Warp Records and has had multiple releases with them.

Mark Lawrence: Produces extremely influential dubstep as Mala. He and Dean Harris (Coki) produce as Digital Mystiks and run the label DMZ.

Anything from **Mark Ernestus** and/or **Moritz von Oswald**: This would include Rhythm & Sound, Basic Channel, Maurizio, Moritz von Oswald Trio with Carl Craig. Also related via the Hardwax record store in Berlin, founded and owned by Ernestus and Oswald; by Peter Kuschnereit and Rene Lowe and their group, Scion; and Monolake, related via the Chain Reaction record sublabel of Basic Channel.

Mark Pritchard: Produces under many aliases, including Harmonic 313, a Detroit-style hip-hop on Warp Records. Also produces as Global Communication with Tom Middleton. Together, they have most recently released an unmixed compilation with an exquisite selection of seminal techno tracks called *Back in the Box.*

Kenny Dixon Jr. (Moodymann, KDJ, Jan): Seminal Detroit producer and member of the 3 Chairs. He rarely does interviews and keeps to himself and Detroit. He is an excellent DJ, often educating his audiences with New Order, Prince, Newworldaquarium, and other more obscure funk and electronic music. His civic dedication to Detroit is impressive, with him giving back to his neighborhood regularly.

Red Bull Music Academy: A respected, reputable music academy sponsored by Red Bull, but without corporate micromanaging. It is an annual two-week educational event occurring at a different site around the world each year. In addition to their core of regular lecturers, they host lectures from influential musicians, instrument designers, DJs, record collectors, and others involved in the global electronic-music industry.

Robert O'Bryant (Waajeed): Detroit hip hop and electronic music artist. Began his career with J Dilla and Slum Village. Then formed Platinum Pied Pipers with Darnell "Saadiq" Bolden. He is a strong advocate of Detroit music and culture and seems to have serious plans for musical involvement with Detroit well into the future.

Harvey Bassett (DJ Harvey): Sometimes described as a disco-punk DJ, he plays wonderful disco edits, as well as house and garage. As a young man, he was a drummer for Cambridge punk band Ersatz. His most recent project is under the name Locussolos.

Tim Sweeney: DJ and radio host of *Beats in Space* (BIS) on WNYU. He has guests play music on his two-hour show every week and maintains an extensive archive of years of BIS to stream or download online. He is a choice selector, a DJ's DJ. My favorite is when he plays the whole show, which happens occasionally.

A topic for another book, perhaps, but I find in this genre more than others a thin selection of female artists whose careers have risen to the level of their male peers. Is there a glass ceiling on the dance floor? What other forces are at work? As a journalist, as I look at our selection of guys in this book, am I partly to blame?

I think journalists are absolutely to blame! However, the relative invisibility of women in electronic dance music depends on many other forces than just music writers. I certainly appreciate the opportunity to address this issue in the context of this volume. I have observed that in cultural scenes involving extensive cataloging of data and collection of artifacts, as with comic books and graphic novels, record stores, car culture, gaming, science fiction, and many other scenes, women feel excluded or out of place, whether or not we actually are. I have certainly felt disdain from comic-book-store clerks upon entering and looking for reading materials or games for my children. I have felt the same thing in record stores—that is, until I carried my selections up to the front counter. It can be discouraging to be a woman entering a male-centered environment like that and feel like we just don't belong. I have heard people in the music industry claim that after reaching adulthood, women stop seeking out music, or stop buying it altogether. I'm not sure how true that is, but electronic music is certainly not something that women are easily cultivated into. In my experience, men either assume you don't know anything, or think that your interest in music is hot and turn it into a sexual thing. There is certainly nothing wrong with the hotness, but it's much more enjoyable to be respected on the basis of what you know and who you are before it becomes sexual.

Some influential women in the electronic music industry, past and present, include the following producers and DJs: DJ Minx (Jennifer Witcher), Jennifer Xerri, Kelli Hand, Kate Simko, Erika Sherman, Jane Fitz, Syd the Kid, DJ Heather (Heather Robinson), Punisher (Michelle Herrmann), Theresa Hill, Stacey "Hotwaxx" Hale, and Liz Copeland. Also important to Detroit's electronic music culture are Zana Smith, event promoter and record/clothing store owner, and Angie Linder, owner and label manager for Detroit Techno Militia. Journalists Emma Warren and Geeta Dayal are wonderful writers and speakers; I soak up their words like a sponge.

As you've done your research, have there been any particular surprises? Struggles? Revelations?

I have had a number of revelations while conducting research in Detroit. My assumptions about the origins of this music have changed drastically from very simplistic to much more interesting and complex. I came here wanting to tell the story that Detroit techno was black music, and I assumed that everyone would agree with me. That was certainly not the case, even among African American musicians. The history of this music is much more interesting and complex than I originally imagined.

Frankie Knuckles.

4

Frankie Knuckles, Jesse Saunders, Farley "Jackmaster" Funk

THE FATHERS OF CHICAGO HOUSE

By Greg Rule || *Keyboard*, August 1997

ith "Disco sucks" emblazoned on every other T-shirt and car bumper in the early '80s, a core group of DJs, producers, and musicians bucked the trend and put dance music back on the map. Named for the Warehouse nightclub where Frankie Knuckles spun his way into history, house music took disco to the next level. Diva vocals and four-on-the-floor kicks survived the name change, but many of the live drum, bass, and horn lines gave way to drum machine- and synth-based tracks. "And when we couldn't get that feel with drum machines," says star DJ/producer Farley "Jackmaster" funk, "then we'd *sample* disco."

In addition to Frankie, Farley, and Jesse Saunders, pioneers such as Adonis, Tyree Cooper, Jeff Davis, Chip E., Ron Hardy, Andre Hatchett, Steve "Silk" Hurley, Marshall Jefferson, DJ Pierre, Jamie Principle, Ten City, and Wayne Williams (to name a few) all played historic roles in taking house from a small club to the world. Many of the above are featured in *Chicago Reunion*, a new compilation CD due out this summer on Jesse Saunders's Broken Records label. "The release date for the album is July 8, 1997," says Jesse, "and the tour starts with a special tribute during the *Billboard* Dance Music Summit, and a release party at the Convent club in Chicago where most of the participants of the album will perform."

Today the Warehouse is long gone, but the music it birthed still fuels dance floors across the planet. And like other established genres, house has spawned a family of sub-styles: deep house, hip-house, acid house, garage, handbag . . . the list goes on.

With the *Reunion* CD and tour just days away, *Keyboard* knew it was time to pay tribute to a few of those legendary musicmakers. Not an encyclopedia of house music, this article aims to hit a few key points in the evolution of the scene and reveal a few tips and tricks about how the artists made, and continue to make, their music. So with no further ado, here are three of house music's founding fathers: Frankie Knuckles, Jesse Saunders, and Farley "Jackmaster" Funk.

FRANKIE KNUCKLES

Frankie Knuckles and the Warehouse nightclub were to Chicago House what the Grateful Dead and Haight-Ashbury were to the San Francisco psychedelic scene. Chicago was the birthplace of the genre, and Frankie was smack dab in the heart of it. "When I moved to Chicago in '77," he tells us, "I was playing a lot of the Philly soul stuff, and disco was really big at that point. At the time, Chicago didn't have any other after-hours clubs like the Warehouse. The Warehouse was a lot like the Garage [in New York City]—a big after-hours club, no alcohol."

Disco was still booming in '77, but mainstream perceptions changed a few years later. "When all those people claimed that disco was dead, it didn't really affect me at the Warehouse, except that there weren't too many disco or dance records being put out anymore. You either had down-tempo, heavy soul or country/western." But perhaps it was a blessing in disguise, because the disco drought motivated Frankie to start remixing tracks. "I found myself having to rely on fewer records, and if I liked them, I had to completely re-edit them or rework them to make them work on my dance floor. There were records coming out that were okay, but they just didn't have enough punch to get my dance floor interested."

With tape and a razor blade, Frankie started splicing together new versions of songs in 1979, strategically cutting in breakbeats from other records. Low-tech, yet very effective. "Frankie was phenomenal with that tape stuff," says Farley "Jackmaster" Funk (whom you'll hear more from later). And the Warehouse wasn't the only club to hear Frankie's custom tracks; he took the tapes on tour with him, as well, fast gaining recognition for his custom mixes.

Frankie would soon raise his productions to the next level, incorporating original synth and drum-machine tracks. "The single most important instrument that signified the house sound, in my opinion, was and is the Roland [TR-] 909. It set the standard at the time, and it's still being used. It's pretty much a staple in what I do at Def Mix, working with Satoshi [Tomiie], David [Morales], and Terry Burris."

Speaking of Def Mix, Frankie says the team now has its system down to a science. "It's great, because having worked with them for so many years, they pretty much know me. Satoshi has tagged all these sounds in the library that are my sounds, so if it's gonna be a writing day, for example, he knows exactly what to go for, and he'll have everything up and ready for when I get there. These days, to get the basic tracks down, it usually only takes us a couple of hours."

As producer, songwriter, and remixer, Frankie's discography reads like a Who's Who: Michael Jackson, Elton John, Neville Brothers, Diana Ross, Toni Braxton, Quincy Jones, Chaka Khan, En Vogue, Lisa Stansfield, Patti Labelle, Ace of Base, Janet Jackson, Luther Vandross, Pet Shop Boys, and on and on. Be on the lookout for his work on *Blood on the Dancefloor*, a new remix CD of Michael Jackson singles.

Even though Frankie Knuckles is one of the most sought-after dance producer/remixers on the planet, he still has his heart in clubland. "The club is paramount," he stresses. "Without that forum, it would be very difficult for me to write the kind of music that I do. Being able to test it on the dance floor . . . that's the one thing I really get off on: turning the audience on to something new that I've done."

> "A lot of these dance records coming out today are done by bedroom producers. But back then, it was all different. I didn't have the technology, for one. I had a razor blade, a Pioneer reel-to-reel, and spools and spools of recording tape."
>
> —FRANKIE KNUCKLES

Comparing the past to the present, he has encouraging news for startup dance music artists. "With technology, anybody can set up a studio in their house now, and do it all from there. A lot of these dance records coming out today are done by bedroom producers. But back then, it was all different. I didn't have the technology, for one. I had a razor blade, a Pioneer reel-to-reel, and spools and spools of recording tape."

To learn more about Mr. Knuckles, we recommend starting on the Web. Frankie's official Web site is still a work in progress, but there are plenty of others worth checking out in the meantime. A standard "Frankie Knuckles" search should get you going. Also, next time you're in the Big Apple, you might catch him at Carbon, the club he just launched with David Morales on 55th Street, or on Friday nights at Club Deep on West 28th.

JESSE SAUNDERS

He's known as the first artist to press a house single ("On and On"), but long before Jesse Saunders made a name for himself as a top DJ and recording artist, he was paying dues in the form of piano lessons and sock-hop gigs. Inspired by his musical friends and family (including stepbrother Wayne Williams), Jesse began dabbling in remixes early on. "I'd take my cassette deck," he explains, "put something on, record it for a minute, pause it, cut something in, record something else, cut another thing in, and what I'd end up with were these really cool extended versions. So I started playing those at parties, and they were an instant success."

Things heated up in 1978 when Jesse and Wayne "went down to the Warehouse to see Frankie Knuckles play. I was underage, but I got in. And once I heard that music, it was like, 'What is this?' Because at the time, we were all into the whole gamut from Fleetwood Mac to James Brown and in between, but not disco. When we heard that music, though, it was, 'Okay, this is what we're gonna take to the masses.'"

With disco fast becoming taboo, not everyone was receptive to the new generation of dance music. "Eventually, though," says Jesse, "people who were more progressive, and who saw how free the music was, started getting into it. People were having a good time, and from there it was a snowball effect. By 1979–80, it was the big thing to do. It was the cool thing to be into. And that's when we started calling it the 'house scene' . . . short for the Warehouse."

In the early '80s, Jesse dropped an anchor in Chicago's Playground nightclub. "Chicago was a very segregated city," he says, "and this was probably the first time people from all sides—north, south, east, and west—came together under one roof. It was during this time, and playing all these different styles, that I started using a drum machine [Roland TR-808]. I'd let it play along with the tracks, then I'd mix it in and out, let it run by itself, and start mixing stuff in and out. Also, Jive used to put out these break records with different drumbeats and things, and they had some that would segue from, like, 120 bpm all the way up to 140 or 150. So I'd use that to get way up to speed, then I'd bring it back down to a hip-hop feel, or whatever. I mean, I was playing everything: Men Without Hats, you name it."

One of Jesse's secret weapons back then was a white-label B-side that had snippets of classic bass lines, horn riffs, vocals, and the like, which he incorporated into his set. But when the record vanished one day, "I decided to make my own version. So I bought a keyboard." A Korg Poly 61 for $600, to be precise, which made an excellent companion to his Roland 808, 606, and 303 setup. With said gear, Jesse recorded his way into house history with songs such as "On and On," "Fantasy," "I'm the DJ," "Funk You Up," "Real Love," and many others. Says Jesse: "'On and On' was first released on my label Jes Say Records in January of 1984." And as for the hits "It's OK" and "Love Can't Turn Around," Jesse tells us he "co-produced the songs with Farley ['Jackmaster' Funk], played all the instruments, did all the arrangements, and wrote in collaboration with Vince Lawrence."

Speaking of Farley, the Jackmaster told us that "Jesse was one of the most talented black DJs there was on the circuit at the time. And he knew how to make music because not only could he play keyboards, he could sing. And that's an important point: If you really listen to everybody's music who came out of Chicago, there was only one original person in the beginning of house music, and that was Jesse. He used to make all his own new bass lines and stuff like that, see. And us—me and Steve ['Silk' Hurley] and all of us—we stole 'Let No Man Put Asunder' a million times. We went down a note. We went up a note. We transposed it. But Jesse was putting on his own original bass lines, lyrics, and melodies. He was definitely a serious influence."

> "Chicago was a very segregated city, and this was probably the first time people from all sides—north, south, east, and west—came together under one roof."
>
> —JESSE SAUNDERS

Today, Jesse has accumulated enough songwriting, production, and remix credits to fry a fax machine, but the impending *Chicago Reunion*, a project he spearheaded and executive-produced, stands to rate among his proudest accomplishments. "The idea came when I was writing my book [House Music . . . The Real Story], because I was hooking back up with everybody: Marshall, Tyree, everybody. And so I thought, 'It would be a great idea to do a reunion album, because it's been 13 years since the beginning of this thing.'" Not an album of remakes, *Chicago Reunion* is "representative of what everybody is doing now. I'd like to do a classics album later, but this is about what's happening today.

"After all these years," he continues, "this is the first time that all of us, in any way, shape, or form, have actually gotten together to do anything. And I thought it would be a great idea to show everyone that we've matured, that we can work together, and that there's unity. We're gonna give you a slice of the past, but 1997 style. That's what this album is all about."

RON HARDY REMEMBERED: A TRIBUTE TO THE MAN WHO BROUGHT THE MUSIC TO THE BOX

BY TERRY HUNTER AND STACY MILLER

It's very important when writing about the history of house music to mention the man who really got the music moving in Chicago at the Music Box: Ron Hardy, who passed away in the early '90s. Ron gave many of our house heroes their first spin on the turntables, such as Marshall Jefferson, Chip E., LnR [Larry Thompson and Rick Lenoir], Adonis, Larry Heard, and Robert Owens, to name a few. The Music Box was originally located at 1632 S. Indiana before it moved to its most famous location at 326 N. Michigan, lower level. This was made famous because of its 72-hour marathon parties where Ron would spin, and always had a packed dance floor. Ron was one of the first to experiment with edited versions of the hottest disco classics and was known for playing records backward when the vibe was right. Ron did only what he truly felt no matter what the situation, and he was praised for it. Praised so much that the term "All Right Ronny" because a catchphrase. Ron was truly a DJ pioneer, and there is no question that he paved the way for house music in Chicago. Ron, we love you, we miss you, and thank you for the inspiration.

Today Jesse keeps a high profile both in the club (he's the resident DJ on the second Friday of each month at the Convent in Chicago) and on the airwaves. "I do a radio show every week in Europe on EVO Sonic Radio—the world's first and only all-electronic music radio station. It's called the *Global House Show* and it's broadcast all over Europe via Satellite Astra 1a, Transponder 13, on Saturday mornings from 10 a.m. to 2 p.m. [Greenwich mean time]. I rebroadcast portions of the show [*The Real Story History Mix*] on Groove Radio in Los Angeles, and KDNR in Albuquerque, and we're picking up affiliates in syndication every day."

FARLEY "JACKMASTER" FUNK

Renowned for his breakthrough radio show on Chicago's WBMX radio, and also for his own house tracks (especially for his chart-topping spin on Isaac Hayes's "Love Can't Turn Around" called "I Can't Turn Around"), Farley "Jackmaster" Funk did more than stir the local waters—he was a major force in turning the global tide for house music.

No overnight sensation, Farley worked his way to the top from ground zero—roadying for Jesse Saunders in the early days, for example, because "I was hungry to be a DJ," Farley tells us. "I was so intrigued, I would do almost anything to be in the presence of Jesse and the music . . . I would carry his records, hang posters, hand out fliers. And I liked the girls, of course [*laughs*]. The two went hand in hand."

Farley took the early inspiration he received from the likes of Saunders and DJ Kenny "Jammin'" Jason straight into the woodshed. "Kenny did things with records . . . he was just phenomenal. Listening to him do mixes, I couldn't believe the way he could blend records and stuff. So one of the ways I learned how to DJ was . . . my mom had a record player at home, and if you turned the knob in between FM and PHONO, you could hear the radio and the turntable at the same time. So what I would do is get the same exact record he [Kenny] was playing, put it on the turntable, and try to find the exact same part of the record he had it at. That's how I learned to flange before I even learned how to mix or scratch."

Years of practicing paid off. "The elements that gave me my own identity were the fact that I could scratch and [unlike almost every other house DJ at the time] I would talk over the microphone and hype up the crowd. God bless, that really got me on the scene." By 1978, Farley's star was rising fast around Chicago. First calling himself "Marvelous Farley," he later dropped the 'Marvelous" and became known as "Farley Keith." When he won the annual Battle of the DJs competition later that year, "It really inserted me into the scene." Farley went on to win numerous DJ battles, in fact.

By 1981, Farley was a certified celebrity DJ in Chicago—not only on the club and party circuits, but on the airwaves, as well. "It was Kenny Jason, God bless him, who helped me get onto WBMX, and that's what really catapulted this whole house thing to the level that it is today. We had the highest demographics ever in the history of Chicago radio. I was playing to 3.5 million people with a hot mix show. And we were breaking all kinds of color barriers because the 'Hot Mix Five' were three white guys, a black, and a Hispanic" [Kenny "Jammin'" Jason, Mickey "Mixin'" Oliver, Scott "Smokin'" Seals, Farley, and Ralphi "Rockin'" Rosario].

Farley also put out his own music during the period, and with minimal gear. "The second-biggest record I ever had was 'House Nation,' and I made that on a 4-track." His instruments of choice at the time were a Korg Poly-800, a LinnDrum, and a Roland TR-808. And when it came time to sell the records, he had a built-in audience. "The thing for me was, since I had 3.5 million people listening to me, every time I played a track . . . I didn't know it in the beginning, but I was making people money. So what I did was, I started playing my own records. And I didn't want to toot my own horn too much, but when I did, I *tooted* it. [*Laughs.*] This is how deep it was: When I played my own track, I could walk into a store the next day, and the people would be lined up to buy it. I could get rid of, like, 3,500 records in Chicago alone, just by playing it one time in a mix."

Regarding his biggest hit, "Love Can't Turn Around," Farley tells us it was the first house track to hit number one in England, an achievement he's obviously proud of. But he also wants to set the record straight about what went on behind the scenes. "For over ten years," says Farley, "the press has given me credit for 'Love Can't Turn

JESSE SAUNDERS ON HOUSE SUBGENRES

If you don't know hip-house from handbag, or deep from acid, here's a quick overview courtesy of Jesse Saunders. But first, a word to the wise. "My summation of all this," says Jesse, "is that it's *all* house music. People want to put it into certain categories, and that's fine, but really it's all house music."

Deep House: "Deep house is classics—classic disco music or new songs that sound like the classics."

Handbag: "A softer version of house. They call it 'handbag' because all the women would carry their handbags and dress a certain way when they went out to these clubs."

Acid House: "A way-out, crazy type of house. Heavy on the [Roland TB-] 303 filter sound."

Garage: "This is a term that New Yorkers gave to their style of house music. Back in the disco days, Larry Levan was one of the first guys to start playing house music at the Garage in New York."

Hip-House: "A combination of rap and house. And lots of samples behind it."

Euro: "Very hard, very electronic, very repetitious-type stuff. Fast and hypnotic."

Jesse also gave us his definitions of "techno" ("an industrial or harder, synthetic form of house"), "drum 'n' bass" ("fast-paced, 140bpm or higher, and an almost hip-hop style with heavy bass lines and frenetic snares"), and "trance" ("just what the name implies, it puts you in a trance").

Around' since it was my name on it. But the actual truth is that Jesse Saunders had an equal [writing and production] role in that song."

By 1982, the Playground nightclub opened with the names Frankie Knuckles and Jesse Saunders on the marquee. But Farley says he was soon inserted into the Friday and Saturday evening slot—a position he held from '82 to '85. "Because I was on the radio," he adds, "we drew people into the Playground of all creeds and colors."

In the mid-'80s, Farley changed names again, this time to Farley "Jackmaster" Funk. But it stuck. "I changed it to 'Jackmaster' because . . . Steve 'Silk' Hurley, a close friend of mine, came to me and said, 'I'm fixin' to change my name from Steve Hurley to Steve 'Jackmaster' Hurley.' Steve was blown' up on the radio at the time; people loved his mixes. But, to make a long story short, I was infamous for making a sound called 'Jack' in about four or five successful records that I had out. It was in a deep voice, and I would go [*he roars*] 'Jaaaack!' And I would sample it. So when Steve told me he was gonna take that name, I was like, 'You can't do that, 'cause I'm the Jackmaster.'" Farley proceeded to race to the station and, just minutes before Hurley was set to take the airwaves, announced his new name to the listeners. "I was on the hour before Steve, and I know he was listening to my mix when he was driving to the station. We he heard that, I think he almost hit a pole [*laughs*]. And I'm still sorry for taking the name today."

That competition paled in comparison to what happened in the late '80s, though. When Farley left WBMX and moved across town to rival station WGCI, WBMX hired none other than Frankie Knuckles to fill Farley's spot.

Today, Farley is still on the radio at WGCI, and still making tracks, but his message has changed. "I'm a born-again Christian now, so it's a struggle for me to do secular music. All I really want to do is make music for the praise of God at this point, but to do it in a house kind of way."

And may the big man bless you for doing it, Farley.

Juan Atkins.

5

Juan Atkins

JUAN ATKINS: TECHNO STARTS HERE

By Robert Doerschuk || *Keyboard*, July 1995

Back in June '82, *Keyboard* published a cover story on something we called "the new synthesizer rock." Artists like Depeche Mode, Gary Numan, Soft Cell, and Orchestral Manouvres in the Dark were stripping rhythm down to the basics and playing spare synth lines in chilly timbres. Vocals in these bands hovered in the baritone depths, a league or two below Jon Anderson's boy-soprano range. The whole thing sounded kind of grim, but at least it was fresh, and perhaps as much of a tonic to what had preceded it as punk was shred to guitar.

Important as the story was, we didn't understand how big it would become within in just a few years. We noted the influence of disco on these acts, but the differences between the largely British and African American styles seemed to concern us more than the potential for crossover: "Although the ideology [of disco] hasn't much relevance to the young synth rockers, they are children of a radio era that has saturated the airwaves . . . with disco's pulse."

What we didn't know was that funk and synth-based new music was already finding common ground somewhere outside of Detroit. There, a teenager named Juan Atkins was puzzling out ways of infusing electronic music with the kind of energy that dance-oriented R&B bands generated with real-time musicians. Along with a friend named Rick Davis, who called himself 3070, Atkins formed Cybotron, a duo dedicated to amplifying the ideas of Alvin Toffler and other futurist writers through music. Later, expanded to a threesome with Jon-5, they put out a collection of tunes that Fantasy later released on the album *Clear*.

These early works borrowed heavily from European techno-pop, especially Kraftwerk; the title track on *Clear* echoes a string synth motif from "Trans-Europe Express." But over time, through working with different collaborators and growing more sophisticated with the tools of his trade, Atkins developed a more original vision. His tempos sped up, with more intricate interplay between elements of the rhythm track and the synth. As early as the mid-'80s, Atkins was using sounds familiar to Soft Cell fans in instrumental works that stretched far beyond traditional structure: Recording under the name Model 500, he cut "The Chase" in '86, with percussion and comp parts adding a funky feel never explored by British synthesists. Even earlier, in '85, his "No UFOs" used the kind of high-register syncopated figure, quick bass-drum kicks, and minor-mode theme—Bb–E–Db–E over an Eb-minor chord—that defined the sound soon known to the world as techno.

In any number of ways, techno revolutionized pop music. It brought the do-it-yourself ethic of studio-based synth music down to the trenches and offered young artists an alternative to garage bands. Like punk and other high-energy movements, it came up from the clubs, not down from record-label boardrooms. It permutated quickly; when Atkins took "No UFOs" to Chicago's Powerplant, along with his Roland TR-909, DJ Frankie Knuckles picked up on his energy and helped launch the house music movement. Tapes by Cybotron, Model 500, and other Detroit artists—Derrick May, Kevin Saunderson, Kenny Larkin—became a launching pad for ambient house, deep house, and myriad other machine-based dance/trance styles.

Though each of these variations is distinct, all are clearly connected to the ideas pioneered by Atkins some 15 years ago. Yet, as an after-effect of techno's alternative roots, he is little known to people outside the industry. Other members of our 12 Who Count gang—Bob Moog, Little Richard, Jimmy Smith—enjoy some degree of notoriety. Atkins, though celebrated on the club circuit, remains an enigma to the public at large. Yet, as much as anyone else in this series, he has had a permanent impact on the way keyboard music is played.

It's not easy to find Atkins's material. Although he does have vinyl singles and EPs available on his Metroplex label, nothing is out under his own name, and much of what he's working on now isn't intended for U.S. release; the new Model 500 album, *Deep Space*, is out only on the Belgian label RNS. Yet it's hard to find any dance record that owes nothing to him. Even as techno spreads and dilutes across the face of mainstream music, echoes of Atkins's techno innovations embed themselves into the cultural consciousness of our time.

How would you explain techno music to musicians from a more traditional orientation?

Maybe the best way to address that would be to say that this whole movement started as the techno—short for "technology"—movement. That says that technology, within the past ten years, has enabled a lot of people to make music who maybe ten years ago would not have been able to. It's not a bad thing, because music is sound. If something sounds pleasing to the ear, then what does it matter how much technical skill the person has who produced the sound? If it touches you, then the technical skill doesn't matter.

Were you a keyboard player as a kid?

I learned something about scales, chords, things like that. I'm not a virtuoso, but I learned enough to have a basic concept about music.

Did you play a lot of live gigs?

I was born in '62, so I was around before a lot of this technology, and I definitely had ambitions to make music even before I ever touched a synthesizer. The synthesizer wasn't commercially viable for me until maybe the late '70s. So I was playing with garage bands when I was 13 or 14 years old.

What instrument did you play?

Some drums. Mainly bass guitar. I played with all the neighborhood guys up and down the block. I was in that phase where you had to get four or five people together to make music. I had a taste of that world before making the transition into technology.

When did you realize that you wanted to make that transition?

It was just one of those things where it wasn't so much a conscious decision as a natural progression. I'm usually very open-minded to things. I'm so into music that

I'll take notice of any innovation or progression really quickly. If something touches me, I tend to go with my feelings. So many people really don't trust their instincts; they'll find themselves saying, "I have a feeling that I should have done this," when they should have just followed their feelings in the first place. But a lot of people are used to doing certain things. Maybe they've invested a lot of time and energy in learning one way of doing something. When something new comes along, they tend not to accept it because they spent a lot of time doing it another way. It's the same thing with people who still don't want to accept computers in their office or want to keep doing things without technology.

Did you listen much to the early popular synthesists, like Wendy Carlos?

Yeah, and Isao Tomita, Synergy, stuff like that. It was interesting but, for me, kind of in the background. I didn't pay too much attention to it, but because I was into electronics I was cognizant of it.

Did you have a sense that this technology would apply to what you would someday do with your music?

Yes and no. A lot of things happened without a lot of planning.

Were you listening to people like Soft Cell, the Human League, and early Depeche Mode?

Yeah, I listened to that. Devo, B-52s. Even Grace Jones: "Warm Leatherette," "Love Is a Drug," stuff like that. Of course, Parliament/ Funkadelic. Stevie Wonder, to a certain degree. James Brown.

These people used music technology to very different degrees.

Yeah. Even Funkadelic, in the early days, didn't have a lot of technology. The synthesizer didn't come in until the stuff they started making after 1975.

What was your first actual contact with a synthesizer?

There used to be a store in Detroit called Grinnell's. It was sort of like a department store for music, really geared to the consumer. They sold, like, the first preset organs that came out, with the rhythm buttons where you pressed "Bossa Nova" or "Waltz" and it played that for you, and you pressed "A Chord" and it would play an A chord for you. But in the back room, at some cubbyhole deep into the store, you'd find the electric guitars, the amps, and the mixers. That's where they eventually put the synthesizers. The first one I saw there was a Korg MS-10. I was instantly fascinated by it. Being into music and messing around with various instruments from an early age, I would go down every weekend just to mess around with this thing in Grinnell's, hour after hour.

> "I'm so into music that I'll take notice of any innovation or progression really quickly. If something touches me, I tend to go with my feelings."
>
> —JUAN ATKINS

Specifically, what drew you to it?

It was the idea of being able to create sounds that had not existed. Since I was kind of spacey anyway and into science fiction, it was the perfect thing for me. I was always into spaceships landing and taking off. When the synthesizer came, it put those imagined sounds into reality.

Did you buy that Korg?

Eventually I saved up enough money and did enough wheeling and dealing to get one.

What did you do with it after taking it home?

By this time, we had moved to Belleville, which was a suburb of Detroit. It was a lot quieter there, and the neighbors were a lot farther apart. People who were doing anything with dance music or R&B or funk were especially few and far between, so I found myself in my room a lot, doing experiments on my own. When I was in Detroit, there were guitar players, bass players, and drummers everywhere. In one block you'd find two or three people who played either bass or guitar. But in Belleville, the closest guy I could do something with was two miles away. I'd have to make an appointment a week in advance to get everybody together at the same time. One could make it one day, but another guy couldn't make it. It got kind of frustrating, because, if you're really serious, music is like a partnership. These people have to be almost like your brother or sister. If you really have a determination and a drive for music, you don't need somebody telling you, "Well, I can't make it to the rehearsal, because I promised my girlfriend that I would go out to the movies with her on Wednesday." So eventually I found myself saying, "Okay, I'll try to do this on my own, as much as I can." It was one of those things where you look at the situation, you make an assessment, and you go with your gut feeling.

How did you use the MS-10?

I'd ping-pong stuff with two Kenwood cassette machines and a little Yamaha mixer. I'd just do overdubs.

How did you create drum sounds?

With noise. I'd close the filter to the point where I had enough resonance to get it right. You could get something that sounded pretty realistic.

Was Kraftwerk a big influence at that point?

I had already been experimenting and dabbling with the synthesizer before I heard Kraftwerk. The funny thing about it was that when I heard them, they were using some of the same sounds I had been making on this MS-10. It made me freeze in my tracks. Coming from Germany, these guys were like a world away. In fact, at that time, it was almost like coming from another planet. But they were using the same sounds I was. And they were so precise! I didn't really have any knowledge of sequencers at that time. I was barely grasping the synthesizer, so I didn't have any clue about the concept of sequencing. I had read certain things about sequencers, but they were never in layman's terms to tell you exactly what they did, like "store notes and play back notes," or how you put the notes in: "Set by a predetermined step pattern." Instead, you'd look on the back of a Giorgio Moroder album and see that he used a [Roland] MC-500 Digital Microcomposer. They didn't refer to it as a sequencer; they gave it this big technical term.

Well, what does that mean for somebody who doesn't know anything? That tells me that I have to go take computer classes and study data processing. Now, taking a data processing class is not going to tell you anything about sequencing. But this is what I thought I needed, because of this language. So when I heard Kraftwerk, of course that's what they were using, but I didn't know how they were making these notes so precise. My thing was really raggedy by comparison. I didn't have the ability to make my notes fall precisely where they were supposed to fall. It was electronic and it was weird, but nothing was too precise.

Of course, you wanted to do something different with your groove than they were doing with theirs.

Yeah. I had my funk and dance thing.

Doesn't it seem ironic that many of today's synth artists are using technology to subvert the kind of precision you're talking about and introduce "feel factor" into their grooves?

It's good that the option is there, if that's what you want. But if you want a live drum sound and feel, get a live drummer. That's why I didn't like the LinnDrum when it came out: It sounded too much like real drums. My thing is, if you're going to buy an electronic drum computer, you want it to sound that way.

So your approach is still to make everything as tight as you can.

Yeah, but everything in the old days tended to stay straight up because we were just happy to get it all working. As people master this technology, of course they'll want to put more of their feeling into it. That's natural, and I don't see anything wrong with it. But for electronic music, while I don't have a problem with putting a human feel to it, I don't like using technology to make music that sounds acoustic. That doesn't really make sense.

While all this was happening, you were going to Belleville High School with two other important techno pioneers, Derrick May and Kevin Saunderson.

Yeah. Derrick is a year younger than me, and Kevin is two or three years younger. But I made my first record in '81, and Derrick didn't make his first record until '87. He was my friend, but he was into sports. He was playing football and looking at scouting reports and scholarships. That was his thing; my thing was that I was studying scales and what-have-you. When I graduated from high school, I went directly to community college, and that's where I met Rick Davis. He bridged the gap of knowledge I needed about sequencers, because he was really advanced in that area. He already had a couple of sequencers and a roomful of synthesizers. All I had was this little MS-10.

What kind of gear did he have?

He had an ARP Odyssey, an ARP Axxe, the first Roland sequencer, and the Roland RS-09 string machine. At that point, though, Rick was really isolated. This was a time when everybody was still wanting to get together and jam. The disco thing was going out, and R&B was coming in. It felt stale. But Rick had mastered the art of doing his own demos, so when he heard one of my tapes, he invited me over. We got together, came up with Cybotron, and did our first record, *Alleys of Your Mind*, which we released on our own label. It was good to play off of Rick's ideas. Some of my better works have come as a result of that kind of collaboration. In fact, one of the biggest records I had on my Metroplex label was *Technicolor*, which was a collaboration between myself and a guy named Doug Craig; because it was me and him, we went under the name Channel One instead of Model 500.

Was it hard to find a place for those early Cybotron tapes?

We didn't have any trouble at all. It's funny how everything hit at the right time. There was a DJ here called Electrifyin' Mojo. He helped make it an instant hit here, although we didn't have national distribution, so we weren't able to push it outside of Detroit. Our idea was that Kraftwerk was really different but there probably weren't enough elements in their music to interface with the R&B or the funk audience. You did have Parliament/Funkadelic, which changed the face of R&B during that period; they were doing something different, but it wasn't different enough. It was my job to bridge the gap between those two styles.

How did you evolve from a sound that was somewhat derivative of Kraftwerk to define the style now recognized as techno?

One of the main impacts on that came simply from the evolution of music technology. Back in the early '80s, you didn't have a lot of polyphonic keyboards, and those that were around cost so much that they were out of reach. If you wanted polyphony on a keyboard, you had to buy something like an RS-09, and that only gave you a string sound. You couldn't make a UFO land on a chord or something like that. So a lot of it was a question of limited technology. I mean, we couldn't even save sounds back then. The sound would vary from day to day.

Even if you wrote down your patch configuration, somehow it never seemed the same each time you set it up.

Yeah, and that was really tedious. What we recorded in the studio never came out like what it was when we had conceived it at home. We would just cross our fingers and hope it would come out better. So as the technology progressed, the music definitely progressed, as well.

To cite one specific example, the hi-hats on some of your early work fell into patterns that seem much simpler than the kind of hi-hat work you did on, say, "Jazz Is the Teacher," with its subtle shifts between swing and techno.

Well, back in the early days, everything was still a novelty, so we didn't think so much about swinging or doing intricate patterns. We were still just learning. The emphasis wasn't so much on details as on, "Let's see if we can get this stuff synced up" [*laughs*]. I mean, we were happy to get any kind of drumbeat down.

That's interesting, since you only used hardware sequencers, especially the Korg SQD-1, for a long time.

But, you know, it was a nightmare before MIDI came in. MIDI didn't actually get going real well until, like, '84. The first MIDI systems had a lot of bugs. In '83, when they introduced MIDI, certain manufacturers weren't working with other manufacturers. You didn't have universal channel selection: Certain keyboards only transmitted on channel one, while other keyboards only received on channel one. It took a while for everybody to get on the same page.

Are you doing software sequencing now?

I'm just beginning to get into it. It's hard for me to ignore it any longer. There are positives and negatives to it, and one of the negatives is the fact that because I was into sequencing at such an early stage, a lot of the first computer-based sequencers just made me mad. I had a Commodore 64 and, man, I almost threw that thing out of the window a couple of times. It would lock up from time to time, and that was because the software was so primitive. In those days, I didn't have the knowledge to save every five minutes. I'd work for a couple of hours before I decided to save, so if something happened, I would lose all that work.

What computer are you using now?

I've got a Macintosh, but I'm still kind of using my [Roland] MC-50. It does the trick for what I need it to do, but I also work with a lot of other things on the Model 500 album I'm doing now. I did about 80 percent of the album in Berlin, and the way I got into it without getting into it was that I would use the engineer to run the software. Even with the software getting better, a person still has to go through four or five steps just to play back an eight-bar track and have it loop. With a dedicated sequencer, you play it in there, you reset it, and it plays back.

So why get into computers at all?

Because I see the advantages. There's a lot of tedious things you have to do, but the possibilities of what you can do have become really powerful within the past three or four years. I can't get away from that anymore. The technology is out there in abundance, and more people are learning to do things with it. So I have to stay competitive.

What's your observation on how techno has changed the kinds of preset sounds you hear in synthesizers these days?

It's had a big impact, but that's not necessarily a good thing. The thing about having presets is that some people tend not to look past them. They don't realize that there's ten thousand other guys with those same presets. If they don't take the time to get past the presets, their sound isn't gonna be any different from what you hear on other records. One of the things about the people in Detroit is that we got into the synthesizer. Our idea was to take the time to get in there. We got things out of the Yamaha DX100 that nobody else did. Because I was into synthesis before these presets, I never could accept using the presets. I mean, I'm a synthesist. The whole concept behind that is to synthesize sounds. If you're just going to punch up a preset, you're not really synthesizing.

"It was the idea of being able to create sounds that had not existed. I was always into spaceships landing and taking off. When the synthesizer came, it put those imagined sounds into reality."

−JUAN ATKINS

Do you still prefer the kind of control over the sound that earlier synths gave you?

The parameter thing got to me for a while, but I can take my time and deal with newer things because there's a lot that digital and FM brought to the table that wasn't available on the analog sound. You can get some fantastic sounds out of the DX100 that you just can't get out of a Moog.

The DX100 has only four operators. Didn't that make it harder to program than the DX7?

That's a perfect example of less being more. Somehow, with only four operators, the DX100 sounded fatter than the DX7. You had fewer areas to manipulate, but the bass sounds were fat, and the lead sounds, man, you couldn't even get on the DX7. You could set a DX100 next to a DX7, and people in Detroit would choose the DX100.

What kind of sampler do you use?

I use Akai. I haven't needed to go beyond the S900, because I don't really sample a lot. If I do, it's gonna be just for the sound, not the pattern, the pass, or whatever.

You never were interested in lifting sounds from records or using found sounds?

No. Being an artist, I don't like the idea of people using bits and pieces of my record to make their record. By the same token, I wouldn't do it to them. I don't think the sampler was made for that purpose. You take the time to get into these things and learn to be creative.

Typically, what kinds of samples would you use?

One thing about samplers is that some of their sounds are a lot fatter than what you get on synthesizers. That's the main reason I got into samplers. They had a lot of drum sounds that you just couldn't get straight from a drum machine. Of course, it fascinated me to sample my voice saying "hello" and play that up and down the keyboard. It's like a toy.

How do you feel about the impact techno made on Europe?

It was kind of devastating. It kind of came out of left field. I mean, now those places in Europe don't seem that far away, because I've been there so many times. But at the time it started happening, it seemed so far removed that I couldn't even anticipate that kind of reaction, so it was definitely a pleasant surprise.

What's your take on all the permutations of techno that have come down over the past ten years—ambient, acid, and so on?

That's a result of the U.K. They tend to be kind of trendy, and I don't mean that in a bad way. They're always looking for something to move on to. One thing about the U.K. is that people there are more open-minded than anywhere else toward anything new or innovative. That constant appetite for different things, for the next trend, is something I can relate to.

Skinny Puppy.

6

Electronic Body Music

FRONT 242: THE AGGRESSIVE EDGE OF RHYTHM AND THE POWER OF RECYCLED CULTURE

By Robert Doerschuk || *Keyboard*, September 1989

Beneath mock rococo chandeliers, before opulent red walls speared with slivers of gilt, four young Belgians known as Front 242 blast a vicious electronic beat through San Francisco's Fillmore Auditorium toward distant balconies where the ghosts of Janis Joplin and Jim Morrison cower apprehensively. The thrumming pulse of "Masterhit," "Funkandafi," "Headhunter," "Agony (Until Death)," and "Never Stop!" scatters these spirits and blows out the historic venue's cobwebs of nostalgia. No history survives the onslaught of Front 242: Wherever they play, the mood is urgent, immediate, simultaneously frightening and exhilarating.

Onstage, from his vantage point behind an Emulator II, Patrick Codenys triggers effects, plays knife-edged riffs, and every now and then looks out at the seething crowd. Despite the frenzy and ear-melting volume of the music, it's easy to imagine Codenys assessing the scene with calm dispassion. His helmet, an ominous dark mask, hides a moonish face, whose features off-stage reflect an uncommon sensitivity and intelligence.

Without advanced instrumental technique, Codenys has made his own wits his main axe. In sampling technology, he has found a tool with which to transfer music into a reflection of modern life. In partnership with Richard 23, singer Jean-Luc de Meyer, and mixing board master Daniel B., he captures the grotesquerie of American televangelism, the turbulence behind bland media imagery, and the violence of alienation in a body of songs that can make listeners laugh, scream, and dance all at once.

Like many contemporary bands, Front 242 builds its sound around drum machines, samples, and sequences. Yet their grooves sizzle with an intensity that eludes most other groups. Though much of their power traces to the fills played live by percussionist Richard 23, the basic beat pounds with enough cold fury on its own to heat up any dance floor. Front 242 weaves sample fragments and metallic thumps around bass lines that galvanize tonic drones with highly syncopated octave leaps. The art behind their noise testifies to an ability to squeeze maximum mileage from minimal rhythmic elements.

This aspect of their sound stems largely from their background in Belgium. The group was formed in Brussels eight years ago as a synth and guitar duo, with tools as basic as the music scene in their hometown. Though inspired by Joy Division, Cabaret Voltaire, and other British minstrels of doom, they considered it their mission to forge a style based more on their Continental heritage than on imitations of English bands. When Codenys and Jean-Luc De Meyer joined the group in 1982, followed a year later by the departure of founding member Dirk Bergen and the arrival of Richard 23, they began building a following, first in Belgium, then throughout Europe, and finally among connoisseurs of underground music in the United States. By incorporating themselves as an artistic association in Belgium, they managed to qualify for government assistance, making it easier to afford updated equipment. Yet the discipline of working with relatively simple gear never left them; to this day, the mainstay of Codenys's setup is an E-mu Emulator II, without any MIDIed appendages.

Front 242's latest album, *Front By Front*, edges them closer to the precipice of mainstream pop success, which also happens to overlook the chasm of lost credibility. Still, it seems unlikely that this band will ever take the plunge toward mediocrity. Judging by their uncompromising fury onstage, and by Codenys's thoughtful ruminations about music and our world before their Fillmore show, they're still perched on that proverbial cutting edge, and will probably stay there until the edge grows dull.

Were you drawn into Front 242 by an interest in playing music, or a fascination with the technology surrounding music?

A little of both. Most of the people in the band were interested in graphic art. When you're in Belgium and you want to do music, it's not like in England or America. It's not easy to run an announcement and have a hundred drummers knocking at your door, because nobody's there! The only way to begin something is on your own. If you need a drummer, you go to a rhythm machine. If you need a bassist, you go for an instrument that you can use to play bass lines. So everybody was involved with machines in the beginning. We actually got together to research sounds. Daniel was working in a keyboard shop, so he's the most technical. But everybody was touching into everything. When I'm working at home, the Emulator is all I need. I just bought the [Roland] R-8 rhythm box, although we don't really need rhythm boxes anymore, with samples.

If you had been born a few years earlier and come up in the pre-sampling era, do you think you would have gotten into music, or would you have stayed with your previous work as a graphic designer?

I think I would have stayed in design. It's funny, though. When you listen to industrial music, the basic idea now is for synthesizers to represent other instruments. But when I got my first instrument, a Korg MS-20, the idea was to build something new. Things have changed very quickly since then.

How much synthesizer programming do you do nowadays?

We still mainly work with old analog synths. You see, a synthesizer is maybe like a TV—a black box with sounds in it. You have to get those guts out of it. If there are still guys finding special sounds with guitars, why shouldn't we keep finding special sounds with analog synths? We have worked with digital and algorithmic instruments, too. We work with DX7s, even though the programming is not so easy. Sometimes we go back to synthesizers that are somewhere between analog and digital MIDI systems, like the [Oberheim] Matrix 1000.

What's your philosophical approach to taking samples?

Our idea is to work with the world. Sometimes we sit in front of the TV and sample from it. Or, if we have time, we go out and take samples. In Sweden, there was this signal we heard, this mechanical sound with the stoplights, that tells blind people when to cross the street; we sampled that. We will record the sound of a woman washing dishes, but we will never go into the kitchen and try to reproduce that sound ourselves, because that wouldn't be natural.

When you're working a sample into one of your songs, is it your intention to use that sample to introduce an element of reality, or to obscure reality?

That's a good and difficult question. There's something about samples that makes things less natural. A sound produced by TV, for instance, is already unnatural because of its association with other sounds. The quality of the sound of a car starting will depend on what's before and what's after. I believe that art in the '90s will be something like that: It will be based on taking sounds and making them less natural. I won't say that people will be copying sounds more. It might be better to call it recycling, because that's a more positive word. More and more people will recycle sounds.

> "I believe that art in the '90s will be something like that: It will be based on taking sounds and making them less natural. More and more people will recycle sounds."
>
> —PATRICK CODENYS (FRONT 242)

You talk a lot about television. That seems to be an important source of material and inspiration for you.

In Front, we speak very often about the media. Something happens in the world, and the media—especially TV—changes it. The same event will be presented totally differently on BBC and on German TV. So already we see this change, this recycling of information.

Does European television provide you with a different type of material for samples than American television?

The main difference is that in Belgium we can catch channels from other countries. European countries are very different from each other, so this sort of work is interesting. The English present things differently from the French, so you understand that the manner of presenting the message is very important. We work in the same way with our samples. Front is just cataloging all these samples and reproducing them with musical support. We don't put any judgment or message on it, but we do work on the way in which we present it. This is very important, because the presentation is what determines how people react. What's interesting is how people find themselves, consciously or unconsciously, in what we do.

In what way?

Well, "Welcome to Paradise" [with its extensive use of the sampled exhortations of televangelists] was an obvious smash in the face. But there are a lot of samples that people will unconsciously recognize because they saw the movie these samples came from. Maybe it's just one sound: They won't be able to recognize the soundtrack from that one sound, but they'll know it. It's familiar. That's another way to seduce people, completely different from the rock and roll way, with guitar solos and all that.

The old rock song structures don't apply in your music, because samples create an illusion of reality, and being bound to familiar structures makes it more difficult to create illusion.

That's right. We make our music more visual.

On one song from Front by Front, you repeat a sample of someone saying, "55 neutral zone." Do you think that a snippet that brief still reveals something about the culture in which that sample was taken?

You have to realize that a lot of American films come to Europe, so everything is mixed, especially in a country like Belgium. As Belgians, we don't really have any roots or strong culture. But that's interesting, too, because we're able to assimilate other cultures very quickly. So a sample like "55 neutral zone" will work in both the European and the American brains.

When you use samples that are really strong, you can relate them to any kind of American theory or science fiction or something like that. Even if people only hear it subconsciously, they will be able to locate it.

Has sampling technology made it necessary for musicians today to communicate a very different feeling about the world than musicians did in the years before sampling?

The approaches to music and to the world of sounds are completely different now than in the past. The main difference is in the limitations. Rock and roll is really based on a formula. It has some rules: You need a bass guitar, a drummer, a guitarist, and a singer, and then you have the magic formula to begin rock and roll. Nowadays, we speak about our opportunities to access the world of sounds. We don't even speak about the abilities of musicians anymore. Just as painting is different from photography, sampling is different from older methods of creating sound. We now have the ability to take anything we want from anywhere we want. Of course, this makes selection the biggest problem. This becomes a question of experience, or of will. I don't want to sound pretentious, but when I'm working with sampling technology, I feel that I'm touching all kinds of artistic disciplines, not only music. When you're watching TV, you have a link between sound and image, and you're more involved in a complete art than in a specific kind of art—rock and roll, for example.

Do you modify this approach when presenting your music in concert?

Yeah. On a record, we always analyze the format we're working in. Studio work involves using effects—echo, reverb, samples, sequences. Everything is generated in an artificial manner, even if the root of the song is a feeling that somebody has, or a clear sample. Onstage, we try to give the songs another life, so the performances become very physical. The performers are dancing a lot, so the guy at the mixing desk becomes very important.

Is it his job to try to make the concert sound similar to the record?

Not at all. It's important to have some references, so that people recognize what you're doing. But as soon as you have those references, you can begin going in different directions. It's the same idea in how we arrange our music. We use rhythm boxes and bass lines because people need a minimum of references. At the moment you have that, you can begin applying more research to your songs.

In another interview, Richard 23 spoke about Front 242's tour several years ago as opening act for Depeche Mode. Richard indicated that he respected Depeche Mode for achieving success in the charts without modifying their original, totally electronic format. Why is this particular accomplishment something that you would respect?

Well, Depeche Mode comes up with very nice sounds in the electronic sector. They present melodies very well. They have a good feeling between what they have in their music and what they present onstage. Also, there are not so many electronic bands doing huge shows, as they do.

But are you saying that achieving that kind of success is more difficult if you're doing purely electronic music?

It is very difficult, because people haven't assimilated it yet. There's also a problem with touring. We are still on this rock and roll circuit, so when we talk with journalists or with people who work for record labels, the spirit of rock and roll is still there. Now, the spirit of electronic music is I wouldn't say clean, but it's about keeping things in order. People are structural in the way they do music, so the way they think is kind of clean. They want to do things precisely, because their music is like that. On the other levels, such as business, marketing, and touring, they like it very precise, too. Yet that's not what the musical world is like.

Certainly you hear this precise approach in Front 242's rhythm tracks. Though you play with a very strong beat, it's also very clean and meticulously constructed.

Well, that's also because we work with Steinberg software, which is very structural. It allows no human error. That's the option you have to take: Either you want your music to be human, or you want to reach a human feeling in another, unhuman way. I remember the first rhythm boxes: They didn't allow you to put three instruments on top of each other because they felt that a real drummer couldn't do that.

That's not at all how we work. I won't say that we want to be un-human, but we do want to do unusual things. For instance, on *Front by Front*, the rhythms are very precise, the structures are very precise, but the total alchemy of the album, the magic of how the sequences go amongst themselves, gives it something human at the final point.

It creates a great sense of power through order.

That's it.

Where do you get your ideas for building rhythm tracks?

Again, because we are Belgians, we decided to base what we do on the idea of what we call white rhythms. Through the ages, most white musicians have been interested in African rhythm because it's still very primitive. But from the beginning, we didn't feel close enough to other cultures to pick up anything in their rhythms that we could feel. So we decided to do our own music, to go toward white rhythms. It wasn't easy, because the instincts of white music are gone. We're just trying to find out what they were.

How far back have you gone in investigating these white rhythms?

I should say that we have gone back into historical white rhythms, but that doesn't mean anything. Who can really tell what they were?

What sort of reception have these efforts provoked from more formally trained musicians or musicologists?

In general, musicians hate Front 242, except jazz musicians. I have a friend, a 45-year-old guy who plays stick [drums]. He's very good, but he can also play all the other instruments. He's tried them all, because he's open. So when he listened to Front 242, he said that we should call what we do "free jazz," or free something. He won't criticize us as much as rock musicians do.

Those guys laugh at the stuff we bring onstage.

Why?

Because we need something like 20 DIs [direct inputs] to the mixer. When they see those boxes coming onstage, they say, "What? Twenty DIs? Are you joking? You're just three people!" Yeah, but this doesn't mean that if you just have one small box, you can't make a lot of noise.

How is your Emulator set up onstage?

We've programmed it so that I have a separate sound for each note. There are some "anti-notes," too. Each song has its own special segment of the keyboard. The funny thing is that on this tour, and on every tour we've done, I've always discovered a sound midway through the tour that was lost at the end of the keyboard.

> "Just as painting is different from photography, sampling is different from older methods of creating sound. I feel that I'm touching all kinds of artistic disciplines, not only music."
>
> —PATRICK CODENYS (FRONT 242)

During the tour, we sometimes change the sounds that we have inside the Emulator. If you start thinking that one song is too much in order, and that there isn't enough improvisation, you can start to feel like a prisoner of the sounds in that song, so you change them.

It's the opposite of how guitarists feel: Guitarists, in a way, are slaves of their instruments. Because they've created personal techniques based on certain sequences of notes. Since you don't have traditional musical technique, you're not a prisoner. That's it [*laughs*].

Could you go into more detail about how you split the Emulator keyboard?

The Emulator is special because it does ping-pong. I have eight channels, so if you assign a sound to two channels, the first time you push on a note, it will go to channel one, and the second time you push on the same note, it will go to channel two. So if you pan left and right at the mixing desk, you have a ping-pong effect.

On my setup, channels one and two are mostly effects and background sounds, channels three and four are voices and slogans, and from five through eight it's more melodic synthesizer or guitar sounds.

Is the Emulator MIDIed to anything offstage?

No, the only MIDI is on the drummer's system. We have three independent systems. Daniel at the mixing desk works tapes like a DI. I work with my own sounds on diskette. And the percussionist works with his samples onstage. Daniel coordinates it all at the desk. He decides who to open and who to close.

So that's where much of the improvisation takes place in your concerts?

Yeah. He's really in the studio when we're onstage.

In our May '89 issue, we ran an extensive article on the so-called cyberpunk movement in electronic music. Front 242 is frequently associated with this style. Do you feel comfortable being grouped with such bands as Ministry, Skinny Puppy, and Severed Heads?

I read that article, and I felt that it was showing mainly an American side to the music. Most of the bands were American. Since '81, though, the guys in Front 242 have been working to reach a certain quality, based only on our subjective opinions. We never felt that we were included in any movement. We were somewhere in between Throbbing Gristle, Kraftwerk, and bands like that, but we wanted to be exclusive, and to have nothing to do with any fashion. It's not a question of fashion for us: It's more a question of doing sound research, and making some sort of a career, and promoting the kind of music we like. We call what we do "electronic body music."

Still, since so much of the music played in dance clubs these days is based around a strong backbeat, as your music is, what is it that makes your approach unique?

First of all, I was very surprised that people here in the States like what we do, because so much of the music you hear in clubs has a lot of black rhythms. Maybe we are seen as kind of exotic. We don't want to be influenced by the English or the Germans, either: We've always wanted to do our music, from our country. We're so degenerated in Europe that we don't know what our roots are anymore. Maybe what makes us different is that we're trying to get back to our cultural instincts, to our primitive white rhythms.

Is there anything in your selections of sounds that similarly distinguishes Front 242?

That's another kind of work. The first step in choosing our sounds is that they have to be powerful on their own, because it has to be tribal. But the way it works in sequences is even more important, because the sequence is the second life of the sound. So, at a certain point, you make rules. Big deep bass sounds have to played in long sequences. High sounds, like cymbals or TV samples, can be more melodic and come in quicker sequences. The main goal is that the total result has to be powerful.

Describe exactly how you create a song, from conception to final touches.

The basic idea is to always be aware of your environment, always pay attention. So if you're in front of your TV, or watching a video, or working with some small unit at home, you might get sentences, special sounds or effects, or a rhythm or a bass line that you like. Sometimes a slogan is enough. The introduction to "Funkandafi" is a slogan; that was the spark that began that song. Maybe that's enough to even begin the structure.

You work on it until you cannot work anymore. Then you put it on cassette or disk and send it to the other guys. They work on it maybe another week and give you a cassette in exchange. And on and on. At one point, after we've heard each other's work, we discuss it all, try to find a common theme, and pick the most interesting songs. Only at that point do we get into the studio and begin to work. And we always work in couples—two persons together.

What's especially interesting is not so much your procedure, but your premise that you must always start by being aware of what's going on around you.

Yeah. That's the root of creativity.

You mentioned earlier that traditionally trained musicians often look down at your band. Are there any final thoughts you'd like to leave for *Keyboard* readers who come from this sort of background?

The best message I can give is that they should try sampling. Piano players are very sensitive persons. The feeling they must have is an extension of the vibrations of their instrument, because the sound of the instrument influences how you think.

If you remove that sound and put another one in, that could transport you to another world. Now, pianists will take five years to develop dexterity in their fingers. That's a difficult job, and very important, too. But if you take that same five years to research sounds, you will have a good background to do music. And if you come to sampling with the technique of a pianist, you would be able to do some very big work.

THE ART OF EXTREME NOISE

By Francis Preve || *Keyboard*, September 2003

In 2003, Keyboard *revisited the artists of electronic body music—this time, not only Front 242, but artists in their circle and who were influenced by their work. —PK*

When I first heard *Twitch*, Ministry's 1986 release on Sire, I realized that synths could be as hard and aggressive as anything a Les Paul and Marshall stack could deliver—even more so because of the unlimited sonic versatility of synthesis and sampling. It was hard to ignore tracks that pummeled your sensibilities while simultaneously making you dance. But in the midst of the aural assault, the emotional content was also loud and clear: For raging against the world, industrial was—and is—often the perfect soundtrack.

It's a logical outcome of the combination of electronics and audaciousness. From the beginning, electronic music has been about using technology to manipulate sound in unexpected and often bizarre ways. Often the results were expressive in ways that went far beyond what a composer could achieve with traditional instrumentation. From the pioneering tape manipulations of Pierre Schaeffer, considered by many to be the father of musique concrète, to the metallic cacophony of Einstuerzende Neubauten in the early '80s. Aggression and aural experimentation have been part and parcel of what has widely come to be called electronica. And nowhere is this more true than with the intrepid synth-and-sampler-wielding explorers of industrial and electronic body music (EBM).

The early '80s brought an onslaught of new technology and innovative techniques for distorting, mangling, distressing, and torturing sound. Some bands, such as the highly abrasive Throbbing Gristle, began as sonic provocateurs, infusing their music with mutated and overdriven instrumentation. Others, such as Ministry, started out as classic electro-pop bands, then transformed themselves into aggro powerhouses, permanently altering—some might even say inventing—the sound of industrial music. Meanwhile, in Europe and Canada, bands such as Front 242 and Front Line Assembly were fusing elements of industrial's bombast with driving synths and hard-as-nails beats, creating the complementary style now known as EBM.

Throughout the '90s, these movements flourished in underground clubs. But they also broke into the mainstream with the success of Nine Inch Nails and Marilyn Manson—which brought the noise to a new generation of listeners. At the same time, new acts Covenant, Wolfsheim, and Apoptygma Berzerk extended the style by fusing their approaches with electro-pop influences. The results became hugely successful in European clubs and subsequently had a big influence on the Gothic scene here in the States.

Though each of these genres stands on its own, there's too much overlap to be ignored, both in terms of approach and the gear arsenal involved. Newer EBM/industrial bands such as Covenant, Haujobb, VNV Nation, and Apoptygma Berzerk routinely cite the same influences as established groups Front 242 and Skinny Puppy. In fact, cross-influences between bands seem to be the rule.

To bring you the real story of what makes the modern EBM and industrial scene so vital, we assembled a roundtable of artists to discuss its past, present, and future. Stephan Groth, known also as Grothesk, the mastermind behind the Norweigan outfit Apoptygma Berzerk; cEvin Key from Canada's Skinny Puppy; Joakim Montelius of the Swedish band Covenant; Daniel Myer from the German trio Haujobb, Ronan Harris of VNV Nation (hailing from London, VNV stands for "Victory Not Vengeance"); and Patrick Codenys and Daniel Bressanutti from the groundbreaking Belgian band Front 242. All of these artists generously agreed to share their insights into where they've been and where they're headed—along with some delicious details about how they go about fusing fury with electronics. Let's crank it up.

Each of you brings a unique approach to sound design and composition within the EBM/industrial scene. Who are your biggest influences, musical or otherwise?

Stephan Groth: The bands that got me into electronic music are Kraftwerk and Depeche Mode. I grew up in the '80s, so everything that happened back then has influenced me in one way or the other. Commodore 64 music and computer game music has been as important to me as the electrosynth pop I grew up with.

The musicians who have inspired me recently are Richie Hawtin (of Detroit's Plastikman and RUSE) and Simon Posford (Alien Sex Fiend, among others). They've taught me a lot about both minimalism and complexity in electronic music programming.

cEvin Key: Kraftwerk, Y.M.O., Human League, Fad Gadget, and Joy Division.

Joakim Montelius: When we were kids, Kraftwerk, Human League, and new wave were it. When we started making music ourselves, we discovered Front 242, Skinny Puppy, and Nitzer Ebb—in fact, it's an honor to be in this article with two great heroes of ours. The third, and perhaps the most important, stage of development was our discovery of underground dance music in the early '90s. From these three basic elements we found a sound of our own.

Daniel Bressanutti: Early electronic music composers, German space rock, and Krautrock. Also, bands such as Gong, Soft Machine, and Velvet Underground were a source of inspiration.

Patrick Codenys: Throbbing Gristle and Kraftwerk.

Ronan Harris: As an artist I find it strange to say that few artists were influences. Instead, I would say that countless musical pieces were. I like electronic music that invokes an emotional reaction, everything from underground trance and techno to dramatic soundtracks and rhythmic noise, and from dark ambient to melancholic pop—music by people who don't care about technique or genres, but who care about getting machines to express emotion. What made me certain I wanted to work with electronic music was the sound—it captivated me. And when I saw people like Kraftwerk, Tangerine Dream, and Giorgio Moroder on TV in the '70s with banks of equipment around them making amazing sounds—I was hooked. As long as the human soul is still in there, I want to hear it. Lately I find myself listening to the likes of Terence Fixmer and Chris Liebing, who define a whole new sound in the techno genre. I like to mix those influences with less contemporary ones.

There's a lot of influence from classical music in our music, too. I like to marry emotion with cold, quantized electronics.

Daniel Myer: Musically, I have to say, it's the gear I work with. I listen to a lot of different music; my fave band at the moment is the Used. I also watch a lot of movies, where everything is an inspiration, but the most inspiring thing is working with the gear and, of course, life in general.

In your opinion, what current bands in the EBM/industrial world are making a difference in bringing the energy and drive to new audiences?

Stephan Groth: Covenant, VNV, FLA/Delerium, and Apop, among others, have succeeded in getting new audiences interested in this music, mainly because of good songwriting that appeals to new crowds. But thanks to Marilyn Manson, Ministry, and Nine Inch Nails, everybody has now heard about industrial music.

cEvin Key: Aphex Twin, Squarepusher, and Autechre are still pushing the envelope.

Joakim Montelius: A few years ago the power-noise movement—bands like Noisex, Imminent Starvation, Hypnoskull—was driving and had an interesting hybrid between dance music and pure noise going on. Right now it seems like they ran out of steam, and again the ball is bouncing on the underground dance floors.

But that's the way it should be, different genres cross-pollinating to give birth to new mutations.

Patrick Codenys: The outsiders—Prefuse73, Tipper, Silicom, Black Lung, Xingu, AOKI Takamasa—these are the bands that are innovating.

Ronan Harris: As far as industrial goes, I would have to say that in the last five years, the Ant-zen label, Hands Productions, and bands like Munich's Noisex achieved more for industrial than they will ever truly realize. They set a whole new standard, gave it an image and an attitude, and they made industrial acceptable. They turned a small elite scene into a large elite scene. They opened minds. They brought a whole new energy to it by taking it to the people and educating without trying.

What's your approach to songwriting and composition? How has it changed over the years? Outline the exact steps you take when writing or producing a new piece, from what inspires you and what gear you use to how you get your final sounds.

Stephan Groth: I started out with a Korg Poly 800 and an Atari. Things are quite different now. Now I work on a Mac with [Steinberg] Cubase and [Digidesign] Pro Tools. These are the biggest changes in the way I work compared to the past.

I always start out with an idea, a melody line, a riff, a word, or a sound. I carry a tiny recorder with me most of the time, so whenever an idea pops up in my head, I record it. I'll fool around in the studio with this idea later and see if it works or not. After that, I'll start with the drums and the bass programming, usually using Native Instruments Battery and the Roland Super Jupiter. It can sometimes take me a whole day just to make these two elements work together perfectly to get the right drive. Then come the riffs, the chords, and at last the vocals.

After the vocals, it's time for the effects and the actual arrangement of the song. This is the part of the process I like the most. The goal is of course to come up with new sounds that haven't been heard before. I run stuff through as many plug-ins and as much hardware as possible. I start out with a sound from my Kawai 100E, my Korg MS20, or some other analog synth and then record it into Cubase or Pro Tools through a TLA FatMan compressor.

cEvin Key: For me, each song is about working on a particular piece of gear to achieve a sound or groove, then collect it into [Emagic] Logic, whereby I can mess with it more, and work with other suitable machines to counteract and create syncopation that doesn't sound like it came from a computer. From there it's about carving out sections that work with details and then enhancing the spectrum sonically.

Joakim Montelius: We don't have a fixed modus operandi. It depends on where the idea came from and the purpose of the song. Either we start with a melody, usually played using any old sound—like piano or strings—to see if it holds or if it depends on the soundscape, or we start with a loop or a beat. In that case, we make the rhythm section first and try to find a melodic element that can carry it to a higher level. But as soon as the basic concept has been established, we start making the sounds, trying out variations and themes, looking for the right "dress" for it. So we keep adding ideas, sounds, sequences, loops, and vocals until we have a full palette of colors.

Then we reduce and subtract until there is a working song with a minimum of details. Everything that isn't absolutely necessary is stripped away, and in the end we have a good melody, a beat, and an interesting sonic world that carries itself.

We sequence in Cubase on a PC, and mix on an analog Allen and Heath desk. We use a variety of hardware synths, samplers, and drum machines combined with software for sounds. We try to keep updated with the latest gear, because it's a source of inspiration in itself.

Sometimes whole new songs just jump at you when you explore new equipment.

Patrick Codenys: We came back to the pure spirit of synthesis, a creative technology that should lead to a new aesthetic. There is no point to try to emulate rock, jazz, or blues with electronic instruments; that's an Anglo-Saxon concept and it is a distortion. With new tools you should create new musical directions. Our new album goes back to the core of a vintage manipulation of the machines. For example, with no memory storage on old analog synths, we need to make instant decisions on the sound design.

> "We came back to the pure spirit of synthesis; a creative technology that should lead to a new aesthetic. There is no point to try to emulate rock, jazz, or blues with electronic instruments; that's an Anglo-Saxon concept and it is a distortion. With new tools you should create new musical directions."
>
> —PATRICK CODENYS (FRONT 242)

Ronan Harris: I write a lot of songs in my head, everything at once—melodies and words. That concept contains the feeling and the sentiment, which are very important in VNV Nation's music. Or I sit in a room jamming with one sound, just writing melodies and songs for myself. In either case, I go to my computer and write out the melody, any words, thoughts, and sound ideas using a program called the Brain (a thought processor) and Emagic Logic Audio. I file it and come back to it another time or continue working on it until I have something finished. I have hundreds of song ideas in that directory now. I used to use a lot of hardware in the studio, though I often restricted myself to two or three good pieces to come up with most of the sounds. I prefer to focus on less equipment while trying to get the most out of it.

Before our last album, *Futureperfect*, I set myself the task of doing everything using a PC. I wrote out a concept for the album describing each piece I had in mind, and then took a laptop with me everywhere to work on sounds and ideas. It was so liberating.

Daniel Myer: We used to start with no computer at all; now we do all the production with a computer. There is no formula to write songs for us. Sometimes we start with a beat, sometimes with a bass line or a sample. Sometimes we just rip another song apart and create something new. Inspiration is in the gear we use, and also in the music we're listening to. At the moment, we work with Cubase on Windows. We work without any hardware; it's all software-based.

Our favorite instruments are [Native Instruments] Battery and Absynth, [Steinberg] HALion, and the Ohmboys plug-ins.

Do you use any sample libraries? Which are your favorites?

Stephan Groth: I try to create my own sounds as much as possible, but I also use samples from Sounds Good, Wizoo, and Native Instruments libraries.

cEvin Key: I like to make my own samples for the most part. I tend to not use too many sampling CDs. I do love the original Mellotron Library, and Battery has some nice drum libraries.

Joakim Montelius: We've always been great fans of the original [E-mu] Emulator II sound library. Those sounds have that gritty and powerful quality that fits so well with our music. Otherwise, we prefer to make our own sounds or steal stuff from others, then recycle it and transform it into something new.

Daniel Bressanutti: No libraries, just TV samples. It's the universal box, the sounds of the planet.

Ronan Harris: Strings are very much a part of our music, and the Miroslav Vitous set made me drool. I managed to get the string CD, and nothing will ever come close.

I bought two other sample CDs years ago, used five sounds from each, and felt cheated. Never again. I also love the [Emagic] ESX24 Analogue Extreme collection. The quality and usability are incredible.

Daniel Myer: We have our own libraries, sometimes we use strings from Halion, but most of the time we create our own loops and stuff.

Sampling and distortion have long been key components for the industrial sound. While they're still an integral part of the genre, I'm noticing more attention to synthesis and dramatic soundscapes, and even an occasional nod to classic '80s electro-pop bands. What's your take on this evolution?

Stephan Groth: Electro-pop is very important to me. I've always integrated a lot of it into my music.

cEvin Key: People are getting back into the classics, and they seem to be over the techno side of things.

Joakim Montelius: I think there's been a generation shift. The people in this article represent two generations. cEvin Key and Patrick Codenys belong to the group of innovators and leaders that inspired Daniel, Stephan, Ronan Harris, and myself to make music. All four of us have similar backgrounds; we found synthpop and new wave, discovered EBM/industrial, and went on to explore dance music more or less at the same time. I guess that's why we—the younger generation—integrate the melodic element of new wave, the grit and darkness of industrial, and the driving beats of techno, house, and hip-hop into a new style. Just like Skinny Puppy and Front 242 used the original industrial sound, punk, and '70s dance music to create EBM and what is known as industrial today. It's all a matter of where you come from.

Daniel Bressanutti: Besides sampling and distortion, plug-in processing became an interesting element of the sound. As for the '80s, I'd say that after recycling old records, mixing existing styles, and using pre-sampled CDs and factory sounds, a lot of artists and DJs realized that they had to go back to the ABCs of electronic music in order to innovate. Which means rediscovering analog synthesis—getting back into your VCO, VCF, and VCA—and that's why we're back to the '80s.

> "This scene would never have taken off without people paying attention to synthesis and soundscapes. The sampler was liberating and definitely contributed much to the sound in the late '80s, but those concentrating on more aesthetic, original sounds were there, too."
>
> —RONAN HARRIS (VNV NATION)

Ronan Harris: It's always been there. This scene would never have taken off without people paying attention to synthesis and soundscapes. The sampler was liberating and definitely contributed much to the sound in the late '80s, but those concentrating on more aesthetic, original sounds were there, too. The "sampler sound" became stagnant, and the copyright laws governing samples put a stop to 90 percent of the source material, so I guess people had to concentrate on making sounds instead of stealing them. Despite this, there were many who avoided samplers. They weren't at the forefront but were very much there.

I would be tempted to describe VNV Nation as one of the bands in the style of sound you describe. I guess that's the age of some of the bands concentrating more on melody and soundscapes. We're in our early 30s, we lived through the '80s, we love electronica for its attention to sounds, and we love our synths. Samplers have an essential place, but when I hear a track with a stolen sound or a sample of a preacher or horror movie, or loops from other music, I cringe.

Daniel Myer: The industrial sound nowadays is more and more pop, and the pop music goes more industrial than anything else. Producers like BT, the Neptunes, or Timbaland are more creative and crazy than 90 percent of the industrial bands today. Haujobb always tried to be different, to create something new, but, to me, much of the new industrial sound is just wishy-washy techno/trance crap that sounds like 1990.

Our readers are always looking for new, innovative ways to distress and mangle their sounds. Can you describe one of your favorite tricks for processing or composing new textures?

Stephan Groth: I use a lot of bit-shifting and distortion. I think the trick is to know your equipment. Even though it's a drag, read the manuals—probably not a very popular thing to say—find out what a piece of gear can do, and try out all possibilities.

cEvin Key: Personally, I like to try various methods in the recording chain, including tube EQ, specialized outboard FX, and quality compression. I then like to take the end result once it's recorded, then tear it apart with a variety of plug-ins and edits with new FX all automated with Logic Audio.

Joakim Montelius: We're big fans of vocoders. Using the same sound as carrier and modulator can give great results. Crappy time-stretching—like the one on the Akai S950—is great for weird modulation. Digital distortion (not modeling, but overdriving digital signals) has a more aggressive, nasty, and piercing sound to it. So has bit-reduction and low-resolution sampling, when you get aliasing and crude waveforms with big gaps for that lovely digital hardcore harshness.

The important thing is to keep the sound usable, to mix the trashed sound with the original to retain some texture and harmonics. Otherwise you end up with just noise. That may be good and well, but if you want it to work musically, it's usually a good trick to mix the sounds. Compressors are great tools for manipulating beats. A properly abused compressor can completely alter a rhythm, highlighting or changing the focus in very creative ways.

Daniel Bressanutti: Playing with a real modular synthesizer is my favorite trick for getting innovative sounds.

Ronan Harris: Maybe it's my age, but I love analog. I tend to find a lot of pro sounds are too clean; they lack any dimension. They make nice building blocks. I like to do things like run digital tracks or sounds from the computer through a triggered modular system and some effects, give them character, and record them back in.

Even in the computer domain you can do this with synth designs in [Native Instruments] Reaktor. I love putting sounds through effects that feed and saturate other effects that in turn feedback to somewhere earlier in the loop and create incredible sounds. If it's not that, then it's finding the weirdest plug-ins I can and processing all sorts of things through them to see what works and what doesn't. Ordinary mixing boards can't do what you can do with a computer. I'm also going retro these days by taking clean sounds and resampling them on an old sampler which has a character all its own. It's subtle, but it works.

Daniel Myer: I love the Frohmage plug-in from Ohmboys. It's some kind of filter-distortion thing. I also like the Waldorf D-Pole. Usually I loop a beat and let the arrangement play, then I record the beat while I play with the knobs of Frohmage or the Waldorf. Afterwards, I cut the pieces that I like and start a new song.

What's your approach to live performance?

Stephan Groth: My goal was always to sound a bit different live than we do on CD. More energy, more rock and roll. I use many live elements, like acoustic drums and guitars, when playing live.

cEvin Key: Have everything as ready as possible to perform what you need, but have new avenues ready to go for improvisation on the spot.

Joakim Montelius: That's always a problem. Our music is essentially pop music, not performance-oriented or improvisational, so we keep it simple. We have a backing track with the basic stuff, and we play the lead keyboard parts live. Sometimes we just add more things on top to keep it interesting. We use lots of vocoders and voice effects live; it gives a nice combination of human interaction and texture.

Patrick Codenys: It has to be the opposite of a studio work. "Live" means energy, power, instincts, and interaction with your audience.

Ronan Harris: Our main focus is to take the energy and emotion in our songs and illustrate it live. The concerts get an amazing reaction on both sides of the pond. There are only two of us, and we decided a long time ago that someone standing behind a keyboard playing the odd melody would not help illustrate that energy. Mark is six feet and six inches tall, and he likes to hit things, so he plays e-drums on most tracks and keyboards on a few others, while I generally run around and sing—or if something goes wrong, I do stand-up. [*Laughs.*] It works! We have a multimedia setup with video screens as a back wall with videos projected in sync with the music. We try to vary our positions as much as possible so it's more dynamic. We're doing one or two instrumental tracks which get incredible reactions. That's something I never expected.

Daniel Myer: I live for my performances. I need the attention, so I love the energy that people give me when I'm onstage.

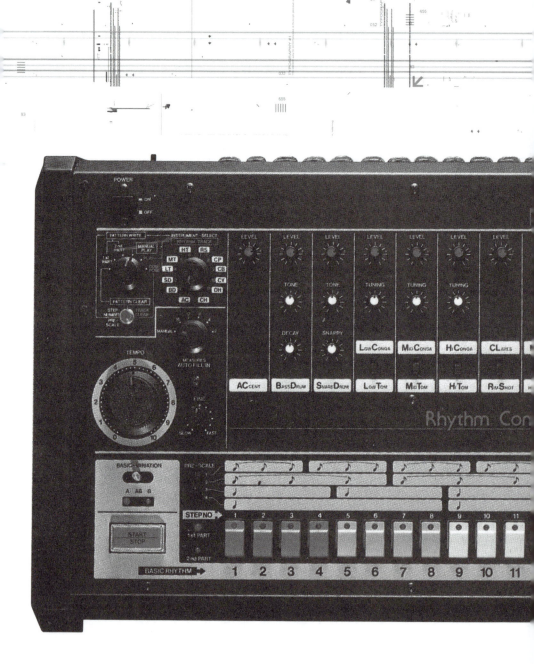

7

Rise of the Machines

ROLAND CR-78, TR-808, AND TR-909: CLASSIC BEAT BOXES

By Mark Vail || *Keyboard*, May 1994

t's hard to imagine electronic dance music without Roland drum machines. In his research into the origin of Roland's magical boxes, Mark Vail goes straight to the source to tell their creation story, behind the scenes. —PK

During the '60s, two entities that we in the electronic music industry take for granted today didn't yet exist: programmable, computerized drum machines and Roland. The development of both came about thanks to one person.

Back then, Roland president Ikutaro Kakehashi ran Ace Electronics, a manufacturer of organs, amplifiers, and rhythm machines. "Maybe you remember the Rhythm Ace," Kakehashi reminisces. "That was my first design. I managed Ace Electronics, and that's when I developed the Rhythm Ace R-1, which I introduced two or three years ago [*he's only kidding*], probably in 1964. It was sold in the U.S. through a wholesaler. It wasn't automatic; it was a hand-operated machine that attached to an organ. This was a golden time for the home organ business. Later, around 1967, we made the Rhythm Ace FR-1, which was the first automatic rhythm machine."

Home organ players latched on to the automatic rhythm concept long before real musicians considered it kosher. (Just teasing, folks.) "Almost all home organs had built-in rhythm sections," Kakehashi recalls. "A stand-alone rhythm machine wouldn't sell at first. Gradually, people started to use them for recording purposes, just to improve their timing. Then musicians began to understand how useful they were, and they finally spread to the music industry market within a period of three to five years."

Meanwhile, Kakehashi had founded another music instrument company, which he opened in April 1972. His initial concern was its name. "Everybody identifies certain companies in the music industry by a letter from the alphabet: 'F' means Fender, 'S' means Steinway, 'Y' means Yamaha, 'K' means Kawai. I was looking for another letter from the alphabet that nobody else was using. I chose 'R.' Then I looked for the best name in places like telephone and history books. Eventually I found 'Roland.'

"Another thing that was important to me—this name must be pronounced the same in any country. In Germany, Spain, France, Japan, English-speaking countries, they all must pronounce it 'Roland.'" Kakehashi may have been sensitive about the pronunciation because his first company's name, which was known in Australia as Ace-Tone, was pronounced "Ice-Ton" and "Acid-Tone" by those native to the Land Down Under.

Rhythm machines were among Roland's first products. The TR-33 was followed by relatively obscure devices like the TR-55, -66, -77, -330, and -700—though not necessarily in numerical order. All of these machines had one thing in common: Their rhythmic patterns were preset. Enter the CPU. By the late '70s, microprocessors began appearing in music instruments. The most notable example was the Sequential Circuits Prophet-5, which made its public debut at the January 1978 NAMM show in Anaheim, California. Ikutaro Kakehashi realized that a CPU could be a beneficial addition to the drum machine and made it so with Roland's seventh rhythm machine. "The CR-78 was the first rhythm machine with a microcomputer," he says. "At that time, the only choice we had for a CPU was between the 6502 and the Intel 80 series. I chose the Intel 8048, because the 6502 was difficult to get in Japan.

"The CR-78 was also programmable. By tapping, you could create a new pattern. You could combine a preset pattern with one that you had created yourself."

Although it wasn't the first programmable drum machine—an honor held by Paia's Programmable Drum Set, a kit that first appeared in 1975—the CR-78 is indeed the first rhythm machine that we know of that featured a microprocessor. The Paia machine used TTL circuitry, not a CPU chip.

According to the CR-78 brochure, you programmed a two-bar pattern one voice at a time, and user patterns could sound up to four of the CR-78's ten percussion voices. You could break each measure up into 8, 12, 16, 24, or 48 divisions. Percussion events were entered using either the standard TS-1 Memory Write Switch or the optional WS-1 programming switch, which allowed the tempo to be slowed down for entry of complex patterns. Battery-backed memory retained user patterns when the machine was turned off. The four voices in a preset pattern could be independently muted using front-panel buttons. An outboard sequencer could be synchronized to the CR-78 thanks to the latter's trigger output, which sent a 0-15V signal.

This at-the-time unique instrument also allowed user-controlled accents on specific beats. "I built many rhythm machines previously," Kakehashi reveals, "but none of them had accents. Rhythm with no accents? Unbelievable! Nobody would buy it. Also, you could adjust the volume level of some of the voices. In previous rhythm machines, all the voices were fixed at a certain amplitude, and you couldn't change the feeling. On the CR-78, you could adjust the volume level of a percussion part such as a cymbal or the maracas."

In addition, the CR-78 offered a rare feature for a drum machine: it could fade rhythm patterns in and out. Separate switches for fade-in and -out allowed three different fade settings: long, short, or off. When you started a pattern with fade-in enabled, the volume would rise from nothing at a rate determined by the tempo. Likewise, when you hit the stop button with fade-out enabled, rather than stopping immediately, the pattern would fade away.

International stars like Peter Gabriel and Phil Collins helped the CR-78's image in the music industry. However, the CR-78 was nowhere near as popular as its successor, the TR-808.

THE HIP-HOP/TECHNO RHYTHM MACHINE OF CHOICE

Although the response was far from immediate, Roland's second programmable drum machine caused the biggest splash on the music scene—long after it had gone out of production. The TR-808 became so popular in hip-hop and techno that you can find renditions or imitations of its sound in all kinds of contemporary sample libraries and synth sound sets. Hip-hop and techno gave the TR-808 a new reputation and life.

Although the 808 still created sound using analog circuits, its sound quality was much improved over that of the CR-78. Five percussion sounds characterize the state of the 808: the hum kick, the ticky snare, the tishy hi-hats (open and closed), and the spacy cowbell. Low, mid, and high toms, congas, a rim shot, claves, a handclap, maracas, and cymbal fill out the 808's sonic complement.

The accent function—integral, as Kakehashi pointed out, in making the automatic rhythm machine musically useful—survived the transition from the CR-78 to the new machine.

What else was new? Thanks to its front-panel layout, which included a graphic design to help the user visualize metric divisions of a pattern's measures, the TR-808 was easier to program. In addition, it allowed step programming of patterns. "The step-writing interface wasn't so new," Kakehashi says, "but it was the first time that we paid more attention to the people who program in real time. It used to be that our customer was the home-organ player. Then people in the music industry started to pay attention to our rhythm machines. Such a musician was agreeable to programming by himself. That's why we developed the step-writing system, so that you could slow the tempo down, enter your rhythm events, and then speed it up and hear the realistic rhythm pattern that you had just created."

> "It was the first time that we paid more attention to the people who program in real time. It used to be that our customer was the home-organ player. Then people in the music industry started to pay attention to our rhythm machines."
>
> —IKUTARO KAKEHASHI (ROLAND FOUNDER)

Besides its improved sound and programmability, the 808 incorporated a number of groundbreaking features, including volume knobs for each voice, multiple audio outputs, and the immediate precursor to MIDI. On the rear of the 808—as well as other 1981-vintage, pre-MIDI Roland rhythm machines (the CR-8000 and TR-606), the TB-303 Bass Line, and the EP-6060 electronic piano (which featured an arpeggiator)—you'll find a five-pin DIN jack that a standard MIDI plug will fit into. MIDI, however, it isn't. Although this connector was for synchronizing devices, Kakehashi asserts that there is a reason for the similarity between this and MIDI connectors.

"We had developed our own communications protocol," he explains. "Inside, it was the same as today's MIDI. At the same time, Sequential Circuits was developing a MIDI-like protocol. We called ours the DCB Bus; they called theirs by another name. Then we started discussing how to develop a common standard. Eventually MIDI came out, but actually more than 80 or 90 percent of it was based on the DCB Bus. Of course, I don't want to say that everything was developed by Roland, because that isn't fair. It was a joint effort. Both companies agreed to implement the best ideas from both companies, so we jointly created MIDI. But when you compare it with the DCB Bus, you can see how similar they are."

Just as many people would love to see the Ford Motor Company remanufacture the '57 T-bird, there are those who speculate that, were Roland to make more TR-808s, the analog beat box would outsell all of its digital competitors.

Hybridicity and Abbreviated Longevity. At approximately the same time that Ikutaro Kakehashi foresaw the value of implanting microprocessor in a rhythm machine, Roger Linn began developing the Linn LM-1, which—upon its release in 1980—qualified as the first programmable drum machine that featured sampled sounds. Kakehashi wasn't prepared to abandon the use of analog sound generation in his rhythm instruments, even by the time the TR-909 was introduced in 1983. However, three of the 909's 11 percussion sounds—crash cymbal, ride cymbal, and hi-hat—were sampled. How long was the drum machine in production? A single year.

"We combined technologies to make a hybrid machine," he explains. "The cymbal in the TR-909 was generated using digital technology, but the kick drum, snare, and other parts were made by analog circuits. We felt that was the best combination, but at that time everyone expected all sounds to be generated digitally. Digital had a better sound quality, and everybody liked to have all digital. Roger Linn developed his drum machine, which generated all of its drum sounds digitally. At that time, everyone wanted PCM, so that's why we couldn't continue to manufacture the TR-909. It was replaced in 1984 by a machine called the TR-707, which had all PCM sounds." Besides being notable for its hybrid sound-generation scheme, the 909 deserves credit for being Roland's first rhythm machine with MIDI.

In addition to sporting three MIDI connectors (not the familiar in, out, and thru, but one MIDI in and two outs), the 909 also featured a DIN connector for synchronizing the machine with older Roland gear. An improvement on the accents concept was also incorporated into the 909. Not only could you accent percussive events that occurred on a particular beat, you could independently accent any sound. And by triggering 909 sounds from a MIDI controller, you could get a wider dynamic range.

Who Deserves Credit? Makoto Muroi, chief engineer of Roland's electronic drum and percussion division, provided the following information: Mr. Nakamura designed the analog voice circuits for both the CR-78 and TR-808. Mr. Tamada, who also designed Roland's MC-8 MicroComposer, developed the CR-78's software. Mr. Matsuoka developed the TR-808's software. Mr. Oue designed the TR-909's analog and PCM voice circuits, and Mr. Hoshiai developed its software.

However, Ikutaro Kakehashi prefers to give credit to design teams rather than singling out individuals. "Many people were engaged. The Japanese system takes teamwork, so there wasn't one person who was responsible. I think the concept to use a microcomputer was my idea, but the real development involved two or three people. Some people worked on the voicing, some people worked on the mechanical design. There wasn't just one person. This is quite different from the U.S. system. In the U.S., very clearly, 'I designed everything' is what many people say. But in Japan, no. So it's very difficult to say who did what. But it's very clear that Mr. Tadao Kikumuto designed the TR-909's hybrid concept. I think on the TR-808, as well. The concept and programming and hardware design were, in many cases, performed by different people."

AKAI MPC60

By Freff || *Keyboard*, November 1988

Unlike for Roland's drum machines, the arrival of the MPC60 was an event on launch. Roger Linn's design was to become legendary, the culmination of a fusion between computing and hardware design. The workflow and layout it introduced can be seen in the way developers and users alike approach software to this day. So, let's travel back in time to see how the MPC60 was received when it landed on Keyboard*'s test bed. It's a reminder that the technological road to the future isn't always smooth. —PK*

For musicians, product evolution is a wonderful thing. There's always something new coming along in the way of instruments, recording gear, signal processors, and otherwise useful musical tools. Furthermore (barring such economic or technical blips as fluctuations in the value of the yen, or shortfalls in DRAM chip production), the trend is toward increased power at lower cost.

For manufacturers, product evolution can be considerably more troublesome. First problem: Evolution means competition. Manufacturer A's products are getting better, sure, but so are those from manufacturers B, C, and D—and maybe faster. Second problem: It takes three necessarily limited resources (talent, time, and money) to hatch a product. The relative proportions of these are critical at each stage of development and marketing. Only after a product is in the market, slugging it out with all the other products, will a manufacturer finally learn if the heavy investment in this particular techno-soufflé will yield dream or disaster.

Third problem: Neither the battlefield nor the warriors will agree to stand still.

ROGER LINN, JUNE 2011

Roger Linn today is no longer at Akai, instead focusing on his own creations, which include returning to his primary instrument, the guitar. I asked him to reflect on his drum machines' place in music making over the years. It's a bit like asking Enzo Ferrari what he thinks of the Formula 1 circuit: operator and machine function together in the result. —PK

"The biggest surprise for me after creating the first MPC was that its sampling was used for entire sampled loops instead of just drums, particularly considering that is contained 13 seconds of sampling, expandable to only 26. It didn't surprise me that new forms of dance music emerged, because dance music seems to be a constant over time. I find it funny that 'disco sucks' was a popular phrase in the '70s but current 'dance music' is cool, even though much of the same musical style and production is used. Interestingly, my original LM-1 Drum Computer was released in 1979, shortly following '70s disco, and one of its first customers was Giorgio Moroder, the producer of then dance music artists Donna Summer and Irene Cara. Giorgio once told me that before LM-1, he would ask the drummer to record 20 minutes of 1/4-note bass drums, then he'd overdub 20 minutes of snares on 2 and 4, then 20 minutes of hi-hats, et cetera, all so he could have the equivalent of a sampled drum machine before they existed. He said it used to drive the drummer crazy.

"It was nice to see many of the ideas I pioneered in the LM-1, like loop recording, quantize, and swing, continue their lives in the DAWs that followed. They were born out of my desire to record musical ideas very quickly without technology getting in the way, and I think musicians appreciated that more and more over time. Of course, even if I hadn't done them first, I'm sure someone else would have, because they were the natural evolution of a trend. For example, loop recording is just like tape overdubbing except without the inconvenience of stopping and rewinding after each pass. And regarding quantize, who wouldn't want to have their timing errors corrected? Regarding swing, that was largely born out of my work at ages 19–21 with Leon Russell, who taught me a lot about why certain recordings feel right and others don't, and how to get them right, including nailing subtle degrees of swing. I didn't anticipate that variable swing would become so important in hip-hop."

The net result of all this is that companies live or die by the degree to which they pay attention to four crucial questions: (1) Who are our customers? (2) What do they want? (3) Between the time our product is conceived and when it finally ships, will the answers to questions 1 and 2 change? And lastly (perhaps most dangerously), (4) What haven't we thought of? Which brings us to Akai's MPC60, a unit that combines a drum machine, a MIDI sequencer, and a sampler in one attractive and fairly portable box. It seems the late '80s are blossoming with such workstation-style products. In this case, the lack of a built-in keyboard makes Akai's preferred nomenclature—MIDI Production Center—more appropriate. Indeed, that name and the unit's $4,995 price tag virtually define the MPC60's primary target audience: professional musicians working in production-oriented studios, where time, rather than money, is the item always in shortest supply.

We should admit our own conflicting reactions up front. Our very first thought, upon examining the MPC60, was, "Why?" Why even design, let alone try and sell, a three-in-one unit like the MPC60 when the marketplace is awash in inexpensive drum machines, samplers, and sequencers (both software- and hardware-based)? When the same amount of money could buy any one of several computers, a MIDI interface, a sync box, a five-star software sequencer, an inexpensive drum machine, and at least a mid-line sampler? Our second reaction, upon using the MPC60 for several days, was, "Oh, of course—that's why." It is an unquestionably professional piece of gear in its attention to conception, design, and execution. It looks good and feels even better: it is, in fact, a tactile pleasure to play and to program. These are qualities that have been given short shrift by manufacturers in recent years, and we're happy to see that the trend might be reversing. In music, means and ends have always been hard to tell apart. It's time we got back to the twin notions that playing an instrument should make you feel something—other than plastic fatigue—and that just how you feel when playing is what throws either gasoline or ice water on the flames of your inborn musicianship and creativity.

> Our very first thought was, "Why?" Why even design, let alone try and sell, a three-in-one unit like the MPC60? Our second reaction, upon using the MPC60 for several days, was, "Oh, of course—that's why."

This is definitely not to say that the MPC60 has no room for improvement. It does. Like every instrument, it has strengths and weaknesses. But the MPC60 also has a curious Rorschach Test quality: Whether you think any given feature is terrific or terrible seems to depend less on the feature than on your own preferred approach to writing, recording, and editing music.

In terms of components, we think the MPC60 is a great sampling drum machine, an acceptable but unfortunately limited sequencer, and a weak general-purpose sampler. In terms of the overall package, we like it a lot and will buy one just as soon as the post office finds our long-lost inheritance check.

Spot some contradictions already, do you? Details shortly. But first, a look at the not-so-distant past and a discourse on the perils (and pleasures) of MPC60 software updates.

Some Relevant History. Few people manage the trick of inventing a whole new class of musical instrument. Cristofori did it with the piano, Bob Moog did it with the synthesizer, and Roger Linn did it with the drum machine. In 1981 he released a $5,500 box called the Linn LM-1, the first-ever programmable drum unit to offer sampled sounds. In retrospect it didn't do all that much, and its sound quality was low, but that's only the judgment of comparative technological history. At the time, the reaction was extraordinary. Then Roger really wowed the crowds with his second unit, the Linn-Drum, which cost about half as much as an LM-1 and did a whole heck of a lot more.

> Cunningly disguised computers don't come any more cunningly disguised than the MPC60.

And then . . . and then . . . well, there's no polite way to put this. In 1984 Roger killed his own company by releasing his third product, the Linn 9000, before its software was ready. Everyone rushed to buy it because of its amazing specs, and everyone got burned, as it proceeded to crash in seemingly endless and extraordinary ways. We're talking serious bugs here, the kind that torment designers in their sleep and recording engineers in their waking nightmares. By early 1986, the ensuing economic chaos had forced Linn Electronics to close its doors, ironically enough just as multiple revisions of the Linn 9000's operating software had finally brought it to the point of real usability. There are still lots of Linn 9000s out there, and these days their owners are a pretty happy lot. Roger, however, lost close to everything. Swallowing more than a little pride, he struck an engineering deal with Akai, in which he would design advanced instruments and Akai would bear the brunt of expenses, production engineering, manufacturing, and marketing. Design, after all, was Roger's actual strength.

Emblazoned across the top front of the MPC60, then, like the stitched ID on a pair of designer jeans, is Roger Linn's name. The MPC60 is his first creation under Akai's wing. In a very real sense, that makes it the Linn 9000 that wasn't: a sampling drum machine/sequencer combination backed by the bucks to do it right. But did it?

Rev, Rev, Who's Got the Rev? For this report, Akai shipped us an MPC60 with Rev 1.11 software ROMs, assuring us it was the latest version on the market. Calls to several music stores confirmed this, so we promptly set to work. To our horror, within the first two days the MPC60 crashed four times, each time in some awful, irretrievable manner that left us with no choice but to lose everything in memory and boot the unit from scratch.

With one exception—locking up the software by trying to play a song that hadn't yet been built, and which therefore contained no data—we couldn't dope out what had gone wrong and replicate it. Things had just fallen down and gone boom. Bugs like these are the worst, because their erraticism makes them difficult to trace and fix.

This was disturbing. It was not what we wanted to find. Painful memories of the early Linn 9000 foremost in our thoughts, we immediately called Roger and Akai to diplomatically broach the topic—and found that we hadn't been sent the latest software, after all. One Federal Express package later, we had the Real Stuff (version 1.12), loaded it into our unit, and continued our test to destruction.

You know what? Nothing blew up. At all.

> We once worked with a 16-bit PCM digital audio encoder for the better part of a year, listening intently every day, and yet we didn't notice at all when it was accidentally switched into 14-bit mode for two days. 14-bit is pretty damn good.

We're sure there are some bugs in there somewhere (finding software that is 100 percent bug-free would be like finding the Holy Grail, and about as likely), but we didn't manage to make them come and bite us. While we weren't happy to run into the 1.11 bugs in the first place, we were thrilled to discover that version 1.12 actually got rid of them. It's a clear indicator that Roger and Akai are going to stand behind the MPC60 and continue to upgrade it. It also encourages us to think that the version 2.0 update promised for the end of this year might actually come out on time and have all the features Roger told us about over the phone (a number of which address limitations we raise in this review). Having been around the block more than once on this kind of promise, we aren't about to compromise our virtue without seeing something concrete. We do have our hard-nosed reputation to maintain. But still—it's encouraging.

ARCHITECTURE AND OPERATIONS

Cunningly disguised computers don't come any more cunningly disguised than the MPC60. Roger Linn rightly knows that many musicians, especially time-pressed pros, have a semirational fear of things that appear to be complicated (whether they actually are or not). Better to make it look simple and straightforward, to give it controls that emulate those its likely buyers are used to, and never mind if they don't quite understand how much horsepower is beneath their hands, or how it does what it does. Akai's designers know this, too: They picked the subtle colors, finalized the design of the flip-up 8-line x 40-character backlit LCD display, and added the crowning touch of padding *à la* recording console across the front. At a time when much gear is on the verge of shrinking until it collapses into a mini-black hole, the MPC60 dares to be the right size for human hands to deal with. Not that it's heavy—it isn't. Moving it from place to place is relatively easy, especially since its indented sidepieces make for a good grasp. Call it a "luggable."

One final note on construction. Kudos to the engineer who laid out the small but effective ventilation slots at the rear of the unit's top and bottom panels. Overheating can make even a good machine act up, so we left our MPC60 on for four straight days to see how it took the stress. No problem.

Specsmanship. Some questions have two answers. For example, if you ask us where the MPC60 stacks up in the Bit Wars, you need to specify whether you want to hear from our ears or our circuithead inner nature. Ears first: It sounds great. The drums on the factory disks, all credited to Roger Linn and producer/drummer Willie Wilcox, were recorded the way we'd like to see more factory samples done—that is, a full spectral range, little apparent EQ, and even less room sound. This is both tasteful and appropriate, considering that the MPC60's target market will presumably want the freedom to warp these sounds with their own signal processors instead of live inside someone else's boundaries. As for the numbers: The MPC60 has a 40kHz sampling rate, 18kHz frequency response, 16-bit A/D and D/A converters, 16-bit sequencer memory, and 12-bit sample memory.

Say what? Call it a late-blooming design choice, one that Roger and Akai had to commit to before they knew that "16-bit" was the buzzword they'd have to market against. The truth is that the MPC60 has 12-bit sample storage but 14-bit resolution, thanks to an adroit memory trick. When it samples, the MPC60 stuffs a 16-bit sample into sequencer memory, then compresses the data into 12-bit form, and moves it into sample memory. The result of these machinations is the equivalent of 14-bit resolution. (We once worked with a 16-bit PCM digital audio encoder for the better part of a year, listening intently every day, and yet we didn't notice at all when it was accidentally switched into 14-bit mode for two days. 14-bit is pretty damn good.)

This memory trick has two side effects. First, though the unexpanded MPC60 has enough memory for 13.1 seconds of samples, the maximum length of any one sample is 5.3 seconds. That's what will fit in the sequencer RAM. Secondly, every time you sample, you wipe out your sequencer memory. Boom. Gone. Akai's advice is that you sample and sequence in separate sessions, and we have to concur. It's somewhat annoying, but when the choice is between saving ourselves a few extra disk loads and superior sound quality, we know which we prefer.

The Drumming Part. It would be surprising if the drum machine side of the MPC60 weren't superior to other aspects of its design, considering the name on the front panel. Roger Linn has been listening to his customers longer than anybody, and he's developed very clear ideas about how a drum machine in a production environment should function. There is, of course, the classic live time-

MPC60 SPECS

Description: Sampling drum machine and MIDI sequencer.

Voices: 16-voice internal polyphony. Up to 32 sounds available onboard at a time, arranged in two banks. Sounds may be doubled to trigger together automatically. Re-triggering a drum or sampled sound does not cut off earlier notes.

Memory: 512K sequencer RAM with 60,000 note capacity. 256K program ROM. 768K sampling RAM holds up to 13.1 seconds of samples, expandable to 1.5 Meg/26.2 seconds.

Features: 16 velocity-sensitive drum pads with programmable level, pan, and pitch. 8-line, 320-character backlit LCD with graphics and contrast control. 31/2" disk drive. Tape transport–like controls, data wheel, numeric keypad, cursor keys, and 28 dedicated function keys. Four variable-use softkeys. Context-sensitive help. 10 MHz 80186 microprocessor.

Sequencer: 99-sequence capacity, each with up to 99 tracks. Each track may be assigned to any one or two MIDI channels. Sequences may be played back independently or assembled into 20 programmed songs, with up to 256 steps per song. Sequences may be looped to play from any bar. Both "on the fly" and step recording/editing/erasing modes available. Automated punch-in/out. Timing resolution of 96 clocks per beat. Per-track quantizing values from 1/8-note to 32nd-note triplet available before and after recording, even while sequence is looped; but quantizing is permanent. Quantized tracks can be shifted forward or backward in time relative to quantize setting. Drum and MIDI parts stored in separate track formats to allow recording of specialized drum functions such as stereo pan and pitch. Pre- and post-sequencing hi-hat decay control.

Audio: L/R stereo outs, eight assignable individual or mix outs, echo send with stereo returns, sampling input, three-way sampling input gain switch, metronome out. 40kHz sampling rate with 16-bit A/D and D/A converters. Samples stored in companded 12-bit format for playback at 14-bit-equivalent resolution. Built-in echo send and stereo returns; effect send level is programmable per sound in separate echo mix.

Interfacing: Sync in/out, sync level control, two MIDI ins with automatic merge to receive both keyboard and sync data, four separate MIDI outs (any MIDI channel can be routed to any single out), RS-232 connector, two jacks for programmable footswitches. Sync to SMPTE, MTC, MIDI clock, MIDI Song Position Pointer, FSK, pulse wave, and quarter-note metronome clicks, Supports MIDI Sample Dump Standard.

Size: 19 1/2" x 18" x 5". 23 pounds.

List Price: $4,999.95. Sampling memory expansion, $599.95.

correction loop record and erase that helped make his earlier creations so popular in the first place. But there is also the built-in echo send/mixer, mentioned above; complex programmable tempo, mix, and pan changes; and extremely flexible voice allocation schemes.

However. We wouldn't be *Keyboard* if we didn't want more from everything we played with, and so we wonder, why aren't the sounds more malleable? Other sampling drum machines, some much less expensive, offer considerable sound processing. We'd love to see onboard digital EQ, multi-stage pitch and amplitude envelopes, even something as simple as a reverse function. These features and others aren't there now; we hope they will be.

The Sampling Part. One-shot samplers are less samplers, by our definition, than they are sound cannons. Load, aim, light the blue touch paper, and stand back! The MPC60 falls into this category. While it samples easily enough, and those samples sound great, there is very little you can do with a sound once you've grabbed it. The MPC60 offers no detailed sample editing or looping functions at all: just start time, end time, and fadeout slope, all in milliseconds. If your goal in life is to replace every snare in your pop song with the snare from somebody else's pop song, you'll love it. But anyone needing a full-function sampler will have to turn elsewhere.

The Sequencing Part. The sequencer in the MPC60 holds 199 sequences in memory, each with up to 99 tracks, and 20 songs of up to 256 linked and looping sequences. Recording is oriented in either of two ways, as stringing together patterns or as linear track recording (the manual is written to heavily favor pattern-style recording). Looping is by sequence, not track, though the loop can be set to begin at any bar. To record a track, you must first choose a specific number of bars you wish to record into. To edit—except for the kind of live erasure described earlier—you must work in step mode.

Clearest indication of its orientation, however, is the way the MPC60 sequencer treats drum tracks vs. MIDI tracks. Drum tracks are stored as MIDI note numbers 0–31 and play (by default) over MIDI channel 16; send a drum track out to a synth and all you'll get is sonic sludge. To be fair, these note numbers can be individually reassigned if you want to take the time. But why chunk them down there in the first place? One of our favorite things to do when creating new drum tracks is transpose old ones up and down against our drum machine until we hear unexpected but useful new patterns—and yet the MPC60 will not transpose drum tracks. We certainly understand the need to approach drums differently than MIDI's more keyboard-oriented terms, but we don't understand why flexibility in that direction must necessarily hamper flexibility in dealing with other user sequencer operations. We made a number of calls to determine how MPC60 owners used the sequencer: commonly, it served as a "sketchpad" for song structure development, after which the sequence would be ported to a computer-based system for fine tuning, global edits, and full orchestration. Whether you will be satisfied with the operation of the sequencer depends entirely on whether its preconceptions and ground rules concerning how to go about recording music match up with yours.

The Verdict. Above reservations aside, we've come to like the MPC60. A lot. Its operating system is clearly still in a state of rapid development, and the inherent potential of its hardware not yet realized, but you know—we find that exciting. An already useful product that still has room to grow is a rarity in these times of hype and hash and pre-release obsolescence. No, its sequencer doesn't yet replace our computer-based system, nor does its sampler replace our other samplers. That isn't the point. This is: Sometimes—and this is especially true in the production studio environments the MPC60 was designed for—having it all in one place beats having it all.

PROPELLERHEAD: PROPELLING CHANGES

By Mark Vail || *Keyboard*, April 1999

Software developers Steinberg and Propellerhead, perhaps more than any others, helped usher in the age of the software synth and all-in-one computer workstation. Mark Vail, best known for chronicling the history of hardware, here reveals how the cult phenomenon ReBirth was birthed in the first place. In the ultimate sign of the software's staying power, and a literal rebirth, ReBirth was re-engineered for Apple's iPad in 2010, complete with some favorite user mods. —PK

Have you been ReBirthed? Tens of thousands have worldwide. In case you've been living in a cave, Steinberg ReBirth RB-338 is a modeled simulation of Roland's TR-808 and -909 drum machines and TB-303 Bassline synth for Power Mac or Pentium PC. ReBirth (reviewed Sept. '97) was developed by Sweden's Propellerhead Software, and since its inception it has caused major commotion in the music industry.

More than its developers ever imagined. "We put the alpha version on our Web site in January '97," recalls Ernst Nathorst-Böös, Propellerhead co-founder and managing director. "It wasn't nearly finished, but we thought that we would have to struggle for months to promote it via our Web pages and going to mailing lists and chat rooms, whatever. Then we started checking the statistics: We had a few hits the first day, the second day we had 200 people visit the site, the third day we had more than 1,000 people, and it grew like that. After a few days, our Internet service provider called and said, "We don't know what you're doing, but you've got to stop doing it, because you're pulling down the whole site.""

In ReBirth, Nathorst-Böös and his cohorts had come up with something special, yet they didn't really know what they had. "The first idea was to get something together that people could use to make music," he says. "There aren't yet that many software solutions that you can load into your computer and in five minutes make music. We know that a lot of our users have never used anything before; they don't have any synthesizers or music programs. They download the demo, get hooked, and then buy the program. For many of these people, it's a starting point.

"The ReBirth song files are small, and they contain everything—all the information required. It's a total-recall system. You load the song and it will sound exactly like it did on someone else's system, which not even General MIDI does. People can just load up Rebirth, make a song in a short time, save it to disk, and put it on the Internet to be shared with a lot of others instantaneously. People talk about the sound and vintage aspects, but we think the core of its success is the fact that you don't have to have a long musical background to get to a position where you can publish yourself."

Over 20,000 copies of ReBirth have been sold so far, and more than 100,000 demo versions have been downloaded via the Internet. Meanwhile, a few aspiring programmers have expanded on Propeller-head's work. "We've had followers, people who like what we're doing and want to be part of it. Some of them have developed freeware utility programs for ReBirth, which you can find on our Web site. We're extremely happy for that. We've borrowed concepts from other people in our products, so that's not at all strange. Besides, it's extremely flattering and very good for everybody.

"After a few days, our Internet service provider called and said, 'We don't know what you're doing, but you've got to stop doing it, because you're pulling down the whole site.'"

—ERNST NATHORST-BÖÖS (CO-FOUNDER, PROPELLERHEAD)

"Then there are Mods for ReBirth. Since version 1.0 of the program, we were using samples for the drum machine sounds. Those are just sound resources pasted into the application file. Same thing with the front panel: The images are just pictures. Anyone with a reasonable knowledge of computers can go in and check them out. But then someone figured out that they could exchange the resources. They took out the sounds and graphic files and put in their own samples and graphic files.

"I can't remember the first Mod that was made; it was red, that's all I can remember. We never got our hands on it, but we saw pictures of it on the Internet. They probably thought it was illegal—it was illegal—but I'm sure they thought we would get upset, so we never got our hands on it. But we embraced that, because, although it was complicated for us from a legal standpoint that they modified the application file, on the other hand, what they did was open up the possibility for people to create their own versions of ReBirth. Then people started creating all these great incarnations of the program that looked really weird. There was a Linn-Drum version that looked like a Western saloon, and there's a Swedish guy who did the Red Top Mod with Daft Punk–like sounds in it.

"These started floating around, and we managed to find a way for people to do this legally; we had simple agreements they could sign. Now, since version 2.0, the graphics and sounds are in separate files—a special Mod file—and we even include a utility for people to create their own Mods. So anyone who has any knowledge of Photoshop and audio-editing programs like BIAS Peak can make their own Mods. There are a number of Mods included on the ReBirth CD-ROM, and if you look on our Web page we have 17 Mods there now.

"In some ways, we've always been one step behind. It's our users who have taken all these initiatives. We didn't open the first Web page with songs on it; someone else did. We also didn't do the first Mod; someone else did. There are all these people all over the world with these great ideas, and it's fantastic."

8

Sampling Nation

"THEY'RE MAKING SAMPLERS WRONG": SIX TECHNO SAMPLE-HEADS DUMP THE DIGITAL GARBAGE

By Greg Rule || *Keyboard*, May 1994

t a time when computers' digital audio capabilities were woefully limited, the hardware sampler was king. Listen closely to the complaints of a roundtable of artists—pioneering innovators, all—and you may see the template for the software revolution still to come. At the same time, the very limitations they cursed became ingredients in their sounds, thanks to tenacity, compositional ingenuity, and sometimes, happy accident. —PK

Hi-tech, dead? Not by a long shot. And certainly not in the world of techno—a genre bursting with synthetic textures, throbbing electronic percussion, and layers of meticulously crafted samples. Like the hip-hop artists spotlighted in Part 1 of our Sampling Nation report (see *Keyboard*, May 1994), techno artists are masters of machines, and samplers are vital tools of their trade.

What exactly are these artists sampling? How are they manipulating their data? What's their take on the current crop of machinery? And do they think it's acceptable to sample passages from other artists? That's precisely what *Keyboard* set out to learn from seven of techno's finest, the centerpiece being a four-man roundtable held recently in San Francisco.

The responses we received were a far cry from those given by the hip-hop interviewees. Generally speaking, hip-hoppers aren't concerned with sample resolution, editing features, and the like. In fact, three of our four artists reported using a sole "dinosaur" sampler to create their hit tunes.

Techno artists, in marked contrast, are generally dissatisfied with the state of technology. Richard James (aka Aphex Twin/Polygon Window) summarized samplers as "shit," saying, "I could talk for ages about all the things they should have on them that they don't." As did Kris Weston of the Orb, who told us manufacturers "are making samplers wrong," and they should consult him "to find out how to design them."

When it comes to sampling material from other artists, or being sampled, the techno contingent took a surprisingly relaxed stance. Richard James, for one, said he didn't care if someone copied his whole track and put it out under a different name, a feeling Mark Gage of Vapourspace related to. He reported that someone took almost 10 minutes of an 18-minute track of his. "As far as I'm concerned," he told us, "once someone puts something out, they might as well get used to the fact that people are going to pilfer." Here, then, straight from the mouths of the artists, are candid comments on the state of samplers and sampling.

KRIS WESTON (THE ORB)

Walking into an Orb show is like walking into a bizarre psychedelic dreamland. "The best gig in the world," raves the British publication *NME*. Whatever the venue, Orbsters Alex Patterson and Kris "Thrash" Weston put on a show that even the mighty Pink Floyd would applaud. The band's discography includes *Little Fluffy Clouds, Adventures Beyond the Ultraworld,* and *U.F.Orb* (on Big Life/Mercury), and *Orb Live 93* (Island). Not one to candy-coat his views, Kris Weston gives manufacturers of samplers a piece of his mind.

You seem pretty dissatisfied with samplers. Why?
There's not enough power to manipulate sounds. Really, what you need is a sam-

pler with a desk inside of it, with full effects and everything, so you could manipulate sounds into something completely different. You can kind of do that with the Roland S-750's filters, but it's still very limited. I think you should have everything in front of you—all the parameters should be immediately available, as in old analog synthesizers and manual sequencers. It's such a human thing to do. It's not human to go through pages.

Is the S-750 your sampler of choice?

One of them, but I also use Sequential's Prophet 2000 and Studio 440, and an Akai S1100.

When you edit, do you do so off-site with computer editing software?

No, we ain't got the gear to do all that.

So you do it all within the sampler.

Yeah. I mean, you still can't do all that much with a computer.

When you're building songs, what role does the sampler typically play in the process?

Well, of course we do things different each time. It all depends on the idea of the song.

Do you use loops for your rhythmic beds?

No, we don't use loops. All the samples we use are disguised; they sound like something completely different, unless you want to use them in the context of having as an obvious sample, which is sometimes nice.

Do you have anything against using loops?

No, not really. There has been quite a bit of that, but they can be good in some ways. Samples that have been used to make another track are totally valid. I mean, why not? Why isn't it valid? But personally, we've been staying away from that.

So you sample mostly from scratch?

Yeah, we do everything from scratch. All the sounds, everything.

Give us examples of sounds you've captured that have appeared on your records.

We sampled an elephant blowing out water, and used that as noise over the top.

Did you go to the zoo to get that sound?

No, that was off one of Alex's videos that he took on holiday. We also took a sample of a horse's sniff and used that as a proper hi-hat. It sounded pretty good.

Have you done any similarly strange things for other tracks?

We do that a lot—fucking around and experimenting with big tubes and shit. More recently, we heard some drums in the park at about four o'clock in the morning. We put mics on the other side of the park, and we were in the process of sampling them when the police turned up.

What's your message to manufacturers of samplers?

Today's keyboards, I don't know what the fuck they're doing, but they've lost it.
A lot of people are going back to the old stuff.
I didn't think they were ever that good in the first place.

RICHARD JAMES (APHEX TWIN/POLYGON WINDOW)

Under the monikers Aphex Twin and Polygon Window, Richard James has re-corded *Didgeridoo* (Outer Rhythm), *Joyrex J4 & J5* (Rephlex), *Ambient Works 82–92* (R&S), *Polygon Window* (Warp), *On* (Sire), and *Selected Ambient Works Volume 2* (Sire). The mad scientist of techno, he designs and builds his own oddball elec-tronic instruments from scratch. Like Weston, he has a nit or two to pick with manufacturers of samplers.

MARK GAGE (VAPOURSPACE)

Mark Gage's debut EP *Gravitational Arch of 10* (Probe/Plus) is colorfully described in his press packet as "a gorgeous, spooky, downpour of tranquility . . . an overload of textures and hard-hitting grooves." At press time, his full-length FFRR follow-up, *Themes from Vapor Space*, was on its way to record stores. Other releases include *Cusp* (Probe/Plus 8) and *Magnetic Gravity Arch Suite* (FFRR). Here, Gage tells us how a sampler "accident" led to a hit song, and how he's already fallen prey to sample thievery.

PAUL AND PHIL HARTNOLL (ORBITAL)

With four releases to their credit, *Orbital 7, Halcyon EP, Orbital 2,* and *Diversions* (all on FFRR), the brothers Hartnoll have been wowing audiences with their "mind-bending, body-invading journey into keyboard wizardry," according to *Billboard*. Here the Hartnolls tell us, in colorful terms, how a couple of their tracks evolved from samples of "old, weird, crap records."

How did you get into sampling?
James: I started out making tape samples until I eventually got one of those kits from Synclair—one of those build-it-yourself things for about 50 pounds. That's what got me hooked on sampling.
How do you marry samplers with your homemade instruments?
James: I use samplers mainly because the gear that I build doesn't respond to MIDI. I have to sample the sounds and use them that way sometimes to get a tighter feel. If I trigger all the stuff I've made with voltages, it has a looser kind of feel. So I use the sampler for tightness, really.
Describe the ideal sampler.
James: It would be a sampling workstation of sorts, but it would be portable and

it would run off batteries. Nothing like that is out there; the closest things might be the [Akai] MPC-60 and [Sequential] Studio 440. But today's samplers, they're just fuckin' shit, really. I designed and built my own sampler for a college project once. When it worked, I reckon it pissed on just about any manufactured sampler. I could talk for ages about all the things they should have on them that they don't.

For example?

James: Too many samplers today are made like DAT machines. Manufacturers don't put enough features on them, probably 'cause they think it'll scare off the users; they think there are probably too many buttons on the thing already.

What features do you think should be standard?

James: Totally variable sampling rates. You should be able to sample from, say, zero to 100k. Instead, they give you four or five rates. You should be able to do loads of digital effects.

Gage: They should be more like synthesizers. It would be great to have lots of knobs for things like resonance, filters, and envelopes—right on the unit itself, instead of jamming it all into one little rack-mount thing, or whatever.

Phil Hartnoll: It's made for bloody convenience, isn't it?

Paul Hartnoll: It's such crap. Who gives a fuck if you're paying 1,500 pounds for a piece of equipment? You know, you want it because it's a good piece of equipment. You don't want it because it fits into a one-rack unit.

Phil Hartnoll: Calm down.

Paul Hartnoll: No, I won't calm down! [*Laughs.*]

How important are samplers in your setup?

Gage: Lately I've been decreasing the role of the sampler a little bit, trying to use more synth technology. I think a lot of people have gone the cheesy route with samplers, using breakbeats, girl singers, and all that. So I've tried to stray from that idea.

Let's segue into applications. Using one of your songs as an example, tell us how you put sampling to use in the studio.

Gage: Primarily I trigger my sampler with the [Roland TR-] 909, using the external instrument mode, which I probably shouldn't say too much about; a lot of people probably don't know about that. For example, the song "The Gravitational Arch of 10" was an entire mistake. I had a disk loaded in the sampler for one of my other tracks, and I triggered the wrong pattern on the drum machine. Immediately I turned on the DAT and started screwing around with the pitch-bend wheel on the [Roland] SH-101. Within about an hour and a half, I had the track finished down to DAT. Things don't always happen that way, though. I mean, it usually starts with a little riff or something, whether it's a sampled riff or a synth thing. It's not like it's divine intervention. Some things can take me two weeks, other things can take me two hours.

Techno folks have been criticized at times for fabricating music from pre-existing samples or relying too much on robotic four-on-the-floor drumbeats.

Gage: It all depends on the person who's operating the gear. I mean, anybody can lay down something, but the question is whether or not it's genuine or different.

Paul H.: I'd like to see those people who complain about that do it themselves.

Gage: Absolutely.

What kinds of things are you sampling . . . any real-world sounds, for example?

Paul H.: Not as much as we want to. We keep meaning to.

Phil H.: We get lots of things from old secondhand records.

Paul H.: Yeah, those really old, weird, crap ones. Sometimes we go through them without even listening, really, sampling ten seconds here and there, and every once in a while we'll cut into something and, "Right! That's the bit I want."

More specifically?

Paul H.: It's hard to single anything out 'cause it's so, sort of random all the time.

Gage: Tell them about "Chime."

Paul H.: "Chime," okay, that was a case of random sampling with an easy-listening record—just sort of starting with a bit about two bars long, and then honing it down and down and down until we ended up with a single-shot sound. Then we started making up a tune from that.

Easy listening, as in Perry Como?

Phil H.: Yeah, exactly. On another track we sampled, Paul brought back a didgeridoo from Australia. He was playing it, a long bit, and we sampled and looped it.

Paul H.: I think to make it more interesting we took two samples of it, panned one left, one right, and played one five semitones lower than it should have been.

Didn't that create a rhythmic mismatch?

Phil H.: It was mostly a drone.

Paul H.: But it did have a rhythm to it. What it ended up being was sort of a triplet figure under the original, and we also put a four-to-the-floor thing against it, which created an interesting rhythm. What else did we sample there? Oh, yeah, that was the one case where we went around with a Walkman, recording sounds. We actually got the sound of an Australian pedestrian crossing, which was a piece of percussion just by itself.

Phil H.: Another track we sampled this vocal a cappella bit and then reversed the thing. It made this lovely melody just by reversing it.

Do you edit within the sampler?

Paul H.: Yeah, we do it all with the sampler.

And you find that adequate enough?

Paul H.: Yeah. I mean, the Emax II has a crap little screen on it, but I found that after a while it doesn't really matter anyway, 'cause you just use your ears.

Phil H.: With samplers, they do tend to have their own unique sort of sound. You know. they all sound a bit different, like all different makes of instruments do. One might presume that a sampler is just a sampler, but I don't find that to be true. The Emax, for example, is quite warm and friendly.

Richard, could you give us some examples of the types of things you've sampled of late?

James: Well. I'll have to be a prick about that.

Excuse me?

James: I don't like to talk about the way I do tracks.

Gage: Come on. Tell us about "Tampax."

James: All right, but that's just a really boring example of sampling. I nicked a bit of a Tampax advertisement, and used it in a track. But I don't want to say anything about the way I use it.

Why not?

James: In this business, it's kind of a geeky kind of music world where everyone thinks their success depends upon their secrets of the trade. In actual fact, it probably doesn't depend on that at all, but I still get chills down my spine thinking about telling people about the way I do things, so I don't. [Ed. Note: James wasn't kidding. When we tried to get an up-close look at his bizarre electronic instruments during sound check, we were promptly escorted off the stage.]

"It's kind of a geeky kind of music world where everyone thinks their success depends upon their secrets of the trade. In actual fact, it probably doesn't depend on that at all, but I still get chills down my spine thinking about telling people about the way I do things, so I don't."

—RICHARD JAMES (APHEX TWIN)

Okay, let's approach the subject from another angle. Did you have to get permission from the Tampax company before using that sample?

James: No. The things I've sampled . . . I've probably only sampled about three or four things ever that haven't been my own material. The last 14 months, I haven't used anyone else's equipment, never mind anyone else's sounds. I just became totally obsessed with using my own sounds, and got to the point where I chucked out all my standard gear in my studio. Now I exclusively use my own gear, apart from things like computers and samplers. But everything that makes a sound, basically, is my own gear.

What do you feel should happen in the courts concerning sampling rights?

James: I don't care. I don't care if someone copies my whole track and puts it out under a different name.

Really?

James: Absolutely.

Mark, what do you think?

Gage: To a degree it doesn't bother me. It probably bothers my label more. I've already had someone take almost 10 minutes of an 18-minute track of mine . . . it was mastered at 45, and they played it at 33 on this big collage CD called *Lotus One*. There was no information given on it, but whoever used it, though, did so interestingly; they layered all this other stuff over it. I think you're not really famous until you've been ripped off.

But then again, musicians need to pay their rent. If they're getting ripped off, why should they sit idly by when they could be getting paid for their work?

Gage: It's up to you, and who you get involved with. There are so many scams in the music industry. I think people should be a little bit more worried about being ripped off by their actual labels than by other people.

Phil H.: Hear, hear!

Gage: I mean, appropriation has been around now for quite a while in audio and video. People should be getting used to it by now. Whenever I use something that belongs to someone else, I at least try to alter it to a certain degree.

Phil H.: I think it's great if somebody samples us, particularly if it's done in a creative way. Then again, if it's crap, then they deserve to get sued [*laughs*]. Nah, I didn't really mean that.

ULTRAMARINE

The music of Ian Cooper and Paul Hammond defies instant categorization. "We hear all the different labels applied to our music," chuckles Cooper, "but I think we're quite happy leaving it like that." Ambient, psychedelic, neo-jazz, techno-lite— whatever the name, one thing is certain, Cooper and Hammond know how to wrench a sampler. And they have plenty of records to prove it: *Ultramarine*, *Wyndham Lewis*, *Folk* (Les Disques Du Crepuscule, Belgium), *Every Man and Woman Is a Star* (Rough Trade), *Nightfall in Sweetleaf* (Dali), and most recently *United Kingdoms* (Sire/Giant). Here, the duo give us a few examples of how sampling was used on their latest.

Hammond: Samplers are absolutely central to what we do. We do the initial writing on an Akai S1000, and build up our songs pretty much with tiny samples.

What kinds of things do you sample?

Hammond: Records, really. Any old stuff. What we're avoiding is taking huge chunks of tracks, because, obviously, it's dodgy legally. So we're not doing that. We prefer artistically to use very, very small snatches of sound, just a single note or a single beat or whatever.

Cooper: To give you an example of the kind of stuff we've been going for, we sampled a lot of early '70s, so-called progressive-rock albums. We found some wonderfully recorded Hammond organ put through fuzz pedals. So we might sample chords or notes from that. Or we might create something from an old scratchy, low-budget reggae album.

So you've shied away from samples that have their own rhythms?

Hammond: Rhythmically, we're a bit looser about how much we take. We do take larger chunks because you can cut them around. You're not tied to a particular tune or chord sequence, and they're less identifiable.

Cooper: There have been a couple of instances on this album where we might have taken a bar or two of something that had an initial rhythm, built up a song around it, and then taken that sample away. What you're left with is something very bizarre that follows no logical rules. There might be some auxiliary snares and hi-hats in unusual places just because there was a more coherent rhythm there originally which we then took away.

Do you edit internally within the Akai?

Hammond: No, we've mucked around with that, but to be honest, it's never been much use to us, really. We like to keep samples fairly crude anyway. We often enhance the vinyl noise on a particular percussive sound, for example, because it adds to the graininess and texture of the sample. So no, we never really got into diddling around to that extent with sample editors.

Cooper: We tend to go the long way around, anyway. If we feel something is going to work, but the timing is a bit out, then we'll chop it up into loads of separate samples. One drum sample might become Drum A, Drum B, C, D, E, and so on—a hugely complex thing.

Are you happy with the state of samplers right now, or do you wish the technology were more developed?

Hammond: I think by and large we are reasonably happy with it, because when you think about it, it is a pretty simple device, really. It affects me like a tape machine in a way; you're just taking small snatches of sound and playing them back in a way that you want. Essentially it's a quite simple instrument. We don't really manipulate samples that much. We kind of chop 'em up and deal with 'em inside the machine and on the sequencer, but we don't tend to over-EQ them and those kinds of things. With most samples, we use the original EQ anyway.

Cooper: I think with samplers, the possibilities are so far-reaching that most people are really only scratching the surface when they use them. It's not as if we've dried up with that particular machine, and, "Oh I wish I had this gadget or that feature." We still have so much to do with the gear we've got.

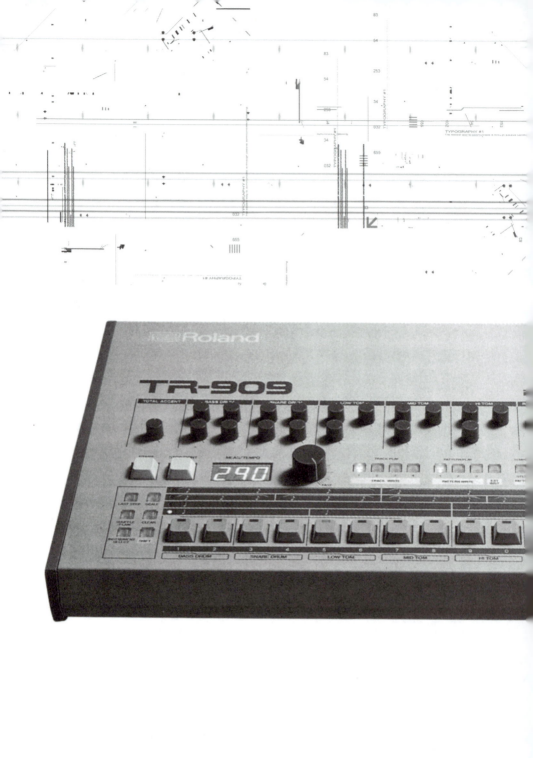

9

Charlie Clouser on Techno

TECHNO HOW-TO

By Charlie Clouser || *Keyboard*, September 1993

efore his influential six-year stint with Nine Inch Nails, before work with Marilyn Manson and Meat Beat Manifesto, before Grammy-winning remixes and TV and game scores, Charlie Clouser taught Keyboard *readers how to make techno. His advice treads from the obvious to the anything-but and, before Clouser had amassed his mind-boggling remix discography, reveals his musical insights and personality. The hardware-centric working methods, composed in a world without Ableton Live, also say a lot about the way in which interfaces impacted music-making methods—including how clever artists twisted those interfaces to their own purposes. —PK*

Live from the techno trenches, *Keyboard* is proud to present excerpts from the studio diary of Charlie Clouser, bonafide techno-madman, the freak behind sampled-preacher-and-astronaut techno rappers Thinking Machine and creepy futuristic supergroup Burning Retna, as well as numerous hit remixes. —Greg Rule

Drums (Sort of). One of the fundamental building blocks of my tracks is analog drum sounds (often culled from the Roland TR-808 and TR-909). But with an analog synth and a sampler, you can build an arsenal of custom-tailored Kraftwerk-style analog drum samples in a flash. Nearly any analog synth will do, but some of the best are the older monophonic ones.

Start with a simple sine or triangle wave. Increase the filter resonance while decreasing the filter cutoff until a mildly howling tone results. Set all of the envelope generator's controls to zero, raise the envelope amount and decay time gradually until the desired percussiveness is achieved, and sample the result.

By toying with the filter cutoff, resonance, and envelope amount, you can create 808 tom- and conga-type sounds. Switch one of the synth's oscillators to white noise and blend it in for snare-type effects. Adding oscillator sync and ring mod (if available), as well as envelope and 110 control of oscillator pitch, will take you into the realm of German clanks and Belgian boinks, as long as you keep the sounds punchy by suitable adjustment of the envelope. To gain even more punch, sample the synth through a compressor.

Oftentimes, when left alone in a room with an old synth, I'll keep a DAT tape rolling as I tweak sounds. That way, I can go back later and find the good bits, as well as apply effects before sampling, if needed. Remember, an average sound can take on a whole new personality when sampled and played at other pitches on the keyboard. Don't pass judgment on a sound until you play the sample back across all five octaves. Reverbs and delays, when sampled and played at other pitches, will often take on new characteristics.

One destructive tip: I once forgot to reset a console and was greeted by the sound of my analog drum tracks pegging the console inputs. The result, a folding, mashed, positively crimping tone—music to my ears, since it was so much larger than before.

Another percussive favorite are what I call "snip" drums: individual drum hits snipped out of breakbeats and drum loops. This lets you create your own drum patterns, or add extra parts to the loop, while retaining the tone of the original.

Here's how I do it: Start with a drum loop from a commercially available, license-free sample library, and then truncate it on your sampler or sample editing program until only a single kick or snare remains. Save that as an individual sample. Next, load the original loop again and then truncate again until a different drum hit remains. Soon you'll have five or six kicks and snares, with a variety of tones, that make a nice matched set. I usually snip up the ugliest, most poorly recorded loops because they seem to have the most character. The more indistinct and thumping the kick drum, and the more tinny and ringing the snare, the better. Map these across your sampler and you've got the tones of your favorite breakbeat, but you control the rhythm.

Completely Looped. When it comes to using sampled loops in a more conventional way, a real time-saver is the step-record function available on most sequencers. If you have a one-bar sample loop that you wish to enter into a sequence, simply enter step-record mode, set the step size to whole notes, set the step duration to a few clock ticks less than a whole note, and play the desired key repeatedly until the required number of bars has been entered. This method is often faster than recording in real time, and the resulting track is already quantized. Generally, each start note that triggers a loop should be quantized, and the note-off should occur only a couple of clock ticks before the next beat. If you've been recording while triggering the loop from the keyboard, do yourself a favor and use your sequencer's editing functions to set that track's note durations and key velocities to constant values; otherwise you may wind up with volume fluctuations and gaps at the ends of some measures.

Matching a loop's tempo to that of your sequence is another story. In order to do this, first create an appropriate test sequence, preferably by the step-record method above, and get it going in infinite loop mode. If your sequence is already running at the desired tempo, and you have entered nice, neat, quantized notes to trigger the loop, you may now progress to your sampler, where you adjust the pitch of the sampled loop until the end of the loop meets seamlessly with the beginning—no flamming or double triggering, and no gap. If you hear a gap or double hit at the end of the loop, adjust the sample's pitch down; if the turnaround is rushed, adjust the pitch up. Have your sequencer loop a carefully entered test sequence and fiddle with the pitch of the loop. By doing so, you can quickly zero in on the right value. But what about the pitch of the loop, doesn't that change? Yeah, it does. So what?

No, seriously, if you have the gear to do high-quality pitch change and/or time compression, go for it (although I rarely do it for strictly corrective reasons). If your loop sample is tuned up 2.43 semitones to line up with the tempo of your sequence, simply pitch-change it down by 2.43 semitones and you're all set. You may not want to do this; a great way to generate frenzy in a track is to use drum loops that are much slower than your song and speed them up without correcting the pitch. The pitch of the drums becomes higher, the sounds get tighter, and the syncopation and swing of the original feel becomes more dramatic.

Bass Hit. The essence of the techno bass sound is purity. Purity of tone, purity of delivery, purity of thought (just kidding). When the track is blasting from a club sound system, with the serious low-end response, the driest, cleanest, simplest bass sounds seem to work best. Part of the reason for the renewed popularity of monophonic analog synths is the fact that any dusty old synth can produce an acceptable bass noise of some type.

> The essence of the techno bass sound is purity. Techno bass sounds don't need to be fat so much as they need to be dry.
>
> —CHARLIE CLOUSER

Believe it or not, techno bass sounds don't need to be fat so much as they need to be dry. A simple, non-effected, clean and dry mono synth sound will rock the house more effectively than some slap-bass sample from a workstation keyboard that's drenched in chorusing and so forth. Do you ever wonder what all those single-cycle waveforms in your sample-playback synth are for? They're for making bass sounds, silly! Even those weak organ-sounding tones can work, if you stack a couple of them and give each slightly different envelope settings.

Of course, they must by dry as a bone and very loud. You can try eliminating velocity sensitivity for more instant gratification. Most sample-playback synths have a flabby pick-bass sample, as well, which is actually useful if you mix it low with some of the other synth tones on top, give it a tight envelope, and maybe control its volume with the mod wheel so you can bring it in at will (adding more thwonk on the attack as needed).

Another important feature found on just about every analog synth is adjustable filter resonance (Q). Curiously, this important parameter is missing from a majority of samplers, sample-playback synths, and digital synths. Besides providing the classic "wa-wa-wow" bass sounds (by having an envelope generator control the filter frequency with high resonance settings), you can use middle-range resonance settings to emphasize a specific frequency range of a sound—adding more punch or thump as needed by substituting keyboard tracking for envelope control.

The real fun starts when you control filter frequency from an LFO (low-frequency oscillator). This provides a regular sweeping pattern that probably won't sync up to the beat. By setting the LFO's rate so that it's almost (but not quite) in sync with your tempo, you can simulate Kraftwerk-style effects where each repetition of a looping synth phrase is subtly different. To create more controlled filter sweep effects, route the mod wheel or slider so it controls filter cutoff and nothing else. Then you can overdub the mod wheel or slider movements into the sequencer and loop a short pattern, if desired, after the keyboard performance has been recorded.

These filter-controlling techniques are useful for an entire range of analog synth sounds, from percussive arpeggiator-type sounds to long, sweeping pads.

Orchestra Hits for Dinner Again? You may have noticed more and more orchestra-hit mutations appearing in techno records.

Usually played in a jerky, stabbing, syncopated rhythm, and a chromatic (if not completely atonal) scale, the sampled hit is here to stay.

The trick is to pick the biggest, fattest hit with a long, full sustain, and then chop off a good bit from the start so the attack is instantaneous and the sustain is full. Loop the sample, if possible. If there's a chord built into the sample, so much the better. Play it from MIDI drum pads, if possible, and try setting the MIDI note-number assignments at random to find unusual scales. This might sound strange, but close your eyes and set the drum pad's note numbers without listening to it.

Then turn up the speakers and jam. I first used this technique in a moment of desperation on a remix of "Can't Help Myself" by Australian art rockers Icehouse. The resulting riff became the foundation for the whole track.

Another staple of the house music genre are chords played very staccato on a piano or a tight synth patch and then sampled. The chromatic transposition of all the voices in the chord gives a song that familiar feel, and if you keep the samples tight and percussive, they'll add a good bit of punch to your track.

Start with a piano sound or a synth sound that has a piano-like attack and release. Sample a variety of chord voicings, but avoid using notes in the lower octaves or they'll interfere with the bass line. If you spend the afternoon sampling different chords, you'll be able to call up samples that fit neatly any track; just make sure that you sample each chord at more than one root note, for example, D, F#, and A minor, so you can find a sample that doesn't have to be transposed too far to get into the key of the song. But why not just play the chords into the sequencer? Playing one-finger riffs on the sampler is a lot faster and will generally yield tighter results than playing the chords manually. This technique won't do wonders for your keyboard chops, but nobody ever said playing techno would help with that.

Trigger-Happy. The all-too-familiar MIDI gating technique (where a track is chopped up by a gate triggered in rhythm with the track) is easy to achieve.

Method 1: If a standard audio gate or a compressor-limiter with a gate function is available, simply call up an organ patch on an unused synth and route the audio signal into the gate's "key" input. Whenever you play a note on the organ patch (with the key input activated), the gate will open, allowing audio through. Play

NOVEAU RETRO: SIMULATING PRE-MIDI TECHNIQUES ON MODERN GEAR THAT HAS NO KNOBS

Arpeggiators. The hypnotic effect created by early arpeggiators was the precursor to today's totally sequenced sound. An arpeggiator simply triggers the notes of a chord one after another in quick succession. Many provided control over key range, the order in which the notes are triggered, the tempo, and so on.

One of the most common uses for this effect is to create rapid-fire, linear patterns consisting of 16th-notes where the pattern changes with the chords of the song. What I usually do is learn the chords and figure out a way to voice them so that two- or four-beat phrases of 8 or 16 notes can be derived. For example, a five-voice chord comes out to 8 notes if played in "up/down" style (where the low and high voices are each triggered only once per cycle). Try it and you'll see what I mean. Then, with the step-record function on, set the step size to one 16th-note and set note length to half that value.

Simply construct the arpeggio yourself, but slowly. Pay attention to the sequencer counter position, and enter the arpeggio up until the first chord change. Then exit step-record mode, figure out another pattern for the second chord (or simply transpose a few voices in the previous pattern), and step-record that pattern immediately following the first one. Working a measure at a time, you can quickly build an eight-bar phrase that can then be looped.

Another popular arpeggiator effect involves using a faster rate to create flurries of notes, usually sweeping up, to lead into sections of a song. For this effect, I usually use 16th-note triplets or 32nd-notes, and set my punch-in point so that I start step-recording no more than a measure before the song boundary I'm trying to accentuate. Even an arpeggio that's only one or two beats long will often work well, as long as it covers enough of a range on the keyboard in that short period of time.

Analog Sequencers. Remember those? Picture a device with three rows of knobs, 8 or 16 columns across, with each column representing one step in the sequence. As the sequencer was triggered, it would step through the columns from left to right, basically giving you three knobs for each note in the sequence. The voltage output of the knobs could be routed to nearly any parameter you wanted. Of course, it's no fun trying to get each note in a sequence in tune when you're forced to use knobs instead of a keyboard, but when you want some undulating, irregular patterns and sequences that sound different each time they loop, an analog sequencer is hard to beat. I've found ways to simulate my favorite analog sequencer effects, honed on a beastly ARP 2500, which melted down years ago.

Let's say you want to control filter cutoff frequency, filter resonance, or envelope decay time. (I'm assuming you have a synth that can route MIDI controller messages such as mod wheel to the appropriate parameter, and a method of generating these messages, such as on an assignable slider on your MIDI controller or on-screen faders if you're a computer user.) First, set up the desired MIDI slider control routings, and then record the keyboard part that you want to manipulate into your sequencer. Then, on another sequencer track that's set to the same MIDI channel, try the following techniques for entering and processing slider data:

• With the step size set to 16th-notes, go into step-record mode and move the slider, advance one step, move the slider, advance another step, and so on. Hopefully your sequencer will record slider movements even though it's in step-record mode. Some won't, and you'll probably have to use a "thin controllers" command (if available) to eliminate excess data. This technique most accurately approximates the actual functionality of an analog sequencer.

• Try setting the sequencer to a very high or very low tempo and record wild movements of the slider. Then set the tempo back to normal and listen to the results.

• For a slowly developing, ever-changing effect, record 16 bars of crazy slider moves, then use your sequencer's "scale time" function to stretch it the length of the entire song. If that function isn't available, set your sequencer's tempo to the maximum and record live slider moves for the length of the entire song in a matter of seconds!

• Use your trusty "thin controllers" command set to extreme thinning on some of that wildly tweaked slider data. If you can thin it enough, you'll get jagged changes in the controlled parameter. If your sequencer lets you quantize controller events, do so, and the changes will occur in sync with the notes. That will produce a similar effect to step-recording the slider moves.

• On a computer sequencer, use the mouse to draw controller data without looking at the measure numbers. Don't draw smooth curves; instead, just click the mouse at random, entering single events. This should produce as jagged a line as possible. I encourage you to use more than one of the above techniques on the same track; the cumulative effects of radically altering controller data get better as you go along. Also, experiment with routing this data to different parameters. Filter cutoff frequency, resonance amount, envelope attack and decay, and oscillator pulse width are all prime candidates. Remember that real analog sequencers often had three or more rows of knobs, so you should definitely try creating more than one slider track, and route each one to a different parameter on your synth.

To achieve the never-repeating effect, make each slider track loop at some strange point—the fourth beat of bar 11, for example—so that it will take about a hundred bars before all of the looping tracks line up the same way again. This technique can also be applied to hi-hat and percussion tracks, and just about anything that won't rub against the key of the song when its loop doesn't line up right.

16th-notes on the organ patch and route guitar, bass, or a pad sound through this gate. Instant rhythms.

The reason for using an organ patch is that it will usually have an instantaneous attack and release with full sustain, allowing you to precisely edit the duration of the "open gate" events. This method provides the tightest, most rhythmic sound. For a gentler, more fluid effect, use a sound with a longer release as your trigger patch instead of the organ. The pulsing effect will be more subtle but no less satisfying.

If you have an old monophonic analog synth lying around, check and see if it has an "external signal" or "external audio" input. Most Moog, ARP, and similar synths have these jacks, which allow you to feed any signal into the input of the synth's filter where the oscillators feed in. Route your audio source (another keyboard or a guitar, for example) into that jack and route your rhythm pattern to the synth's trigger input (often a cowbell sample will work if amplified enough). You'll then have not only a full-featured MIDI-gating effect, thanks to the synth's envelopes and VCA, but the full complement of filter effects discussed above! Imagine filter-sweeping, pulsating triggered fretless bass! What's the world coming to?

Method 2: If you don't have access to a compressor or mono synth, then you'll have to resort to MIDI volume gating. This can get tedious, but it's worth it. In the event-edit mode of your sequencer, enter a volume message of 127 on every 16th-note for a measure. Next, go to another track and enter a volume message of zero on every 16th-note for the same measure. Shift the second track by a 32nd-note or so, and set both tracks to the same MIDI channel. Loop or repeat that first measure on both tracks, and then play along using a pad sound on the same MIDI channel. Hopefully, you'll hear the once-smooth pad sound chopped up in perfect rhythm. By sliding the second track back and forth in time, you can change the length of the gate events. And by erasing single events from the first track, you can create holes in the pattern. It's worth spending an hour or so doing this. Save a variety of patterns in a file that you can use as a template later. And don't forget that most multi-effects processors that have real-time MIDI parameter control (Lexicon PCM-70, Alesis Quadraverb, and Boss SE-50, for example) will let you control the master volume of the signal going through it via MIDI volume. This allows you to MIDI-volume-gate any signal, not just MIDI synths.

Last Word. Of course it would be great to have a whole bunch of vintage gear all under control of the master computer, but the reality of owning and maintaining a pile of temperamental, perpetually out-of-tune pre-MIDI synths is more than a hassle: It's a career. With a little prodding, however, a totally modern synth setup can simulate many of the best moments of synth history. On the other hand, I wouldn't want anyone to go through life without at least one analog, polyphonic, MIDI-capable synth, and many of the above techniques are most satisfying when implemented on such an axe.

When you combine these techniques with those designed to simulate life in the pre-MIDI days, you can get pretty close to some of the good-old-time synthesis heard on many techno records. Check out recent releases by Depeche Mode, Erasure, and so on. If any of you out there misuse these techniques, don't you hurt yourselves!

The Orb.

10

The Orb

INSIDE THE AMBIENT TECHNO ULTRAWORLD

By Robert Doerschuk || *Keyboard*, June 1995

If music is a response to the temper of our times, then the Orb is exactly what America needs. Things are getting a little too cut-and-dried here: Complex problems beget weirdly simple solutions—kicking people out of the country, putting them in institutions, shutting down institutions, or just saying no. As the guiding force of the group known as the Orb, Alex Paterson sees things differently. His music is all blur and fuzz. Scraps of sound fade in and out, drifting over fields unbound by the barbed wire of verse and chorus. There's rhythm, and it's as regular as anything on the prosaic dance charts. But so are heartbeats regular, though life swirls through and around them with beguiling imprecision. Shapes are hard to identify in Paterson's world. Voices fly about, sometimes as sharp and intrusive as a mosquito's whine, more often muffled and unintelligible; someone is talking, but we can't quite make it out. Occasionally the aural clouds lift and we hear something more clearly—something ugly or scary, a snakehandler's snarl, or fragile, a child's tale. We hold our breaths and listen, afraid of losing this picture of innocence as it sinks into a sea of reverb, the sound of a dream dissolved by the light of awakening.

There's a lot more going on here than ambience. Many of the artists tagged with the ambient label update the ideas pioneered by Brian Eno and, especially, Harold Budd. Through space and suggestion, they define a style that celebrates inertia, or even creates almost a sense of paralysis before a moment of beautiful oblivion. But there's an optimistic tinge to the Orb. It surfaces in the organ motif from "His Immortal Logness" on *Pomme Fritz*, a simple, roller-rinkish tune that seems drawn from some half-remembered childhood scene. It blossoms in synth parts that fan out over teeming noise pastiches. Even the prickly staccato synth and rhythm interludes in the Live 93 version of "Blue Room" is more tickle than sting.

Then there's *Orbus Terrarum*, the latest Orb exercise. As noted in last month's review, Paterson combines a vivid timbral ear and improvisational sense to create an album of great organic power. One could imagine its pulses, spacey reveries and fragmented monologs as a kind of interior soundtrack, a score for a ballet of brain and biology—an almost uniquely human document.

Not much of Paterson's style draws from pre-punk rock or the familiar electronic icons. Its energy is a streamlined variation on the ambient dance discs he spun as a DJ at Paul Oakenfold's club, Land of Oz. Its sense of movement stems from his experience as roadie and occasional performer with Killing Joke in late '79; the slow, unfolding pace owes much to Paterson's experience as an A&R staffer for Eno's E.G. label, beginning in the spring of '88.

In those days, Paterson was working closely with Jimi Cauty, whose music was being published by E.G. Together they launched the Orb catalog in the summer of '88 with "Tripping on Sunshine," an experimental piece intended for use on ex–Killing Joke bassist Youth's *Eternity Project One* album. Other releases followed: They pressed and quickly sold 1,000 copies of a four-song EP built around samples recorded in 1981 from broadcasts of KISS radio in New York. In the spring of '89 they unleashed "A Huge Evergrowing Pulsating Brain That Rules from the Centre of the Ultraworld," a haunting meditation on a sample taken from the late Minnie Ripperton's "Loving You."

Several months later, Paterson and Youth collaborated on "Little Fluffy Clouds." With its thumping beat and spaghetti-western harmonica hook, it hit the charts hard. After Cauty left to work full-time with KLF, Thrash became Paterson's partner and helped lay the groundwork for the group's live debut in April '91.

Since then, the Orb has performed throughout the world, on occasion as post-punk quartet covering the Stooges' "No Fun" but often in more ambitious settings. From Glastonbury Plain to pre-dawn sets at Woodstock II, Paterson and assorted colleagues excel at live remixes that embrace and absorb the natural world into which they are released. After an Orb marathon, it doesn't really matter whether the crickets you're hearing are real, sampled, or in some strange place between.

We met with Paterson in L.A. Thrash had recently departed the Orb, leaving Paterson in charge. He was putting a new lineup together, with plans to tour the U.K. from March 15 into April, with European dates following in May, American club gigs in June, Japan in July, and more concerts in Europe after that. As we spoke, the group consisted of Nick Burton, Simon Phillips, co-writer and producer Thomas Fehlmann, and Andy Hughes, engineer and, according to Paterson, designated sex symbol. We began by zeroing in on what American audiences can expect from this year's incarnation of the Orb.

How does the Orb's approach to performing differ from the approach taken by more traditional bands?

Everything is already on DAT, basically. We have a multitrack onstage, because we try and take the feel of the band in the studio onto the stage, rather than go onstage with instruments to copy what you've a ready heard. Technology has given us the freedom to buy three DAT machines for the cost of a thousand pounds, so in essence we've got a three- or four-track studio up there. Will there be any instruments onstage? I might have my ARP 2600, because that's what we used for the bass part on "White River Junction" [from *Orbus Terrarum*]. It's been MIDIed.

You'll have a rack of modules, as well?

A rack of effects, mainly. Andy's got his rack of effects, and I put my effects through whatever I want to do with two turntables, three cassette machines, two CD players, and a couple of DAT machines. That creates quite a racket.

Effects seem to play a key role in how you improvise in concert.

Well, yeah. If you listen to an Orb record, there's never really an ending; it just leads to another record. You've got to change the DATs live, so if you just leave an effect running you can do that.

You can do the same thing by using looped samples as transitional elements.

Right. "God wants to love and use you": That's an example we've been using recently in our shows. That's a pretty phenomenal vocal, and we just leave it running in a loop. I've got my own Akai S1100 in my mixing desk; DJs are a little more technical than they used to be when they were just playing two records. I've got two ten-second samples I can use through a digital delay any time I need to stop the record. When we first started doing shows, we used to use just a DAT machine. But when I'd play it onstage, people would say, "That sounds so different tonight. What track did you play that in?" And we'd be playing the same DAT every night! We'd just be changing effects.

The DAT, then, would include the basic rhythm and chords.

In the old days, it would contain the whole track. In the new days, you can strip it all down to just the metronome. It depends on what you're trying to do.

We're bringing real musicians into technology now, whereas we used to do it the other way 'round. The hardest thing we're doing right now is to get a bass player and a drummer who are open to what we do-ing and can play in time with everything on the DAT.

Simon and Nick seem to be having problems try-ing to understand what the hell is going on. It's easy enough with technology to move something in 7/8 over something else in 4/4. But to get humans to do that is difficult. Depending on the people you hire. But, look, I'm not hiring these people. They're my friends. We're going to tour, which means we're go-ing to be living together for a year. You can't hire people for that. That ain't gonna work. They'd end up in their own tour coach, wanting loads of money and not getting on with other people. It's very diffi-cult to stay friends with people when you're on tour.

> "You've got to have some humor on these records, and words can put a smile on people's faces. In essence, I'm doing what a lot of journal-ists—dare I say?—want to do, and that's to take the piss out of some-body."
>
> —ALEX PATERSON (THE ORB)

Traditional bands improvise through solos. When you've got your DAT running onstage, how do you improvise?

I'll take some effects out. The engineer on the other side of the stage brings other effects in. Chris [Weston, aka Thrash] used to do that as our engineer, but then he decided he didn't want to engineer anymore; he wanted to concentrate on doing the music with me. Chris got to the point where it was very much like, "Well, if you're doing that with the music, I don't like it. I want to be doing this, and then I'll like it." It was pretty sad. He's left the band now. Nick, Simon, and Andy, as a live band, are very strong. Nick and Simon have been touring with us since 1992, and Andy has been in the studio as an engineer with us since just after *U.F.Orb*. He was the engineer on *FFWD* [available on the English label Inter-Modo]. He got himself more and more involved. Then Chris wanted to become the engineer again, and be the songwriter, and not have anybody else involved. I told him, in no uncertain terms, "Get your own band together. Sort your own life out." So he left in early August. At the end of the day, Chris might feel a bit grieved about leaving the band, but it was his decision.

What kind of a role did he play in Orb concerts?

Well, he stopped doing them two years ago. He didn't want to go on the road. Andy just got gradually involved, and a bit of antagonism was going on. So when Chris finally left, Andy just stepped into his shoes.

What qualities does your current co-producer and co-writer, Thomas Fehlmann, have that let him play a major role in your creative process?

He's a very dear friend. And he's got the same idea that I have, that music isn't just something to dispose of. We don't want to make disposable records. We're fed up with them. You pick up a Led Zeppelin record, you know exactly what you're gonna get. It's gonna be the same kind of integrity we'd like to have in putting the message across on an Orb record. We may have achieved that on the new album. At least we gave it our best shot. But I think that, like a Led Zeppelin album, it sits on its own. The difference is that you kind of know what's going to happen on a Led Zeppelin record; on an Orb record, you don't. You hear something in one speaker, then you walk to another speaker in another corner of the room and it sounds completely different. But you don't know that until you get over to that speaker and listen to it three times. So it's really nothing like a Led Zeppelin record, except in that I've got to have some kind of focus to make it not just, "Oh, I'll listen to that album and forget about it."

Some of the strong beats on earlier Orb albums seem to reflect your punk roots. How did you evolve from that background to the position you assign to rhythm in your music today?

I'll mention one band: Can. That's the easiest way to answer. He [i.e., Holger Czukay] changed my way of thinking in the sense of what he was up to. I admit I was a very late learner of Can ways. They were always hidden under the perception that Kraftwerk started up. Kraftwerk was an amazing band, too, which leads me to the whole German feel of music in the early '70s. I mean, Stockhausen brings out the non-rhythm side of the music, but that same quality is still there. I sat down one night with Richard James, played some Stockhausen, and talked about it for half an hour.

Which Stockhausen piece was it?

The one that was made in 1959. I'm quite attracted to it because of the fact that it was made the year I was born.

Your rhythm tracks create an almost ethnic feel, often through intricate patterns that avoid emphasizing the backbeat.

That's true of the new album, but we've done music where it's much more obvious where that bass drum is gonna come down.

How do you get that organic quality in your rhythm parts?

That's from putting the noises through any outboard effect we might have handy. That makes them sound completely different. A bird noise can be turned into a cuckoo clock, as an example. We don't always do that kind of thing deliberately, but on *FFWD* we did—so deliberately that we called the track "What Time Is Clock?" We'll take raindrops and use them, too. There was a hole in the roof of our studio, and every day it would rain. Every day we'd have to take all the gear out, then put it back in when the rain stopped and carry on recording. One night we decided to record all the raindrops. That turned into a rhythm pattern.

When did you begin exploring beyond the ambient idea?

I was working with Jimi. We'd spent the weekend before programming these really shit drum sounds. I was rapidly going off the idea of using drums, because I wanted to create a music you could play after the clubs, music that was modern but that you didn't have to dance to. The only way you could stop people from dancing was to take the bloody drums away. That night I went out to an amazing club or party, call it what you want, in a big tent near the sea. I ended up on the beach the next afternoon. Then Jimi and I went back and did "Loving You" [the Minnie Ripperton vocal sample used in "A Huge Evergrowing Pulsating Brain . . . ," from *Aubrey Mixes and Adventures Beyond the Ultraworld*]. I was so chilled out by the fact that we'd spent the afternoon by the sea after doing this club all night that it was like, "We can take these drums out!" The ambient noises in there created the environment where we'd been that morning.

Before launching the Orb, your involvement with music technology was minimal. You were a drum tech, for example, with Killing Joke.

It's easy enough to say I was just a drum tech, but actually I was the only roadie they had. I ended up with the drums because that's what I enjoyed most: tuning drums, playing around with drums, annoying people with drums. Still do. Besides, we were the first band ever to use [Clavia] ddrums. I was the first roadie who ever tried to pull ddrums into a live kit, because the drummer looked like an idiot playing the stupid electronic stuff. He wanted them to look like the sound was coming out of a regular drum kit, which really pissed me off. I wasn't a bloody carpenter. Still, [Killing Joke drummer] Paul was very open to hearing me. If I wasn't getting the bass drum in time, he'd still hear what I was trying to do. When you listen to Can, you can hear what he was trying to do: loops that you can do in a computer now.

Do you see what the Orb is doing as a bridge between, say, Stockhausen and more accessible styles?

I know exactly what you mean, but if somebody reading this says, "Oh, I've got to buy that Stockhausen record because it must be really good," they're gonna get a cruel awakening.

But you have no problem combining radically disparate influences in your music?

That's right. It's like being a painter. You see something that you want to put in a picture. It becomes a collage rather than just a painting. Americans are very good at doing these things through society, picking up bits from Europe, from South America, from here and there. That's what we're doing at the musical level. I mean, I had the first Led Zeppelin album coming into my head when I was eight years old. So I've always thought, "I like John Bonham, I like Sly Dunbar, and I like Brian Eno. I wonder what that all sounds like together?" That's what the Orb is, even today.

Did you ever go through a period of playing real-time music in bands?

No, but I've always been surrounded by music. I had what I regard as a musical home. My brother was a really good musician. [Producer/Killing Joke bassist] Youth and I grew up together. We went to school together, shared flats until about four years ago. He was trying to teach me to play the bass guitar when I was 15 or 16, but I was more into basketball than music at that time; my fingers were always in bandages because I kept dislocating them. [Paterson holds up two somewhat twitchy ring fingers.] In fact, these two fingers still have their own minds. Forget it: If I'm playing keyboards, it's with my thumbs and index fingers. That's peculiar, but it's just one of those things.

So sequencers and related developments in technology must have been the catalysts that let you begin making music as the Orb.

Well, to be honest about it, the Orb at first was basically about taking lots of drugs and going clubbing. I had been trying to run my own label with Youth, but people were telling me that since I was also working in the A&R department at E.G. I should be more involved with the label that was paying me. Then Jimi and I decided that we should get a band together. I saw that as my lifeline, because Jimi had a 16-track studio and his publishing company was E.G. So the people at E.G. said, "We'll turn a blind eye to you working with Jimi, because if you come up with anything successful we'll publish it." They also turned a blind eye to me running a company with Youth, because Youth was signed to E.G. Publishing, as well. So those were the breaks that took me into the realm of making music. The technology had been there, but I was a late developer.

How did sampling affect your work?

It really gave me my main purpose with the Orb: What can we do with this sample? What effect can we put into it? How can we hide the saxophone from *Blade Runner* and put that into a track that went into the Top 20 in Britain without anybody recognizing it? There's a kind of beauty, a kind of cleverness, in that: People will go, "What did I just hear? That ain't in there!" But it is! It's like taking the drums in "Little Fluffy Clouds" from a drum break that went on for about three minutes on an album by a very important singer who died recently. No one would even think of going into that type of music to find it in the first place.

You rely a lot on spoken-word samples to set moods and provide segues, though they're often mixed down to the point of inaudibility.

That's true, although we didn't do that on the first album [*Adventures beyond the Ultraworld*], which was three weeks of hard work: Get the album out and keep it under budget. The new album is two years of blood, sweat, tears, and loads of money—more money than I ever would have imagined I could possibly get my hands on when I was younger. And getting the words in the right places.

> "It's just something to chill out with at the end of the day. It's nice to know that people can cuddle up, kiss each other, and make themselves at home listening to the Orb."
>
> —ALEX PATERSON
> (THE ORB)

Where did that money go on this album that made it different from less lavishly funded Orb projects?

Into our manager's pocket. Let's put it that way.

Have you got a better manager now?

I've got a caretaker manager, a close friend.

How did you begin thinking of spoken-word samples as devices that could enhance your music?

Intuition. That's the only way I can put it. You've got to have some humor on these records, and words can put a smile on people's faces. In essence, I'm doing what a lot of journalists—dare I say?—want to do, and that's to take the piss out of somebody. For example, "Spanish Castles in Space" [from *Aubrey Mixes*] has a sample I took from an album in Russian. This bloke was talking about what kinds of fishes he had in his fish tank. You can imagine the reaction this will get when you play it in Russia.

Where do you find your speech samples?

Mainly from the lovely TV and radio networks you've got here in this lovely country. I record two hours of DAT while sitting up in a hotel room, bored. Then I'll go home, put it in a sampler, and find the nice ones. It could be two hours of crap, but sometimes I'll find something great. Remember that sample on "Little Fluffy Clouds"—something about a morphine drip in someone's stomach? That comes from a religious program. That's just an example of this society you live in; we wouldn't have some evangelist punching somebody in the stomach and yelling, "See? No pain! No pain!" Pow!

Fundamentalist religious diatribes are familiar material for samples these days.

Yeah, but we got in trouble once for using something from the Koran. We were using samples of passages from the Koran on one tour, and we were told, "If you don't stop, we're gonna declare a *fatwah* and destroy every gig you play." In fact, when we were playing this record onstage in Brighton, these guys started trying to strangle our tour manager. I was putting the Koran over the top of, I think, "Outlands" when this message came up on my mixer: "Take the Arab record off. Now!" I thought someone was joking. Then I saw these three Arabs holding my tour manager up in the air and screaming at him.

What about bird chirps and other real-world samples? Do you get many of them from third-party sources?

I used to. Not now. It's an excuse to get away.

So if we hear a train on an Orb record, it's not taken from a sound-effects CD?

Certainly not trains. There's a very big train line just 300 yards from my house. At about three in the morning this huge train comes running through, so there's this really low rumble going on. One night I left a DAT on outside my bedroom and got it on tape. It's also got the sound of some kids talking about whatever they could possibly think up. I have all of it on this two- or three-hour DAT, and I play it live at gigs.

What purpose does Orb music serve? Is it entertainment? Is it a kind of commentary on our world?

It's just something to chill out with at the end of the day. It's nice to know that people can cuddle up, kiss each other, and make themselves at home listening to the Orb. It's not like, "Right, I'm gonna get into the Orb and go for it tonight!" It's a much more personal experience than that.

In that sense, do you see the Orb as playing a major role in defining ambient music?

Look, we're not making ourselves to be the "guardians of ambience." We're not throwing down this gauntlet and saying we're the best band in the world. We're just doing our own thing and creating what we want to create. I like to think there's someone out there making music in the '90s that I can enjoy, just like I enjoyed sitting at home and having a listen to Can records. But if there isn't, I'll do that music myself.

Orbital.

11

Orbital, Meat Beat Manifesto, Underworld

PLUGGED!

By Greg Rule and Caspar Melville || *Keyboard*, October 1996

*A*merican festivalgoers' *sometimes on-again, off-again love affair with synths and electronic dance music was most definitely "on" in 1996.* Keyboard *visited the two-day, eight-band Organic '96 festival in California's San Bernardino National Forest, at a peak in the U.S. rave scene of the mid-'90s. The descriptions may bring back waves of nostalgia for those who saw the scene—*

and also featured bands who were able to ride the wave of dance music's popularity. There are also signs that some of the trends wouldn't last—take note of the prescient L.A. Times *writer who wonders, correctly, if the rave would have the staying power the Grateful Dead had. Before years of anti-rave laws reined it in, though, the party continued. —PK*

By winter, the Snow Valley resort is a haven for Southern California downhill skiers, but on this midsummer night, the site played host to a pack of rabid ravers who turned its grassy fields into a modern Dust Bowl. The smartest guy in the lot was the one dispensing dust masks for a buck each. A short hike up the main ski trail, though, and it was pure heaven: panoramic mountain view, star-filled sky, and cosmic laser-beam swirls from below. Back on Earth, there was no shortage of mind-altering experiences. The attendees were also an eyeful: drag queens with more face paint than Tammy Faye Baker (the winner wore a three-foot blond beehive), grown men and women sucking pacifiers, and those ecstatic youngsters who kept their heads buried in the bass bins all night. Can you say hearing loss?

For us synth-lovin' types, the scenery—colorful as it was—took a back seat to the action onstage. If ever there were doubts about the health of synthesizers on the live-music front, this event should put them to rest. Not since Emerson and Downes in their prog primetime have we seen such mammoth synth rigs at a concert event.

ORBITAL

Paul and Phil Hartnoll (collectively Orbital) plied their techno trade at Organic with a keyboard rig the size of Texas. Taking the stage at 2 a.m., the stage awash with dry ice and Varilights, the brothers would have been invisible had it not been for their custom high-beam headlight visors. Like radioactive frogs bouncing behind banks of blinking hardware, Orbital doused the crowd with liquid electronica—a soothing contrast to the searing breakbeats cranked out by the Chemical Brothers. Prior to the performance, it took a bit of arm twisting to persuade the Hartnolls to do an interview; fresh off the plane from England, at the start of a hectic mini-tour of the U.S., they were much more interested in tucking into the free grub backstage than answering questions from the press. But we persisted, and after a brief intervention from press officer Sioux Z, and with the mellowing effects of their recently consumed dinner taking hold, we were granted an audience.

Taking advantage of the late-afternoon sun and the spectacular view of the San Bernardino National Forest, we hiked up one of the dusty slopes, perched ourselves on top of a rock pile, fended off lizards, topless women, and security guards, and got down to business.

Where are you from?

Phil: From Sevenoaks, Kent [a small country town outside London].

What was your entrée into music? Were you DJs?

Paul: Musicians, although we didn't play much of anything. I used to play the guitar, badly, and then we'd play it along with the electronics, fuzz pedals, wah-wah, that sort of thing. Then I gave up on the guitar.

Phil: I learned the saxophone for a while, dabbled around, but I wouldn't say I was a musician; I just had a real love for music.

Did you go out much, to clubs?

Phil: Not much, really, not in Sevenoaks.

Paul: We did, actually, that's a lie, because there was one place that was really good called the Grasshopper Inn. It was around 1986. That wave of rare groove stuff just before house kicked in, when it was all James Brown loops and hip-hop. And then around '88 or '89, house started coming there, as well.

So you received a pretty broad musical education through that club?

Paul: Yeah, and also from a friend who used to do pirate radio and had the largest collection of Chicago house you're ever likely to see.

Did you find that you had to move out of Sevenoaks at some point?

Phil: I moved to London and did silly jobs up there for a while. Paul stayed in Kent.

Paul: I stayed for a while. Our parents left to run a pub down the road, and I stayed. Around that time we were collecting more musical equipment. It wasn't really feasible to have a studio in a paper-thin-walls flat in London, and we had spare bedrooms in Sevenoaks where we could put a studio. I was appreciating living in the country, too, then, with the aid of cannabis.

What kind of gear did you start out with?

Paul: The first thing we had was this Latin percussion drum machine—a Korg. It was a little silver thing.

Do you still have it?

Phil: Oh, yeah, it's still there in the studio.

Paul: Then Phil bought a [Korg] Poly-800, so we used to play about with those two and my guitar. Then he got a [Korg] 707; he had to sell his sax to get that, but the electro bug had caught on in our house. This was about 1985, when electro was big, industrial funk stuff on Factory Records out of Manchester. Then Phil decided to go to America, and he lent his keyboards to a friend instead of leaving them with me!

Phil: I didn't really think. This person just asked me, so I said yes.

Paul: It didn't really matter, though, because I had some money, and I was able to buy a drum machine and keyboard of my own. I'll tell you what happened—just to put a little slur on Soho Soundhouse, I decided I wanted to get a [Sequential] Six Trak. The idea of six sequences, a six-part multitimbral thing, I thought was great. In Soho Soundhouse I saw that, as well as the 707. They were selling the Roland 909s for $400. I could afford both, but I was told by the sales assistant, "Oh, no, you can't run Roland and Sequential Circuits MIDI stuff together. MIDI only talks to the same company." Basically the idiot couldn't figure out how to sync up the two things. So being completely wet behind the gills, I bought the Poly-800 knowing that was a good keyboard, and I got the 909, but I was very dubious about it 'cause it wasn't as good as the 707, or so I thought. When Phil got back from America, we put his stuff together with mine. Him lending his stuff to someone else turned out to be a good thing, because it forced me to get my own stuff.

Where did you go in America?

Phil: I was in Manhattan mainly, in search of hip-hop culture. I thought I would find all the records, all the culture, but it wasn't really like that. I did tape a lot of good music from the KISS FM live mixes, stuff like that. When house really started hitting, we didn't find it that unusual really.

Paul: It just sounded like electro and Hi-NRG combined.

At what point did you lay your first viable pieces of music down?

Paul: I bought a four-track early on, so I was making tons of tapes back then. We've been 12 years dabbling in home recording, but it's hard to point to a time when those recordings became viable. Early on we weren't sending our stuff around. We felt it wasn't ready, but eventually some friends of mine took a couple of tracks to this DJ who did a radio show—Jack Man Jay, his real name is Kevin Marsh—and he took them to Jazzy M, who used to do London Wicked Radio. He played them. That's when we really started taking tapes around.

Were you always called Orbital?

Paul: I had a couple of tracks under the name DS Building Contractors.

And the first Orbital release?

Paul: Was in 1989: *Chime* on London Records.

At what point did you come into contact with sampling?

Paul: After we were burgled, and they stole loads of our stuff. With the insurance money we bought an [Akai] S700 sampler.

You were self-taught?

Paul: Yeah, there was no one else to teach us.

Let's fast-forward to the new release, In Sides. You've gone for some very organic sounds this time. Is that a dulcimer we're hearing?

Paul: Yeah. We actually approached it as trying to make a record that was shorter.

We're a little sick of the overall playing time of an album being 74 minutes instead of 45. I think it can work better shorter. So we thought, let's do a shorter album, lots of tracks, much more uptempo, much more dancey, really jolly—and of course that didn't happen at all. We go into the studio with an idea, and often it turns out completely different, but that doesn't matter. That is a dulcimer sample. We sampled four different notes and then split the notes onto two sides of the keyboard so you can play them with your fingers like a real dulcimer. We did things like velocity to start point and velocity to pitch point and velocity to filter—which vary ever so slightly so the sound is more natural.

So you spend a lot of time crafting the sounds and samples?

Paul: Yeah, it's important with the dulcimer, for example, because if you just had it on a regular keyboard, it wouldn't sound authentic.

Define each of your roles in the studio process. Is it a 50/50 split, or do you each specialize in certain aspects?

Paul: I specialize in holding the mouse.

And Phil specializes in trying to get it off you?

[*Much laughter all 'round.*]

Paul: We both specialize in staring at the screen and discussing everything. What often happens is we have two keyboards up and running and I'll be fiddling around with chords while Phil might be working on a lead. All of a sudden it'll be, "Ahh, stop, do that again," and we'll work it out like that.

What kind of drum sounds do you favor?

Paul: I enjoy breakbeats and I enjoy drum machines; I just enjoy it all, but with this album we got a friend of ours, Cloone, who is a drummer and put him in a big studio, which we never normally hire, and recorded him on 15 different mics, onto an ADAT, and some other DATs.

Playing to a click track?

Paul: Sometimes, although being a drummer, he doesn't like playing to a click. So we got a day of him drumming so we could make our own breakbeats, which is enjoyable because you really have to work to make it sound dynamic. It was fun to be able to take the bass drum out or put it in really loud or with reverb. We also just got a [Roland] 808, because we couldn't stand to be without it any longer. We used to have to borrow one, but we had to have our own. So that turns up a lot beside Cloone's breaks.

Did you tell him what type of beat you wanted him to play, or did you leave it up to him?

Paul: Well, he kept asking us, and we just said do what you like. We did get him to use brushes and a couple of different snares.

Phil, take us through your studio setup for this record.

Phil: Oh, God, there were a lot of samples on this record.

Paul: No there weren't, not that many. The [Oberheim] Xpander shows up a lot, the ARP 2600 has a nice airing this time. The Roland modular turned up on this album, as well.

[At this point the technological discussion is interrupted when Phil spots a gecko on a rock, and a naked woman sunbathing a few yards away. After much craning of necks, we continue.]

Did you use any new gear, like the Clavia Nord Leads or Korg Prophecies?

Paul: Yeah, we have a Prophecy, but we didn't get it in time to use it on this album.

And the sequencing?

Paul: We use [Emagic] Logic Audio, which is fine except it can't handle long tracks the way we do them; we have to do tracks in four chunks. I don't know what's wrong exactly; we've had a lot of people come and look at it, but no one seems to be able to figure it out. We might have to send it to the big man.

How many albums are you on now?

Paul: Four.

Phil: Seven. We've got a seven-album deal of which we've made four.

What gear do you use onstage?

Phil: Oh, blimey.

Paul: We've got three [Alesis] MMT-8s, with two spares because I have to change one halfway through the set. They have shit memory.

Do you use them for their supposed feel?

Paul: Yeah, the feel is really tight, and I like the way you can turn them on and off and then have the same thing in there, like a drum machine. We've also got an [E-mu] e64, an EMI, a [Roland] Jupiter-6, R-70, 808, 909, and R-8, a [Novation] Bass Station, a Prophecy, and an Xpander.

You're brave to take that old beast on the road.

Paul: It's been very reliable, actually, apart from freaking out a couple of times in Europe.

To what extent are you able to improvise?

Paul: Well, with the MMT-8s in pattern mode, you can go 4 bars, 8 bars, 64 bars—it completely varies, and we just punch things in and out. You get quite good at it. You get to learn what works. You can end up using mutes and MIDI echo to create breaks that aren't really there.

How would you describe the experience of translating a studio venture onto the live stage?

Phil: A pain in the fucking arse.

Paul: The only way you can do it is in real time. I make a line of phantom folders and put them in order 'til I have the whole set there, backed up about a thousand times.

Are you happy with where your career has taken you?

Phil: Oh, yeah.

Paul: It's more than I ever dreamed of. I always thought it would be great to be as culty as Cabaret Voltaire.

Give us an insight into what it's like working with family.

Paul: Well, we don't know what it's like working without family. Our mum does our books, so it's a real family business. Knowing each other so well, it's easier to say, "That's crap," and not have that weird ego thing.

What do you hope to do in the future?

Paul: Film soundtracks, definitely. We've had a few tracks in films, but I want to write the whole bloody score. I hope you're listening, Terry Gilliam.

MEAT BEAT MANIFESTO

He's revered for his work with Meat Beat Manifesto, but Jack Dangers is also rattling cages as an ace producer/remixer. He's got a platinum client list that includes Nine Inch Nails, David Bowie, Depeche Mode, David Byrne, and many others, and a vintage vault to die for. Onstage, Meat Beat did what no other outfit at Organic did: integrate keyboard technology with live drums, sax, and guitars. The result was a unique and captivating live set, despite their early time slot. Backstage, *Keyboard* got a chance to talk turkey with Dangers about his live show, his home studio setup, and his new Meat Beat platter, *Subliminal Sandwich* on Nothing Records.

When you were gearing up for this new record, did you have a specific concept or theme in mind?

No, no concept really. The only concept, if you could call it that, was that I didn't want to do this album to a deadline. I just wanted to work on it until it was finished. The tour we just got back from in Europe, we only did eight shows, and before that, the last time we'd gone out was in 1992. So I wanted to get out of that album–tour–album–tour loop. I wanted to get a bunch of new equipment and learn it. I was an Atari and Cubase person, and I wanted to get into the Macintosh. So I got a [Macintosh] 950, [Digidesign] Pro Tools, [Emagic] Logic Audio, and I just sat down and learned them over a period of two years. That's what the new album is.

How painful was the learning process?

It went very smoothly, considering I was completely Macintosh illiterate. I surprised myself. When I moved to San Francisco from England, suddenly I realized I was in an area where all these hardware and software companies were. So it was inevitable. I had to get into it. I had to upgrade. I had to seriously sit down and figure it all out.

We hear your home studio is a bit like a mad scientist's lab.

[*Chuckles.*] Yeah, a lot of old gear. I use it for a pre-production studio, and once I've got everything ready, I'll go in [to another studio] and mix it. I mean, I have mixed stuff there, as well, but it's mainly a pre-production room.

What's in it?

I've got a couple of [Alesis] ADATs, a Mackie 8-bus mixer, a Macintosh 950 with [Digidesign] Pro Tools and Sound Designer, Logic Audio, a Summit tube compressor, a Lexicon 2020 analog/digital converter, and two preamp/EQ channels from an old Neve that everything goes through. Synthesizer-wise, I've got a huge Roland modular system that used to belong to the Human League; they did *Reproduction* and *Travelogue* on it. I've got a Roland Jupiter-4 and Jupiter-8, and an old Vocoder Plus, an ARP 2600, and a Theremin from Big Briar [Robert Moog's hardware company].

Did you make a conscious effort to use all-new sounds or samples on this record?

No. In fact, sometimes I repeat things on purpose. It's kind of like a signature. There's a little thing on "Nuclear Bomb," for example, that resurfaces on "Assasinator."

Where do you draw creative inspiration—from other bands?

Musically, not so much. I get more inspiration on a social level. "Nuclear Bomb" was written at a time when there was a lot of stuff on the news about black-market uranium trading, and how Europe and America were getting together and buying it so they could put it in a silo in Carolina, or somewhere. And the whole thing about the super dollar in the Middle East, the forgery of $100 bills. Things like that things you hear on the news or read in the paper.

Walk us through the making of a Meat Beat track.

Sometimes it all stems from a lyric idea the idea of the song. But technically the beat is always one of the first things to go down, the foundation, and then comes the bass line. "Sound Innovation," the very first track on *Subliminal Sandwich*, for example, started with a loop I made from this obscure Swedish vibraphone player's record. I can't even remember his name. There was this funky beat, so I chopped it out, sampled it into the [Akai] 3200, and made a new pattern out of it. Then I put the bass line down using Logic Audio.

Synth bass?

No, on that track I recorded a bass guitar straight to the hard drive. I was originally a bass player. I am a bass player [*laughs*].

How do you go about getting your loops to lock up?

I use [Steinberg] ReCycle a lot for that. It's quite simple that way.

So you edit your loops quite a bit.

Yeah. With loops, one thing I like to do is get one loop and [audio] compress the hell out of it with the Summit. Then I'll get another loop, match it in tempo with the other, and put it in the [E-mu] Emax. Even though I've upgraded now, I haven't lost any of my lo-fi sensibilities. I still put things in the Emax and resample them into the 3200.

Listening to *Sandwich*, it sounds like you sampled plenty of non-rhythmic material too, like ambiences and vocal snippets.

The atmospheric samples were gathered from different soundtrack pieces, and I put them through a patch I made on the Eventide DSP4000; it's a pitch conversion patch that takes it up a million miles away from the original signal, and I just use the wet signal. I cut out the dry, so it completely alters it. From there it goes into the sampler.

Do you usually print your sequenced tracks to tape, or keep them virtual?

It depends. Sometimes I don't even bother putting them on ADAT; I'll just send them through the Summit, put it through the Lexicon, and to DAT.

When you do put things to tape or, say, into the sampler, do you record effects?

Oh, yeah, I like working with limitations. That's the way I grew up. I grew up working with an Atari, and with drum machines triggering samples, so that's just a throwback to all that. To me, if you're sampling something, and you like the sound, you should go for it. That appeals to me.

> "I like working with limitations. That's the way I grew up. To me, if you're sampling something, and you like the sound, you should go for it."
>
> —JACK DANGERS (MEAT BEAT MANIFESTO)

How long from beginning to end does a song usually take you to do?

About five solid days, working around the clock. I usually just work until it's finished. Same with remixes. I spend probably five days doing a remix, except once. Once I went into the studio and did a remix in a day for MC 900 Foot Jesus. I was on tour, and I couldn't do it any other time. That was hard, because I like to spend more time on it. I know some people who do, like, two a day [*grimaces*]. I'm into quality rather than quantity.

Let's talk about the live show. How much of your studio comes out on tour with you?

Well, I've got the Theremin up there, and the ARP, but the modular is too big to travel with.

Who will be onstage with you tonight?

There are four people onstage: John Wilson, who plays sax and various prepared and weird guitars [processed] through an ART multi-effects unit, a Zoom processor used for ring modulation, and Godley & Creme's wacky guitar invention called the Gizmotron, Lynn Farmer on drums, and we've got Mike Powell on keyboards, samples, and Theremin. And me.

What's your role onstage?

I'm mixing the show. There's a sequencer that's running the synthesizers, and I've got all the channels coming into a 16-track Mackie.

I've also got a bunch of outboard gear up there, like the Eventide DSP4000, an old tape echo, and a compressor. I've got a couple turntables, and I run some old breakbeat records through a [Lexicon] JamMan and loop them. I've got one ADAT that spits various spoken word stuff, sub-bass, and the SMPTE that runs the sequencer. The sequencer, a Roland MC-50, is running the samplers [Akai 3200s], the vocoder, everything, basically. The only reason I use the ADATs is because it frees the samplers of being bogged down with really long samples.

A lot of the show is improvised. We make a lot of it up as we go. You can tell when we're getting out, 'cause it turns into a big wall of noise [*laughs*].

We know how you feel about vintage synths, but what do you think of the new-breed stuff?

Yeah, pretty good. Haven't tried the [Clavia] Nord Lead yet, but I got the Prophecy. You can get some good sounds out of it. It's still digital, though. It's got a digital crispiness to it, but the control surface is really good.

Have you programmed your own sounds with it yet?

Not too much yet. We only got it two weeks before we went on tour. Mike's been using it, though. He's programmed a few sounds that you'll hear tonight.

What's up next for you?

The next album will be out sometime in the first half of next year. We're doing a couple of new tracks tonight. [Suddenly a familiar synth sound blasts from the stage. Jack spins around. "Hey, that sounds like my vocoder they've got up there."]

> "Even ambient music can have a groove in the sense that it is something that draws you somewhere. It makes you feel that you're actually on a journey, as opposed to making you feel as though you're stuck in one place, looking at the same wallpaper."
>
> —RICK SMITH (UNDERWORLD)

UNDERWORLD

One of the highlight performers at Organic, Britain's Underworld whipped the crowd into a techno frenzy, With two technologists whose heads seldom emerged from their phalanx of keyboards and audio gear, and with a roving frontman who provided guitar licks, vocals, and occasional Korg filter squelches, the band's show walked a delicate line between modern mixing and traditional rock showmanship.

Part space rock, part techno, Underworld is one of the fastest-rising stars on the electronic music scene. Their debut disc (*Dubnobasswithmyheadman*) scored big on the European front, and now their follow-up (*Second Toughest in the Infants*) is gaining global praise from fans and critics alike. Rick Smith, one-third of the Underworld braintrust, had this to say about life on the hi-tech highway.

What's the genesis of Underworld's hybrid sound?

We love electronics, so whatever we do is going to be electronically based, but we've had years of dabbling with acoustic instruments, and I haven't got fond memories of some of the writing problems with them. Trying to translate things to other musicians.

How do you write?

Well, we write constantly. We don't just go into the studio for three months and do an album. We are basically writing from the time the last album's been released.

Do you write in a home studio?

Yeah. The studio has been in my spare bedroom for about eight years, and funny enough, just before Christmas, we moved it.

When you're building a track, is it usually from the bottom up?

Every tune starts from the groove, really. There's one piece that's almost ambient on the record [*Second Toughest in the Infants*] called "Blueski," and that's just kind of guitar, but even then the idea was to build a groove around this Dictaphone sample of a guitar.

Dictaphone?

Yeah. Just an acoustic guitar, and we stuck a microphone up in front of it and into a Dictaphone.

So when you talk about starting a song with a groove, it's not necessarily drumbeats you're working with.

That's right, but most often it is, because our greatest passion is dance music over and above anything else. So most often it starts with a rhythm section as we understand it—drums. I feel, though, that even ambient music can have a groove in the sense that it is something that draws you somewhere. It makes you feel that you're actually on a journey, as opposed to making you feel as though you're stuck in one place, looking at the same wallpaper. Some drum tracks can make you feel like that: "Oh, dear, this is going nowhere."

When you lay down drum tracks, do you prefer patterns or loops?

I love breakbeats; I like that sampling approach where the sampler is a window into a piece of sound. Into a space. I've been using [Steinberg] ReCycle to chop up and reassemble samples in radically different ways, then I might tune 'em up and down, and time-stretch 'em a bit. And even though your original groove is gone, you've still got these tiny little snippets of another space. I really love that. Same with guitar samples or whatever. Again, they're all windows into another time and another place.

SITES AND SMELLS OF ORGANIC '96

Dennis Romero (*L.A. Times*): "I think the main question is whether festivals like this can replace what the Grateful Dead have left behind. I'm not so sure. Everything in this culture is not about artistic culture but money culture. It's about the bottom line."

Bob (runs the Space Ball): "This was designed by NASA for training the astronauts for the Gemini and Apollo missions. What it does is create a condition called spatial disorientation. It's a giant gyroscope with a seat in the center. We've never had anyone throw up, and we've had some pretty drunken people on it. It's a great ride. My kids love it."

Aaron (runs the Brain Machine): "I've been doing this since 1991 around California and all over Europe, at raves and concerts that have a psychedelic edge to them. No drugs are necessary for this. It was designed for meditation and relaxation purposes. It uses frequencies to hemi-sync your brain. William S. Burroughs has been credited as one of the inventors. He called it the dream machine. Basically, it's a giant LED system which adds up numbers and then clicks them out in lights, synchronized with sound."

Jody (body-piercing booth): "This is the first rave we've done, and it's been pretty good. It's a tribal thing. It's aesthetic and it has shock value. I'm freezing my ass off here."

Zac (backstage brute): [In response to the question of why he's working here.] "Why does it matter? You can't get in without an all-access pass."

Chris (San Diego): "We just decided we were gonna go all out. We've got ourselves some friend-ship bracelets, and we're going to be here 'til the end."

Jimmy: "I'm from Dublin, but I live in Santa Monica now. I'm here to cause some mischief."

Anonymous: "Beautiful, awesome."

—Caspar Melville

As you're working on a song, do you usually hear a sound in your head that you try to reproduce with your instruments, or do you like to experiment blindly?

Visual things have always fired my imagination, and often it's pictures rather than sounds that really get me going. In terms of experimentation, yeah, absolutely. There are glorious things that happen in mistakes, especially if you can recognize the difference between a good mistake and a bad one [*laughs*]. But you know, those are the moments when it shocks you. "Where did that come from?" I'm all for capturing the moment.

We don't really have one way of approaching things. I'm nervous sometimes about saying, "We do this," because it's the spirit of something that writes a tune, not necessarily the logic behind the putting of it together. So a lot of the tracks are different in the way they come together inasmuch as the head that writes them is different that day. Some of the pieces came together in three or four hours; others I worked on for months. There are other pieces, like "Rowla" from *Second Toughest*, which took months, but in itself was only a few hours; it was months inasmuch as I knew what I wanted to do but it wasn't happenin'. So four or five attempts later, it finally all came together—this simple, single-synthesizer-and-909 approach.

You mentioned using ReCycle earlier. What other tools are in your studio?

I use Emagic Logic on a Macintosh, and Digidesign Session 8, which was about the cheapest hard-drive system we could afford. We've had that now since the last album. Before that I was using Creator, the C-Lab program. I'm a complete fan. I love what you can do, and how you can get inside things with it. Pulling things apart.

Do you use tape at all during the pre-mix phase?

No, not much anymore. Up until about a year and a half ago, all we had was an Akai 12-track [tape] machine, and we've finally stopped using that now. So unless we're using something off DAT here and there, everything goes onto the hard drive or is sequenced.

Do you prefer to mix on a big desk?

All the stuff is done in the home studio here. Everything goes through the Soundcraft Series 600 desk we bought about 12, 14 years ago. We're still using it. I had a couple of channels modified, and the master outputs, but apart from that it's still the standard all-Soundcraft desk. It's got 32 inputs and a really crappy EQ, but it's got something about it that binds sound together.

What's your approach to the live show?

Karl [Hyde] and I have been playing live together for about 12 years—and about seven or eight years before we met Darren [Emerson]. We did everything from small club tours, to a tour of recording studios going live to radio, to a tour with the Eurythmics with a seven-piece band, which was a really miserable experience. Very depressing.

Why?

Lack of enthusiasm for the music, really, a feeling that the demos, which were done on the computer, were better than the live results. We were translating things just for the sake of it. And meanwhile, back in Britain, acid house was going crazy. We could feel it, but we didn't feel we were a part of it. We were kind of playing

> "You know, when the audience is excited, we might stay with a drum groove of a song for ten minutes simply because we can sense that nobody wants to move from there. They're enjoying the journey, and the last thing they want is to be hit with a huge chorus and then the middle eight."
>
> —RICK SMITH (UNDERWORLD)

things by rote. So when it came to playing live this time, we had two main criteria: one was we'd never lose money, because we'd always lost money playing live, and the other was that we'd jam. It seemed the audience always got excited when there were mistakes, and when things went howlin' off. You'd have to improvise, you'd have to be on your toes, and your recovery would be very exciting. The audiences thought it was great.

So with this band we wanted to approach it more from a DJ vibe. Being more flexible. That was the starting point. The problem for me was how to program it. How to make it feasible. You know, being able to make electronic music but still have the ability to jam. To be able to shape the parts or the mix. One of the biggest things that can affect dance music is the mix—the way the dubs are approached, and what you don't use as much as what you do use. You know, when the audience is excited, we might stay with a drum groove of a song for ten minutes simply because we can sense that nobody wants to move from there. They're enjoying the journey, and the last thing they want is to be hit with a huge chorus and then the middle eight.

So you assembled a rig that allows you to make changes to the song structures on the fly.

Yes. Basically it's an open-ended system where there's a master synchronizer, a Roland SBX-80, which runs the Macintosh. We use a couple of Powerbooks with Emagic, and they're running an Akai 3200, which has lots of samples in there. We don't take a lot of keyboards out with us because, logistically, we wanted to travel light and be able to set up really fast. And then there are a few other synths, like a Technox, a Roland 909 which is pumping away merrily, a Roland 606, a vocoder, and we're taking a Nord Lead with us these days 'cause it's such a fantastic instrument and you can fool with it live. Everything's running in sync. There are no set parts, and all the decisions are made at the desk.

There must be a lot of interaction onstage between the three of you.

Oh, yeah. We talk to each other, we laugh, we argue, we take the piss out of each other—all that. [*Laughs.*] I think that's part of being a band, as opposed to a group of people standing there trying to re-create an album sound.

Aphex Twin.

12

Aphex Twin

STILL HACKING AFTER ALL THESE YEARS

By Greg Rule || *Keyboard*, April 1997

He's one of the most brilliant (and bizarre) electronic musicmakers on the planet. But how in the world does Richard "Aphex Twin" James find time to record, tour, and build his own instruments? Filterboxes, drum machines, custom keyboard modifications, and even a sampler—there isn't much he hasn't tried. "When it worked," he said of the latter in May '94 [see "Sampling Nation," page 104], "I reckon it pissed on just about any manufactured sampler." And nearly three years later, we're happy to report he hasn't changed a bit. Richard is still a tinkering maniac, but now his focus has shifted from hardware to software.

"I've got three Macs," he tells us, "two laptops and a PowerPC. I use all the sequencers on the market, but at the moment I've been solely using my own program to create new algorithms." And not with Opcode's Max. He's been building the algorithms from scratch. "It's like using a programming language. A bit like Pascal. I've been doing it for about three months, so it's all quite primitive, but it's looking really interesting.

This language . . . you can bring in your own samples and mess around with them. And it's got DSP functions you can't get anywhere else, but you have to program it in. There's no fancy sliders, although they're easy to construct. I've made loads of graphical interfaces for things.

"It was pretty interesting watching people dance to my algorithm."

−APHEX TWIN

"The algorithm I just finished," he continues, "is a percussion thing that lets you swap and change the sounds. It does bass, as well, but it's really acidy. You can leave it on for, like, an hour, and it really comes up with some mad shit. I made it learn to gradually change [the music] over time." While he doesn't plan to market his software, he has been showing it off at recent gigs. "I just finished a tour, and I used it for one of the tracks. It was pretty interesting watching people dance to my algorithm."

His touring rig consists of, get this, "One laptop computer, a little mixer, and an effects unit. But soon I'll be eradicating the mixer and effects. So basically it'll be one computer. It does everything I did before with live samples and sequences. I've put every element down on a digital track [in Digidesign's Pro Tools], so I can mix between tracks."

Speaking of Pro Tools, "It's wicked," he enthuses. "You don't notice it's there, which is what you want with computers. It doesn't get in your way." While he's purchased most of the third-party plug-ins for it, Richard, true to his tinkering image, has also created one from scratch. "Within about two weeks I came up with one with this programming language I've been using. It's really, really cool. You can loop between sections, and loop individual tracks the same way you could with a sequencer. And I've got this thing on there so you can re-synthesize each track, change its pitch . . ."

Talking to Richard about his homemade software almost derailed us from the main purpose of the interview: to discuss his new self-titled album on Sire. *Richard D. James* is like nothing we've heard before, and frankly, we're still not sure whether we love it or loathe it. It's a bizarre 15-song blend of feeble synth sounds and jagged jungle loops. "Most of the album was done on my Mac, basically. Even the keyboard sounds were all pretty much computer-generated. Native audio." And when Richard sings, the sound gets even weirder. Give "Milkman" a spin, for example. "That was modulated on the computer," he says of the twisted vocal track.

Richard's drum programming is particularly impressive—rife with triplets and unpredictable stops and starts. "I think the main influence is Luke from Wagon Christ. He really inspired me to get into it more. I used to do lots of crazy triplets and stuff at a slower pace, but he really got me into doing it at a faster pace. He gave me the spark to do it faster, but now I'm trying to take it to all extremes, basically."

Richard's jungle influence comes from "any of the drum 'n' bass and breakbeat artists. It's nothing new to me. I've been into breakbeat culture ever since it started, through hip-hop, hardcore, and jungle. So I've always been into nicking other things, recycling 'em, basically mashing 'em up and making something different. I just like to mash things up a bit more than most people, that's all."

One of his favorite mashing tools is Steinberg's ReCycle. "Yeah, it's quite a wicked program. The most useful thing about it is it creates a bank on your sampler and gives it loads of sample names. And that saves you an hour, at least. You can cut something up into, like, 90 samples, and transfer it over SCSI in a minute. That would take two hours normally."

And not just for breakbeats—Richard uses ReCycle for melodic material, as well. "I might play a violin or a trumpet scale into Pro Tools—every note I can think of—and then bang it into ReCycle, chop it up into little bits, bang it into the sampler, and you've got a complete bank of sounds in your sampler in about five minutes."

Richard and his laptop are currently on tour in the U.K., but he hopes to circle the States sometime later this year. "This is the next step for me," he says of his strange new sound. "It's like the first step for a much bigger step that I hope to take later on.

Chemical Brothers.

13

Chemical Brothers

WATER INTO ACID: THE CHEMICAL BROTHERS BLOW UP

By Greg Rule || *Keyboard*, June 1997

Trace the course of music evolution and you'll find a handful of key history makers at each link in the chain. From the classical masters to the pop icons of the last few decades, there have always been, and will continue to be, those who rise above their peers and become the symbols of an era. Only time will tell who earns that distinction from today's group, but in the burgeoning world of electronic dance, keep your eye on a pair of young men from England known as the Chemical Brothers. Tom Rowlands and Ed Simmons, still in their 20s, are fast becoming a global phenomenon.

After taking in one of their live shows, it's easy to see why. Fusing elements of techno and hip-hop, and shoving the mix down the throat of a fuzz box, the Chemical Brothers bust through speakers like a brass-knuckled fist. Their sound is hard, rough, and relentless, and it boils with energy and attitude. In a music market still coming to grips with the return of synths to the mainstream, this English package is a most welcome arrival.

How did the Chemicals get their start? Like many great partnerships, Rowlands and Simons came from two disparate yet complementary musical camps. "I started on piano when I was eight or nine," Rowlands tells us. "I played the guitar and stuff, and was in bands at school. I always had a drum machine because I liked the fact that I didn't have to rely on anybody else. You could go into the bedroom and have this machine play for you. And then I got a sampler, and suddenly I saw this whole other way of making music, and it seemed so exciting to me."

Rowlands made the fateful connection with sidekick Simons at college. "Ed comes from a totally different background. He wasn't that technical or musically based. He had a more DJ approach, which was a good thing, I reckon. If you have two people who are musically obsessive or technically obsessive, you kind of lose that thing of what's good and what's not. You get so far removed from it."

The duo soon began playing together, igniting rave after rave, and then one day Ed propositioned Tom. "He asked me, 'What if we made our own records?' I said, 'Well, we can, because I know how to make them.' And it was like that, really."

Talk about getting off to a good start. Their first single, "Song to the Siren," went straight to hitsville. "We made that song in my bedroom on an S1000 and a Juno 106," says Rowlands, "and it was mastered on a Hitachi hi-fi. You can't believe how we made that record then. At the time it was just a rough idea, but I think it came across quite well—that DIY kind of thing. And that's the good thing about this kind of music: It can be made, and you don't need all this great equipment, and you don't need to be a band rehearsing and gigging around the country. You can just go to your bedroom and make it."

Make it they did.

> "That's the good thing about this kind of music: It can be made, and you don't need all this great equipment, and you don't need to be a band rehearsing and gigging around the country. You can just go to your bedroom and make it."
>
> —TOM ROWLANDS (THE CHEMICAL BROTHERS)

We exchanged handshakes with the Chemicals backstage at the Organic festival in late '96 [see "Plugged," page 139], but Tom and Ed weren't in the interviewing mood at the time. When they proceeded to knock our blocks off later that night with their awesome live set, and then again three months later in San Francisco, we knew this story was worth chasing. Eight months later, *Keyboard* finally got a chance to roll tape with the Brothers when they visited New York in early '97.

Brother, actually. Since Tom is the half who likes to talk gear and techniques, and since Ed was doing his best to appease a hungry flock of press vultures, *Keyboard* went one-on-one with Tom, who took us behind the scenes in the studio and onstage.

CHEMICAL COOKBOOK

Your sound has been described as a hybrid of techno and hip-hop. Is that a fair assessment?

Well, when we started playing together, Ed and I hit upon this idea of making records that combined, yeah, techno and hip-hop, which no one had really done to its fullest extent, we thought. And that's been the basic premise for our records— this combination of things. And now we think we've taken that quite far, and we're just going off in different things.

Has your method of making music changed much since *Exit Planet Dust*?

On a basic level, it's that we've had more time and flexibility. I think the difference between the two records is the way we've treated sounds. We were getting into it on the first record, but I think we spent a lot longer just messing around with the sound, and having longer to work on specific things, really, whereas before, the songs were made quicker.

Describe the environment you recorded in?

We have our own little studio set up around a Mackie 8-bus and a pair of DynAudio N2s with the ABS Sub Bass system. Just a little project studio where we write, and some things we record onto a Hi8 [TASCAM DA-88] 8-track. If we like the sound we get in there, then we use it. But generally for the more complicated tracks where there's more stuff going on, we go downstairs. Our studio is based in this complex in Southeast London, a place called Orinoco. We have our room upstairs, and they have a proper studio downstairs with a big Neve console. So we mix on that.

Does the process typically begin with a drum loop?

No real method, really. A lot of the tracks do start off with, we'll hear an interesting little snare sound, or an interesting loop, and we'll take it. We use [Steinberg] ReCycle a lot, and that's one thing, on a technical level, that's made our life easier. We used to spend a lot of time chopping up breaks by hand. Like, we'd do a remix for someone, and the first day and a half would usually be spent chopping up breaks and making them fit and groove. And now the program does it for us, which is brilliant.

So that's been a big advancement for us— the ease of being able to chop up breaks like that.

Is vinyl your main source for loops and samples?

Yeah. I mean, we'll hear things, sample it, play around with it, and start adding our own stuff to it. A lot of it is actually me playing guitar and bass on the record. And then some tracks, like the last two, are written around a guitar and a sitar, which I played, and then we made a loop out of. But generally, I like the sound you get when you sample things from all different contexts and put them together. You end up with a sound that you can't get any other way. You're sampling from eight completely different sources, and they've all been treated differently, and you put them all together.

MANGLERS

You guys have become masters at murdering sounds.

Yeah. We don't make clinical machine music, even though I'm a great fan of bands like Kraftwerk and such where everything is so precise. I really like that. But one of the major things we've done from the beginning is use rough guitar effects. We've got quite a large collection of Electro-Harmonix pedals and stuff like that. They always put a bit of a bite into things, which you don't really get from your new, latest Roland-effects-unit-type thing. I think when people were making effects and pedals back then, there was a wild edge to what they were doing. I think it was more experimental.

Is there one particular pedal that gets the most service?

The [Electro-Harmonix] Bass Microsynth, which is quite a fierce pedal. And we use the Frequency Analyzer a lot, which has got the wildest filter I've ever heard; it's the most extreme thing. I was reading some literature about it the other day, and it was meant to be used on brass. I can't imagine any horn player playing through it. [*Laughs.*] If you put a bass through it, or drums, it just sounds wild.

It's funny how some of the most popular equipment was originally intended to serve a completely different purpose. Roland's TB-303, for example.

I'm sure the engineers never imagined it becoming the defining voice of trance.

I know. Whoever thought that was going to mimic proper bass? It's just amazing. I mean, if that was intended to replicate a bass player, then why are the filters so extreme?

What's your take on the new crop of synthesizers?

Too many machines today are boring. This idea of having to replicate the sound of, I don't know, a great piano or whatever. I mean, if you want that, get the real thing. For us, synthesizers are for making sounds that no other machines can make—not for copying other sounds. It's all about making sounds that no one has ever heard before. It's an exciting thing, and it gives the records an edge. I mean, we spend hours . . . We've got an ARP 2600, and we spend days playing around with it. I like that kind of thing.

What about the new virtual analog synths?

I remember speaking to Underworld a while ago, and they had just gotten one of the [Clavia] Nord Leads. They were saying how amazing it was. But we haven't bought any of those things yet. No [Korg] Prophecy or Nord or any of those, and I don't know quite why that is, because I'm sure if I did buy one I'd be quite impressed. Part of it is me being wary of mass-produced . . . Everyone is going out and buying the Prophecy, and everyone is going out and buying the Nord Lead. It's cool, and I'm sure I'm hearing those noises on records and thinking they're good, but I suppose I'm more interested at the moment in . . . the most exciting piece of equipment we've got at the moment is the ARP 2600. We're really getting into that. It's not very controllable, but some of things you can come up with are wicked. And we've also got this guy in Germany who's made some things for us. He makes these things called Shermans: the Sherman filter Bank and the Sherman Chaos Bank. He only makes, like, 50 of each of them, and they're just wild. They sound really good. Extreme.

What does the Chaos Bank do?

[*Laughs.*] It's a little modular synth setup, and it comes out with the most unearthly noises. I think he's building a big modular system, and I think this is one part of it. It's worth checking out.

And you're sampling maniacs, of course.

For ages we've been using Akai samplers, and just recently we went out and bought the new E-mu range. We're just getting into that—into the synthesis/sampling engines of those machines. Just the way you can patch things together where the LFO is controlling the start point of the sample. Stuff like that. A lot of our sounds are done through that cross-patch page in the E-mu. A really good way of working.

You mentioned using ReCycle earlier. What other software programs do you use?

> "For us, synthesizers are for making sounds that no other machines can make—not for copying other sounds. It's all about making sounds that no one has ever heard before. It's an exciting thing, and it gives the records an edge."
>
> —TOM ROWLANDS (THE CHEMICAL BROTHERS)

We use [Digidesign] Pro Tools when we compile a record, but the one thing I'd like to get into more is having the ease of moving large chunks of music around. At the moment what we do is, a lot of the things on the record are quite sectional. They were recorded at different times, because we wanted to get that feel of certain old records where things were edited together from different takes. Say a Beatles record, or whatever: You can hear a completely different sound from section to section. So what we were doing was recording sections. We'd do, like, two days recording a track, put it on a DAT, and then work another two days on the same track with a totally different setup. And then without Pro Tools, what we did was use our large sampler arsenal to put a lot of the information in, and then play with it as if it were loops. It is quite cool, because you get that feeling as if it were different records being cut together, when in fact it is your own music. It's quite a laborious process, 'cause you've got to make the equivalent of like four records to get it.

Once all of the loops and pieces were stored in your samplers, how did you control them?

We use [Steinberg] Cubase on a Mac. We've got an [Akai] MPC3000, as well, which we sometimes use for the feel of it. It's good to be able to hit things [referring to the MPC's front-panel trigger pads]. We only got the MPC about a year and a half ago to basically play live with. But then when we started playing live with it, we realized the things you can do with it that you can't do with a computer. Being able to bash the pads . . . In fact, one thing I want to get is that E-mu Launch Pad thing, which looks quite cool. Having real-time controllers, and a fader, is quite cool for us. It's a DJ kind of thing, because you have the fader controlling the volume and stuff.

When using effects, do you try to perfectly match the delays with the bpm of the song, for example, or is it more a feel process?

It's just whatever feels right. I mean, I can never find my bpm tempo chart. It just doesn't matter, really. Sometimes I'll set the Roland [Space Echo] delays, and you get a loose kind of feel. The way we make drum loops move, the way we put movement into them, is to put a lot of little short delays on them, and then play around with the delay times. And then when you get everything grooving together, you record it. As long as it sounds good, that's all that matters.

THIEVES?

Much continues to be said about the legalities of sampling from other artists. What's your view on this issue?

Our approach, especially on this record, is to disguise it. We like the idea of the sample culture. In the late '80s, you had those records where people were just bare-faced stealing, things like De La Soul and stuff. I thought it was quite a liberating thing. I really liked it. You could sit these things next to each other, and people knew what they were. But the thing is, you can't do that now, really. And so, since we've been making records the main thing is to take a source sound and make it something else that it wasn't. You start with a sound that you generally know, and think is cool, and then you move it somewhere else. And we cut it up so small. If you play the things [we've sampled] to the people who played them, they wouldn't be able to tell it was them. That's an exciting thing. I like the feeling of having a recorded sound, and in essence, you're recording it again. You know, someone took it that far, and now you're taking it somewhere completely different. And when you start mixing up different things, you end up with things that you'd never think of. It's a good way of working.

What's your approach to recreating your recorded music on the concert stage?

Our basic view is that when we play live, we strip things down. We get rid of a lot of stuff that's on the record. When we play, we want people to dance, and get locked into that thing. So what we do, the actual nuts and bolts of it, is we loop up lots of our tracks. We have three samplers—an MPC3000, an [E-mu] e64, and an S3000—which are all fully expanded. And on those, we have loops of our songs that we've made up at home. And then we have an Akai MPC3000 running in sync with a TASCAM DA-88.

What material do you keep on tape?

More of the treated-type stuff that we haven't got enough sample space for. So what we do is, both are in sync, and we cut between stuff on the sequencer and stuff on the DA-88, which for us is quite a flexible way of working. I mean, a lot of times the DA-88 is just muted. If we're on the bus that afternoon, and we have the idea of extending a section, we can just extend it in the MPC. For us, that's the exciting thing about making the music live. And it's something that's really shaped the way we make records. It is a testing ground, so to speak.

It is a place where you can try out different things.

How is the data organized?

In the MPC we have "bands"— programs in the samplers—that all correspond to a particular bpm. This band is 120 bpm, and then there will be a definite point in the sequence where the bpm changes. Maybe it gets knocked down to 111, or up to whatever. So we have loads of loop-groups of our tracks that all work at these bpms. And basically us playing live is cutting between different stuff of ours, or remixes we've done, or anything we can load into the sampler that afternoon. If it's at that bpm, then we can flip in whatever. Then, along with that, on the MPC we have loads of keyboard lines and stuff running through to, like, the Juno 106.

What drew you to the MPC as your primary live sequencer?

It's a great thing to have live, 'cause you can just jam on it. It's cool. After playing live with it, you come back and sit in front of the computer, and you lose a bit of that intuitive thing. You can't hit it. [*Laughs.*] But then there's other parts of it that I find really annoying. I've been brought up in [Steinberg] Pro24 and Cubase, and I have to see the songs, and like that, especially with complicated arrangements. It gets quite difficult. But then live, when you're just working in blocks of bpms, it's quite easy.

Is there a certain approach you take each night in terms of the bpm sequence?

We have a variety of sequences that we programmed at home, so we can say, "What do you fancy tonight?" That type of thing. But generally, we spend a lot of time sorting out what we're going to do. We know in each section. I'm in control of the sequencer, and Ed knows that it I go into a certain section, he'll know what's coming up next and can change the patches and stuff on the Juno. The thing is, we've made music so long together, and we've DJed so long together, that it's quite locked in, really. That one thing about electronic bands who play live: They always feel this pressure to take what people refer to as "real musicians" onstage. That wouldn't work for us, because that's not how we make our music. Even when we bring in live musicians, or when we play stuff on the tracks ourselves, we always, always loop the things up and get them in the sampler and treat them that way. That's when we're happiest, doing things that you couldn't physically do. We like the way it sounds. Someone once said to us, "Why don't you get a live drummer?" And we said, "No. The drums we use are not physically reproducible."

> "Someone once said to us, 'Why don't you get a live drummer?' And we said, 'No. The drums we use are not physically reproducible.'"
>
> —TOM ROWLANDS (THE CHEMICAL BROTHERS)

Leave that stuff to Jack Dangers, eh?

Exactly, which he does quite well. But we're just on another tip, really. We like machines. We like that control you have.

Live drummer or not, there's no lack of energy on your stage. You both seem to wring the notes out of your machines.

Yeah, it's cool. Our music is exciting, and that's the spirit of it. That's why it's good to play it live. You can crank it up, and that's how people should hear it—and in a room with a load of other people who are having a good time. A lot of our songs are based around that kind of feeling. And then when you get to play it live, it's a really good feeling. How can we not get into it?

Your setup is a pile of gear and spaghetti-like wiring a bit dangerous-looking, actually. Any disasters to report?

[*Laughs.*] Yeah, we've had a few. Nothing really that bad, but a few nights when the DA-88 wouldn't work. Moisture and stuff. But, luckily, we're flexible, so we can just play off the MPC.

Unless it crashes.

Yeah, it's a difficult thing to take these pieces of equipment which are fine in the studio, but don't do so well when they get sweaty and dirty. It is quite a testing thing. The MPC, one time, got smashed up coming through the airport. It was a mad scramble around to get stuff. We use SyQuest 2705 [removable hard disk cartridges], and all our stuff is on that. I suppose we're a bit foolish for not having DAT backups, but we don't. I think we'll get more safety-conscious on the next tour, but we've always managed to get through. People don't understand. They think, "Ah, you're using machines, nothing goes wrong." But if you've got a band, and, say, the bass drum mic gets knocked over or something, at least you've got a lead singer who can tell a few jokes—or do an acoustic set. But with us, if someone kicks out the power, we're looking at a major disaster.

We did this gig once supporting the Prodigy. [Singer] Keith Flint came out when we were playing "Chemical Beats," and he started dancing around our stack and knocked out the power lead to the mixer. Suddenly there was nothing. That was probably the worst moment we've had onstage.

How is the sound handled at your live shows—do you send a stereo feed to the house?

Most of the time, yeah, because the real integral part of the performance is how we're mixing it. So all we send out is a left and a right, and some different effects output auxiliaries and stuff. The guy who does our front of house plays around with it, and all he has to do is make sure it's loud enough and that the general EQ is okay. A lot of the sound check is spent making sure everything sounds right. We know how things sound through our little Sennheiser headphones, so we try to get the monitors as close as we can to that.

When we did a tour in England, we were able to get a big sound system that had Pink Floyd's old desk out front, and a jog wheel for rotating sound around. So for that we sent out lots of different things. Delays were colliding around the room, and stuff. Pretty cool.

Your collaboration with Noel Gallagher was an interesting and successful venture. Where do you see the Chemical Brothers heading in the future?

I'm sure the record company would like us to do more of that, but we've done that now, so . . . Obviously we'll continue to collaborate with people, because it's something we enjoy doing, and it's good when people bring different things in to the sound. We like that, and that's why we enjoy doing remixes: getting to jam with other people's ideas, and putting your own twist into them. But we don't want to get into that thing that a lot of techno people tend to get into when they're making records, which is, "We need to have a voice on this song," or "We need to have this element on this song." And they end up with an album full of collaborations. You're left thinking, "Whose record is this?" But there are no hard-and-fast rules.

If someone comes to us next week and says, "Do you fancy doing this?" and it's a good idea, then sure. Why not?

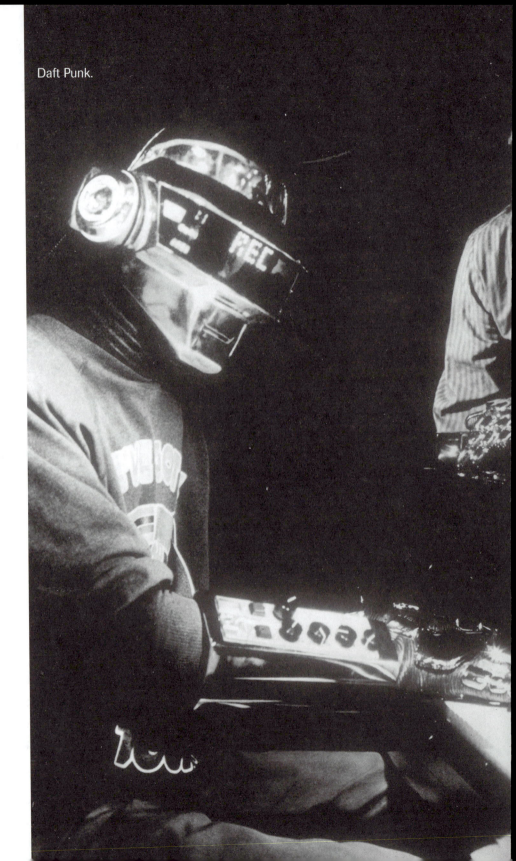

Daft Punk.

14

Daft Punk

ROBOPOP: PART MAN, PART MACHINE, ALL DAFT PUNK

By Chris Gill || *Remix*, May 2001

Hermetically sealed within silver and gold robot masks and gloves, Daft Punk could be accused of making themselves into poster boys for faceless, machine-made dance music. And that would certainly be the case if the Paris-based duo of Thomas Bangalter and Guy-Manuel de Homem-Christo simply delivered a lifeless heap of stiff robo beats, predictable riffs, and monotonous bass lines on their long-awaited sophomore effort. But with its tongue-in-cheek '80s

rock overtones—which include convincing synth emulations of Van Halen–style guitar pyrotechnics, progressive-rock baroque-fugue figures so pompous they'd make
Rick Wakeman blush, and cheeky body-popping electro beats that haven't been heard
since the last Cinemax screening of *Breakin' 2: Electric Boogaloo*—Daft Punk's latest album, *Discovery*, is probably the freshest and most invigorating effort by a dance music
act since—well, Daft Punk's debut LP, *Homework*.

It's somewhat ironic that the duo have reinvented themselves as humanoid machines. "We did not decide to become robots," silver-domed automaton Bangalter
explains dryly. "There was an accident in our studio. We were working on our sampler, and at exactly 9:09 a.m. on September 9, 1999, it exploded. When we regained
consciousness, we discovered that we had become robots." In stark contrast to
their mechanical-man couture, Daft Punk have issued an album that promises to
breathe new life and vitality into house music.

Ever since Daft Punk burst onto the scene, many house music artists have followed every move they make and have toiled to duplicate their signature low-tech
sound. With *Discovery*, Daft Punk have foiled the competition by completely rear-
ranging the formula.

Although Bangalter and de Homem-Christo claim they were physically altered
by some obscure millennial bug, their music has benefited from the injection of
a human element that's even rarer in these days of sequencers, samplers, and
simulated synths. Initially, the duo called upon house music heroes Todd Edwards
and Romanthony—whom Daft Punk had previously praised in their name-checking
tribute "Teachers"—to lend soulful vocals to the songs "One More Time," "Face to
Face," and "Too Long." Next, Bangalter and de Homem-Christo stocked their studio
with vintage Fender Rhodes and Wurlitzer electric pianos, funky '70s effects pedals, and long-forgotten '80s drum machines. Much to their surprise, they also discovered that the accident had given them an insatiable desire to actually play their
instruments instead of merely programming them. But perhaps the most shocking
development was the duo's venture into territory where no dance music has gone
before: the solo.

Daft Punk may have reinvented themselves with *Discovery*, but their music still
delivers just enough familiar elements to keep their more conservative fans happy.
After all, most of the sounds that characterized their '90s singles—filtered disco
samples, massive 909 bass drums, vocoded vocals, and swirling phase-shifter textures—have become so characteristic of modern house music that Daft Punk might
have pulled the plug on their musical career if they abandoned them altogether.
In fact, one can more readily excuse the rather pungent *fromage* of the Barry Manilow samples on "Superheroes" when they're immediately followed by the nasty
disco-diva loops and pounding four-on-the-floor drive of "High Life."

Anyone who is surprised by Daft Punk's newfound fascination with musicianship and songs should look back about ten years to when Bangalter and de Homem-Christo played bass and guitar, respectively, in a trio called Darlin' with their friend and current Phoenix guitarist Laurent Brancowitz. The group enjoyed marginal success when Stereolab released one of their songs on a multiple-artist EP and invited Darlin' to play some opening gigs in the United Kingdom. A reporter for *Melody Maker* witnessed one of these gigs and described Darlin' as "daft punk" in a review of the show. Going back even further, Bangalter was barely out of diapers when his father, Daniel Vangarde, was producing and writing songs for disco acts such as the Gibson Brothers, Ottawan, and Sheila and Black Devotion. That was back in the glory days of disco, when drummers—rather than drum machines—pumped out the rhythms that inspired dancers to shake their booty.

Bangalter must have experienced some sort of fraternally inspired divination when he stepped into a dance club with de Homem-Christo in 1993. Shortly afterward, both decided to abandon their string instruments in favor of synths and samplers. A year later, the renowned independent Scottish house label Soma discovered Daft Punk and issued the duo's first single. In early 1995 Soma released Daft Punk's second single, "Da Funk," a stomping house hit featuring the funkiest riff to hit dance floors since George Clinton manned the *Mothership*. The Chemical Brothers commissioned a remix, and Virgin beat a path to Daft Punk's Paris doorstep with a record deal. Suddenly, these daft punks were the darlin' of the United Kingdom's burgeoning underground dance scene.

Virgin released Daft Punk's full-length debut, *Homework*, in 1996. Although Bangalter and de Homem-Christo were still in their early 20s (Bangalter was born on January 1, 1975, and de Homem-Christo was born on August 2, 1974), together, they soon became one of the most powerful creative forces in dance music. Almost everybody wanted to sound like Daft Punk, and even though many pop music stars approached them with generous offers for remix makeovers, the duo declined. Instead, Daft Punk devoted their energy to producing a stunning live show and making innovative videos directed by Spike Jonze, Michel Gondry, Roman Coppola, and Seb Janiak (all of which were compiled on the *D.A.F.T.* DVD, released in 2000). Meanwhile, Bangalter released several solo efforts and tracks by Roy Davis Jr., Alan Braxe, and Romanthony on his Roulé label. De Homem-Christo also jumped into the record-mogul role by establishing the Crydamoure label and releasing singles by Le Knight Club (his collaboration with DJ Rico), Paul Johnson, Buffalo Bunch, and his brother, Play Paul. Selections from Crydamoure's 12 singles are available on the recently released Waves compilation.

Even while on break from Daft Punk, Bangalter continued to achieve phenomenal success. Collaborating with Alan Braxe and Benjamin Diamond, he created perhaps the biggest dance music hit of 1998, Stardust's "Music Sounds Better with You." In the same year he inadvertently dominated dance charts with his remix of Bob Sinclar's "Gym Tonic," released without Bangalter's consent. The success of these tracks only increased Bangalter's desire to complete the second Daft Punk album. In late 2000, fans were finally treated to Daft Punk's first new track in nearly five years, "One More Time." Effectively a bridge between the old and the new Daft Punk and Stardust, the single gave listeners an ample helping of exactly what they wanted and a taste of what was headed their way.

Even with the release of *Discovery*, Daft Punk isn't sitting still. Just before the album's release, they announced the launch of Daft Club. Every Discovery CD includes a club card bearing a number that provides personalized access to a Web site, where surfers can download new tracks and other exclusive material. And the digital duo will certainly embark on another world tour, although plans for the live show are still under discussion.

Bangalter promises that Daft Punk will continue to deliver many surprises during the coming years. "We never like to do the same thing twice," he says. "It's more fun and entertaining for us to do something different, whether it's wearing masks or developing a persona that merges fiction and reality. We're happy to give back to the masses."

Discovery evokes the sounds and styles of the late '70s and early '80s. Did you initially decide to pay tribute to that era when you started working on the album?

Thomas Bangalter: This album has a lot to do with our childhood and the memories of the state we were in at that stage of our lives. It's about our personal relationship to that time. It's less of a tribute to the music from 1975 to 1985 as an era, and more about focusing on the time when we were zero to ten years old.

When you're a child you don't judge or analyze music. You just like it because you like it. You're not concerned with whether it's cool or not. Sometimes you might relate to just one thing in a song, such as the guitar sound. This album takes a playful, fun, and colorful look at music. It's about the idea of looking at something with an open mind and not asking too many questions. It's about the true, simple, and honest relationship you have with music when you're open to your own feelings. Electronic and house music has shown how it's possible to destroy the old rules, so it comes from an open-minded approach in the first place. But it has started to set its own new rules. We wanted to destroy the new rules that define house music today by doing something that is more in the house music spirit rather than the house music style. The spirit of house music is about questioning yourself and trying different things. Electronic music is about creating exciting new sounds. A lot of house music today just uses samples from disco records of the '70s and '80s. In some respects, house music is a revival of that style. We don't want to make music that is considered just a revival. While we might have some disco influences, we decided to go further and bring in all the elements of music that we liked as children, whether it's disco, electro, heavy metal, rock, or classical.

You can even hear elements of progressive rock on a few songs, like "Superheroes," for example.

Bangalter: The classical arpeggios are very obvious on that track. We wanted to convey the feeling you get from certain movies. We wanted to make something that sounded like Queen's music for *Flash Gordon* or like what you hear when you're watching an old science-fiction cartoon like *Wizards*.

You've also broken away from the standard house music instrumentation. For example, you used Oberheim and Linn drum machines on several songs instead of the usual 808 and 909.

Bangalter: We used an Oberheim DMX and a LinnDrum a lot. There is a Sequential Circuits Drum Tracks on "Short Circuit." It's not like we're going against what other people are doing. We're just opening up the music to new ideas. The instrument itself is not as important as the way we use it. Instruments come with certain instructions in the manual, and many people can't look beyond those rules. People ask us why we like to use vocoders or electric keyboards from the ' 60s, but to us instruments are just tools. The idea is more important than the instrument. One of the cool things about the house music spirit is that it inspired musicians to use instruments for things they weren't designed to do.

> "When you're a child you don't judge or analyze music. You just like it because you like it. You're not concerned with whether it's cool or not."
>
> —THOMAS BANGALTER (DAFT PUNK)

You had a hiatus between Homework and Discovery where you both concentrated on your own labels, Crydamoure and Roulé. How did those experiences affect the outcome of this album?

Bangalter: We spent most of 1997 touring and doing our live show. The first half of 1998 we focused on our own labels and working on our DVD. In 1999 and 2000 our time was split between making music for our labels and recording the new album. We make music together, and we make music separately. The first album was done in the same process. It's an experience of being independent and having an outlet.

When you're working on a piece of music, how do you decide whether it's going to be a Daft Punk song or material for one of your other projects?

Guy-Manuel de Homem-Christo: We have the same tastes in music. When I make records for Crydamoure, it's a different style than what may end up as Daft Punk music. I know what Thomas likes, and he knows what I like. Crydamoure is not so production oriented, even if it's not too far from Daft Punk. The Daft Punk material is more orchestrated and slightly different. I may be working on a sample for Crydamoure, and maybe no one else can hear the difference, but we know. It's very precise.

How do you two collaborate?

Bangalter: It's pretty wide open. There is no formula to our music. But we almost always start by working separately in our studios and coming up with ideas on our own.

de Homem-Christo: I have a studio with DJ Rico [Eric Chedeville] that I use to do my work for Crydamoure. Thomas's studio is where we do the bulk of our work for Daft Punk.

What is the difference between your studios?

de Homem-Christo: They're pretty much the same. I have a lot of the same equipment and instruments. The main difference is that he has more effects and mixing things.

Bangalter: My studio is bigger. It is more like an old studio, more of a professional studio.

What do you record to? Analog tape? Hard disk?

Bangalter: We use sequencers to control a lot of different samplers and synthesizers. Every sampler has a different sound, but my favorite is the E-mu. We have Roland, Ensoniq, and Akai samplers, too. A lot of times we'll try a sound in all of our different samplers to see which is best. Our sequencing is done either on an E-mu SP-1200, an Akai MPC, or a PC with Logic Audio software. We do not work on things in just one way.

This album sounds like it features a lot of live performance, too. The "guitar solo" on "Digital Love," for example, sounds like something you played instead of sequenced.

Bangalter: That was a mix of elements. It was done with the help of technology, with the help of sequencers. We're interested in making things sound like something other than what they are. There are guitars that sound like synthesizers, and there are synthesizers that sound like guitars. The other goal is to create spontaneity. Even though we're not that good, we played a lot of things ourselves. With the help of technology, you can manufacture skills you don't have. That's one advantage of having a home studio. It takes a lot of time to put together music that way, and that's not always a luxury you may have in a regular studio. You might have one or two months to record an entire album in a regular studio, but in a home studio you have more time to experiment. We also like the idea of the solo. No one plays solos in their songs anymore, but we wanted to include some on the album.

What do you look for when you select a sample to build a song with?

de Homem-Christo: We usually look for something simple. We'll just be browsing and something just happens. But it's very rare when we find something that inspires us. If a song doesn't happen fast, we move on to something else. We come across maybe one good sample every six months or so. We used only three samples on this album, and everything else is played.

Bangalter: If you listen to 50 records a day, you may find three good samples out of all of them. Of the two we find a year, we then have to worry about making something good out of them.

A lot of our songs start with samples, but we also have songs like "Too Long" where we wrote some chords first and took more of a song-based approach.

The songs on *Homework* were mostly based around loops and grooves, whereas this album primarily features traditional-style songs. How is this going to affect the way you perform live on the next tour?

Bangalter: It's too early to tell. On the last tour we worked with different layers. Everything was synced up—the drum machines, the bass lines. The sequencer was just sending out the tempos and controlling the beats and bars. On top of this structure, we built all these layers of samples and various parts that we could bring in whenever we wanted to.

There are a lot of electric pianos on the album. Did you use a real Wurlitzer and Rhodes?

Bangalter: All the electric pianos were real. It's funny—technology allows you to simulate things, but you just don't play things the same way as you do when you have the real thing.

Are effects pedals still a big part of your sound?

Bangalter: I use everything. I have a lot of Boss pedals, but I also like to use all-in-one effects boards. It's amazing what you can do with just an 808 or 909 when you play it through those things and experiment with the sounds. Again, it's a matter of using things for something other than what they were designed to do. For example, some pedals are designed for bass, but they sound incredible when you play a guitar through them instead. It's all about whatever rules you are willing to break. Whenever we get a new pedal, we try it with everything we have. Sometimes that can help us come up with an idea we never had before.

You use vocoders and phase shifters on many of your tracks.

Bangalter: People always ask us what vocoder we use, but every one of our vocal tracks uses a different vocoder effect. We have the old Roland one [an SVC- 350], Auto-Tune, and a Digitech Vocalist. We take the same approach with phase shifters. Every track on this album uses a different phase shifter. We have a Mu-Tron phaser, a Moogerfooger pedal, an old AMS phaser, and an Ensoniq DP-4. With the older items, you can have several of the same model and they all sound different.

We also use vocoders in ways most people don't use them. Auto-Tune is great for fixing vocals, but we use Auto-Tune in a way it wasn't designed to work. A lot of people complain about musicians using Auto-Tune. It reminds me of the late '70s when musicians in France tried to ban the synthesizer. They said it was taking jobs away from musicians. What they didn't see was that you could use those tools in a new way instead of just for replacing the instruments that came before. People are often afraid of things that sound new.

How did Romanthony feel about the heavy processing you applied to his vocals on "One More Time"?

Bangalter: He loved it. He has done a lot of different things and he always tries to innovate, which is what we like to do on our records. He never had his voice treated like an instrument like that.

You gave Romanthony's career a boost. How did you get involved with him?

de Homem-Christo: We met him at the 1996 Winter Music Conference and became friends. Before that, we mentioned his name on "Teachers," thanking him for his influences. We wanted to invite him to sing with us because he makes emotional music.

Bangalter: We wanted to work with Romanthony and Todd Edwards on our first album. They didn't know who we were at the time, so it was very difficult to convince them. When we met Romanthony in Miami, he told us he was very into what we were doing, which made us very happy.

de Homem-Christo: What's odd is that Romanthony and Todd Edwards are not big in the United States at all. Their music had a big effect on us. The sound of their productions—the compression, the sound of the kick drum and Romanthony's voice, the emotion and soul—is part of how we sound today. Because they mean something to us, it was much more important for us to work with them than with other big stars.

Bangalter: They are the house producers who were the biggest influence on us. Working with them was a way for us to close the circle. It was very important for us to do that, because they are part of what we do. Now that we've worked with them, we are free to explore other areas. It will be interesting to see what we'll do next. Now we can work with other people.

You probably get a lot of offers from other artists.

Bangalter: Yeah, but some people are afraid to approach us—and those are the people we usually are most interested in working with.

You haven't done too many remixes lately. Now that the album is completed, will you be doing more?

Bangalter: We're not doing any remixing. We've done only one remix in four years: Scott Grooves's "Mothership Reconnection," which was something we agreed to do a long time ago. We did a lot of remixes before we recorded our first album, but since then we've concentrated on recording original tracks. It's more a question of scheduling and priority. It's not that we've not been interested in doing that. Remixing is an interesting concept.

de Homem-Christo: It's not always constructive. It's different every time. Sometimes when the track you're given is good, there is no use remixing it. For us it's more interesting to start from scratch. The best remixes we've done were those where we took just one element and made an original track from it.

How do you feel about all the credit you've received for boosting the popularity of French dance-music artists?

de Homem-Christo: There was not so much going on before. Because the scene was not so big, we met a lot of the musicians. It's great that people in France are making music now, because before there was nothing. Now there are ten or more French artists who are making great music, and everybody is doing different types and styles of music. I wouldn't call it a French touch, because the French touch really does not exist. A lot of French artists are involved with electronic music, but the only connection between us is that we're all French. We're not making the same type of music, and there isn't any traditional French influence. France is now connected with house and electronic music, but it's all part of a bigger scene. If someone was to tell you that Cassius was English, you wouldn't know the difference. The country is not as important as the music. It's a worldwide movement.

Richie Hawtin.

15

Richie Hawtin and John Acquaviva

THE SOUNDS OF SCIENCE: RICHIE HAWTIN PUTS THE TECH IN TECHNO

By Chris Gill || *Remix*, December 2001

lthough techno innovator Richie Hawtin still enjoys success recording as Plastikman and running the Plus 8 and Minus record labels, for the past three years he has focused on DJing. Hawtin's DJ-mix album *Decks, EFX, and 909* (NovaMute, 1999) showcases his innovative performance style, in which he processed records with live effects and programmed accompanying rhythms on the fly with a classic Roland TR-909 drum machine. For his latest album, *DE9: Closer to the Edit* (NovaMute, 2001), Hawtin took the mixing concept to a new extreme, cutting more than 100 songs into small loops and layering, splicing, and editing them to create an entirely new piece of music.

While DE9 offers listeners a peek at the future of the DJ-mix album, Hawtin's current live DJ performances are giving clubgoers a glimpse at what lies ahead in the fast-evolving realm of live remixing. Interestingly, a combined hardware and software product from N2IT Development called FinalScratch made both of those developments possible for Hawtin. FinalScratch allows DJs to control digital files stored on a computer from a vinyl record encoded with digital data. FinalScratch's software made it easy for Hawtin to extract loops from songs while he was gathering raw material for the album. Offering the ability to store thousands of songs on a hard drive, to slice each song into dozens of discrete elements, and to edit and rearrange those songs any way he sees fit, FinalScratch gives Hawtin license to venture away from playing records linearly and to create unique remixes instantaneously as he performs his sets.

> "The people who are really pushing it are the people who do a hybrid between live performance and DJing. They're reevaluating and reinterpreting music right in front of you."
>
> —RICHIE HAWTIN

Hawtin remains focused on new music-software developments that promise to enable him to take his live-remixing concepts even further. Although he doesn't feel that vinyl is obsolete, he does feel that the DJ's role is going to change significantly in the coming years. "The people who are really pushing it are the people who do a hybrid between live performance and DJing," says Hawtin. "They're reevaluating and reinterpreting music right in front of you. Audiences are going to want to hear a DJ do more than mix a couple of records together on two turntables once they realize what is going on."

You're taking loop mixing to a new level on DE9.

I'm using technology to reevaluate my ideas and trying to approach them in a different way. Hopefully it will let me do something a bit more intricate, which usually is what technology allows you to do. In some ways the album is much like a DJ performance. All I'm doing is layering one track over another, but instead of layering them in a linear fashion from the start of one to the beginning of the next, I've been able to cut each track up into smaller components and build new ideas by overlaying, inter-mixing, and inter-splicing loops. Remixing is taking someone else's track and reinventing it. I tried to reinvent the whole album by using different pieces of other people's tracks.

You must have listened to quite a few tracks in great detail when selecting the loops.

Yes and no. Because all of the tracks had been in my DJ crate for a while, I already knew what tracks I wanted and had ideas about what worked together. As you mix two records together, you may discover that they make a really cool rhythm, but that disappears as you go into the next record. I remembered how certain tracks complemented each other; that's what I zeroed in on first. I also liked the feel, groove, or bass line of other records, so it was quite easy to choose parts. The most time-consuming part was recording those things into the computer. Some of them were already in there for use with FinalScratch, but even then I had to cut and slice them down to what I wanted. It took me longer to edit the tracks than it did to find them.

What made you decide to take a loop-based approach on this album?

I've been thinking about doing something like this for a couple of years, but FinalScratch made me get back into experimenting with that idea. A lot of loop-based software has been developed over the last couple of years—things like Sonic Foundry's Acid and [Image-Line Software's] Fruity Loops. I was trying to see if there was some way of using these to create something larger in scope than some of the programs were able to do themselves. I was using the software to give me parts and usable pieces. One of the advantages I've found with FinalScratch is that it's very easy for me to re-edit people's tracks, to take loops and breaks out or to take certain sections and repeat them to make a bed track that I could work with. I'd mix those tracks with other ones. The more I did that, the more I thought about it, and the more I started to think about music in a nonlinear fashion. It was more of a collection of parts that could be reassembled in any way I wanted, as long as I had the technology that would make that possible. I'd move loops around for one track, then move loops around for a different version of another track. I wondered what would happen if all these elements became just components in the mix. Would that still be a mix album? Would it be DJing? Or would it be something entirely new?

How did the whole mix come together? Did you have a start and end point in mind?

I did. There's a track at the end that I always ended my special sets with, and I always wanted to get that into one of my mix CDs. That was the point I wanted to get to: the point of no return. I was playing with certain ideas for the beginning, but everything came back to continuing where *Decks*, *EFX*, and *909* left off, which was a Burial Mix [label] record [Rhythm and Sound's "Never Tell You"]. I started this album with a track by the same people, which had a similar type of dub feeling. I wanted the albums to be different but complement each other. The first album started off quite intense and broke down, mellowed out, and got weird at the end. I wanted to start this one that way, build it back up, and then bring it back down.

It's fascinating how seamless the whole mix is. Sometimes you don't realize that it's a compilation of a lot of different tracks.

The album was a little bit longer at first. It was approaching 70 minutes. I cut it down further because I wanted to keep a certain pace. I explored a few ideas, then went off to something else. I didn't want any one track to play so people would go, "Oh, there's that track." I wanted it to be a little bit of this track and a little bit of that track. I wanted to have a forward progression and a real momentum. Suddenly it starts, and then it's done. It takes on a life of itself, and that's what I wanted.

Were any parts difficult to piece together?

Not really. I had the beginning and end and moved forward through it, putting things together that seemed to complement each other. At certain points things came in, and I knew what would work with it because it worked in my set. Even when I record my own tracks, I work as fast as possible and don't worry about minute details. Then I go back and do the micro-editing and chop things down. Most of my recordings and compositions are longer at first, and then they end up shorter.

Is Pro Tools your main editing system?

Now that Pro Tools has integrated MIDI, tempo mapping, and grids that can lock MIDI to tempo, it came into its own for this project. I was able to bring a lot of loops in and drop them into different grid paths. I could change my grids to 32nd-notes and get in there quickly to edit the loops. In the past, I would have had to do that by looking at the waveform and scrubbing over it. I wasn't necessarily doing anything I hadn't been doing before, but progressions in the software enabled me to do things much more quickly and efficiently—things like using Acid to bring everything back to the right tempo. Because I was able to use a program like Acid to lock up some of the loops, it enabled me to focus my attention on other areas.

How did you discover FinalScratch?

I and a friend of John Acquaviva saw it a couple of years ago. We're always looking for new technologies and ideas. We thought it sounded cool. We had no idea how well it would work. We'd seen other things like Video 15 that you hear about over the Internet, so we were a bit skeptical. John was going to Holland a couple of weeks after he heard about it, so he was able to check it out. He gave us a report back and said, "It does what it's supposed to, but there's a lot of latency. But the actual theory is working. If they can reduce the latency it should be interesting." We stayed in contact with them. Initially John was more into it than I was, because he still wanted it even with the latency. He picked up a really early version, but I don't think he ever got it to work. I wanted to wait until the latency issues were worked out. There was no way I was going to play a record with a five-second delay. Finally, one day N2IT contacted us and told us that the latency was reduced. When I saw it, it was unbelievable. John got the first revision of the new prototype, and I got the second. We've been taking it through the paces ever since.

What type of PC are you using?

A Pentium III/600 MHz Sony VAIO—one of the super-slim models. I have a 20 GB hard drive, which is about the biggest you can get for a superslim, and 128 MB of RAM. One of the best things is being able to sit on a plane and go through all my new records.

How many MP3 files do you carry with you now?

I have about 2,500 tracks.

Do you still bring much vinyl to gigs?

I've been trying to get down to one crate, but I'm still carrying two crates with me now. The only reason I do that is because I've been traveling back and forth so much that I haven't had time to catalog what is on the computer. As soon as I figure that out, I'll be down to under one crate. My sets are ranging from a minimum of 30- to 40-percent FinalScratch up to 80- to 90-percent FinalScratch. I did a one-hour set the other night, and I didn't play any records at all. I just hooked up the computer and did my set. It's definitely liberating. Having all those choices can be overwhelming, but it's amazing once you get used to it. There are so many possibilities, such as having the ability to re-edit tracks and loop tracks that I can mix in a special way. I have loops of my breakdowns so I can elongate them from five seconds to two minutes if I want. It enables me to put on a better performance. I can take things further than I was able to do with the whole *Decks*, *EFX*, and *909* show over the past couple of years.

All of that must have significantly affected the way you DJ.

It has, and it will do more as I have more time to work with it. I've been doing some edits on planes, but I haven't been able to re-edit the material as much as I would like. I don't want to play the regular version of any record anymore. I want to edit everything, even if it's just a slight change. Someone may hear it and think it's the regular version, but then they'll hear a little part that they don't remember. I want to get more into that. It's really offered me new possibilities.

Are you currently doing very much live-effects processing?

It's all with outboard equipment. FinalScratch is only playing back the music. I'm not using any plug-ins. I have a customized Allen and Heath Xone:62 mixer that has extra sends and other modifications. I'm using the Electrix Repeater, which is one of the coolest hardware products I've seen in a long time. I used a prototype about six months before it came out. I didn't use the really early versions, because they crashed all over the place, but it's really solid now. I used to use an Ensoniq DP/4, but I've moved over to a Lexicon MPX500, which is much cleaner and of-

FINALSCRATCH

TECHNICAL ITCH: JOHN ACQUAVIVA GETS HIS FINALSCRATCH
BY STACIA MONTEITH *REMIX*, DECEMBER 2001

The times, they were a-changin'. As recently as 2001, Remix *could marvel at the notion of a DJ spinning turntables but leaving the vinyl at home. The technology in question, Dutch developer N2IT's FinalScratch, would come to be marketed by Stanton and Native Instruments under the name Traktor Final Scratch; competing products from developers like Serato would follow. Linux support was eventually dropped, along with visions of an open-source, community effort, though some open-source DJ tools persist today (notably Mixxx). But in 2001, one sees the genesis of the digital vinyl era, through the eyes of two artists—Acquaviva and Hawtin—who helped shape both the tool and the scene. —PK*

John Acquaviva enters Los Angeles's Spundae and quickly assesses the sound system. He places two dub plates on two turntables, plugs in a small box, and boots his laptop computer. With the flip of a switch, he fires up an arsenal of 3,000 tracks, giving him the ability to throw down any obscure disco song or sophisticated Brazilian percussion track he wants, even if he's in the middle of a straight-up house set. Acquaviva used to lug two record boxes (about 200 records) to every gig, but now his sets are no longer limited to the amount of vinyl he can carry with him, thanks to FinalScratch.

Acquaviva, alongside fellow techno icon Richie Hawtin, is the first to experiment with a new vinyl-to-digital interface called FinalScratch, the brainchild of Amsterdam-based N2IT Development. Basically, FinalScratch allows a vinyl record (here, a dub plate containing digitally encoded song information) to control a digital file. An A/D converter box, called the Scratch Amp, connects to and provides an interface between the turntables, mixer, and computer. DJs manipulate the records just as they would any other 12-inch. "For me, as a DJ, the turntable is a much better controller than a mouse, CD, or touch pad," Acquaviva explains. "You can pick the needle up and see the response on the computer screen with a song, and the waveform display helps me find the break." The digital file can be MP3, WAV, or audio CD. Acquaviva finds he can get powerful club sound quality just by using any of the larger MP3 bit rates, such as 192- or 256-Kbps.

Acquaviva sees many practical advantages with FinalScratch: "If you're doing demos for labels, DJs, or producers, you don't have to make acetates or burn CDs. It's great for me because I use Sonic Foundry software like Acid Pro and Sound Forge, and I'm constantly doing new mixes. I used to rip ten different CDs for ten different mixes. Now if I want to play my latest mix during a gig, I just click on it."

Acquaviva also finds benefits in the realm of production: "It has motivated me to do more edits. Often a track just needs to be reshuffled. Now DJs can play their own mix of a song, whether they're simply mixing two copies or producing their own new elements. If I don't like my own mix,

I can go on the airplane tomorrow and re-edit it over headphones. I'm just starting to scratch that surface. If FinalScratch becomes the standard, it will be amazing."

FinalScratch was developed on the BeOS operating system. "BeOS is the best real-time system," says Acquaviva. In 2002, FinalScratch will be developed on an embedded Linux system. "Linux is such a great operating system," he says. "Once it's in Linux, N2IT wants the community to improve it. I think Linux is ideal for this technology, because sharing ideas is what the electronic-music community is about." FinalScratch is nearing the end of its prototype stage. Although the pro version is still produced only on a micro scale, a consumer version, compatible with both PC and Mac operating systems, is set to premiere in early 2002.

fers me better sampling delays. My whole show is running on completely different boxes and hardware than it was three years ago when it started.

Are you still using a Roland TR-909?

The 909 is being phased out a little bit, because people have had trouble finding them for me. I don't like to carry too much with me, so I'll rent things. The Repeater and FinalScratch are about all I take with me now. The 909 really works. It's amazing, and people love it. Some people are disappointed that I'm not using it that much anymore. I'm looking for something that is like a 909 that I can really interact with spontaneously, which is what's so great about the interface on that unit. The problem with a 909 is that its sound bank is limited. I could use it with a sampler and have it MIDIed up, but I just want to use one box. Right now, everything comes down to size and weight. We're at the mercy of the airlines.

Part of the allure of being a DJ is not having to deal with hauling a lot of gear around and doing sound checks. The reason why a lot of clubs like to book DJs is that they don't have to worry about bands and sound checks. Unfortunately, if you are booking me, you do still have to handle that. A lot of places have to rip their DJ booths apart because we're bringing in our own mixer. The only things we usually use are the turntables. I have a sound technician who travels with me. Some clubs were a bit apprehensive at first, because there was more work involved.

Some DJs are a bit lazy, because they don't want to take that extra step. They just want to play their set for a few hours and then leave. Those days are numbered. DJs and promoters have to wake up. There's more work involved with what I do, but it offers everyone a greater experience. When I was a kid and I went out to see Derrick May or Jeff Mills, the best moments were when they did things that I had no idea what they were doing. Back then it was a simple matter of changing volume or pitch—that was the cutting edge. But it was fresh. I want those experiences again. I want to give people those experiences. You can't do that when you're just mixing two records.

One of the most exciting developments of the past ten years is the concept of live remixing. The manufacturing community is starting to come out with products that support that concept. The Repeater is basically like Acid in a hardware box. It allows you to grab samples, loop them, and change pitch and tempo. I'm looking at Ableton's Live software, which seems like it will allow me to do what I did on the *DE9* album live. It also records your gigs. Sometimes I come up with ideas while I'm working in front of people that I can't re-create later. This software will let me pull that performance back up so I can refine it and perfect it for an actual release.

> "When I was a kid and I went out to see Derrick May or Jeff Mills, the best moments were when they did things that I had no idea what they were doing. Back then it was a simple matter of changing volume or pitch—that was the cutting edge. But it was fresh. I want those experiences again. I want to give people those experiences."
>
> —RICHIE HAWTIN

Where do you get most of the records that you play?

All over the place. I'm getting more records than ever sent to me; not all of them are good, though. Everywhere I am, I go record shopping. I'm listening to more demos than I ever used to. Even though I'm not signing as much as I used to on my label, now I have the potential to load it into FinalScratch and play these demos live. One of the biggest tracks I'm playing right now is a demo that some kid from Holland sent me. I sent him an e-mail, but he hasn't gotten back in touch with me. I just wanted to let him know that it's a great track. It's not what I'm looking for for my label. It's a bit more clubby, but it works perfectly in my set. When I was in Montreal, I found this demo that someone from Montreal had sent me. I loaded the track up and played it that night. I was hoping that the kid would have been there, but unfortunately he wasn't. That would have been crazy. He just finished the track the week before, and there I was playing it. That's how fast things are moving. People are posting MP3s on FTP sites, so I can download them and play them if I like them. I've had some songs three or four months before they were even pressed on vinyl.

Recently, certain styles like house, progressive house, and trance have become popular, yet techno remains underground. How do you feel about that?

Techno will always be somewhat underground because of its progressive nature. What's happened with the other styles is that someone will have a good idea and then everyone will milk that for six to eight months. When that happens, the music stops developing. When ideas get stagnant, the mass population has more time to catch up with things and starts to appreciate those ideas. It's hard for the mass population to appreciate something when it's constantly changing. It's too hard for companies to promote and commercialize. Someone has to grab hold of our equation and move it into the mainstream. When something like progressive house becomes more commercially viable than what I'm involved in, it becomes a bonus for us. That means that more people will get into what we're doing. My music has the funkiness of house and the weirdness and electronic progressiveness of techno. Some of the tracks on my *DE9* album were pressed in runs of only 800 copies. I consider those things on the cutting edge of electronic music right now.

What is one of the most significant changes you've noticed in the scene during the past couple of years?

FinalScratch is the first thing I've seen that bridges the gap between the digital and analog worlds, the new world and the old world. Being able to perform with digital files has caused me to re-evaluate everything I play. Being able to have an entire studio on a laptop is amazing. [Propellerhead] Reason is quite liberating. During the past five years a lot of manufacturers have finally realized how big this market is and that they can make products for people who produce this music, whether they're groove boxes or DJ mixers with effects built into them. All these weird things that we used to only dream about ten years ago are widely available now.

I'm going to use the advantages I have to let people know about things. Whether it's FinalScratch, creating *DE9*, or using effects with turntables, sometimes the only way people are going to find out about it is if they read about it or hear about it from some artist. I like to use my position, whatever that is, to try to forward things. That's what keeps me involved. I'm interested in making tracks and music, but in a progressive way. People who have a progressive frame of mind are the people I get along with and appreciate.

BT.

16

BT

THE MIND OF BT

By Stephen Fortner || *Keyboard*, December 2005

T is a model of the artist in the new millennium, collaborating on software as well as music, making his sonic signatures into tools. Stephen Fortner spoke to BT about a then as-yet-untitled release that would become *This Binary Universe*, and an early look at the software that would—years later—be released as iZotope Stutter Edit. —PK

"Basically, my house is a hard drive," laughs Brian Transeau. Though BT's referring to the more than eight terabytes of computer storage at his home studio, the place actually does look like a hard drive, its sparse cubic forms and corrugated metal walls boldly rebelling against the Spanish-tile status quo of residential hills near L.A.'s Griffith Park. "It was designed by Frank Gehry [the architect behind Disney Hall and Seattle's Experience Music Project building], and I think even the realtor didn't know that when I first made an offer."

It's hard to think of anything more fitting than one innovator creating art from inside the artwork of another—though "innovator" only begins to describe BT. From his work with Tori Amos almost ten years ago on "Blue Skies" and producing *NSync's "Pop," to Emotional Technology's juxtaposition of trancefloor soundscapes and pop songcraft and his acclaimed score for the Oscar-winning film *Monster*, BT has become the face of electronic music virtuosity, a techno-mage with formal training to match his DJ and synthesis chops, a massively overclocked brain, and the childlike enthusiasm of Shaggy from *Scooby Doo*. "Like, wow, man, you gotta hear this," he'll say. "You'll totally freak out!"

Listen we did, thanks to the opportunity to be first to hear tracks from his fifth studio project. In addition to this creative endeavor, he's also been working on a dance-oriented album, and he just signed on to score the romantic comedy *Catch and Release*, starring Jennifer Garner and slated for April 2006 release. But this is something else entirely. Labels such as "ambient" or "modern classical" fit for a few seconds, then the next passage in the song blows away the last, taking any attempt to classify along with it. We can't restrain our editorial opinion: This as-yet-untitled magnum opus is fine art that works on many levels, mind-bendingly deep but a pleasure to kick back and just listen to. In a hundred years, it could well be studied as the first major electronic work of the new millennium. It's that good.

NEW MUSIC

"I get such a rush listening to this, even after working on it for hundreds of hours," says BT. Even so, he's a little cagey about the project's release details. "I've got a title, which I'll keep to myself for now, because I'm not sure whether it'll be of the record or the project itself. I might not call this a BT record, per se." Seven compositions, each about 15 minutes long, combine acoustic instruments, synth parts played real-time from keyboards, and "cut-and-paste, musique concrète-type stuff," he explains. "But the really cool part is that it involves seven short films by people ranging from a CalArts student to famous animators. Come summer, we're going to take this out with drums, a string quartet, electric cello, and myself. Live, in 5.1, with projection, baby! We've talked to the Hollywood Bowl, who are very excited, and I've always wanted to play spaces like [Washington D.C.'s] Corcoran Gallery. While some of it is very rhythmic and makes me want to move, I want people to be able to just receive without feeling like they have to dance or be in a club mindset."

Unlike the after-the-fact surround mixes often done for pop CDs, this work was composed for 5.1, and begs to be heard that way. BT cues up a track where expansive piano chords (all from Synthogy Ivory) fold into impossibly complex, evolving textures, suddenly going up in a mushroom cloud, breaking into granular desolation, then resolving back into walls of sound layered over beats that constantly evolve, one minute a march, the next, trip-hop. The emotion coming from the speakers is so undeniable that it feels like sacrilege to listen with your eyes glued to Logic's play wiper. So I closed mine.

"After this, my new 'normal' album sounds more like indie bands," he says, "which are what I listen to primarily, than my previous work. It's got beautiful jangly guitars all over it, like Death Cab for Cutie or something. Imogen Heap is going to sing on it—I get goosebumps just thinking about her voice. I've always wanted to take those elements and put them in a context that makes sense on a dance floor."

> "The grandfather clock in my parents' house played those pentatonic Westminster chimes every quarter hour. Mom also took me to church a lot, so resolutions like the plagal cadence and Picardy third are prominent, too. Trevor Horn, New Order, and Depeche Mode were where I went to school."
>
> —BT

BT traces the musical sensibility that's permeated all his work to a surprising origin. "The grandfather clock in my parents' house played those pentatonic Westminster chimes every quarter hour," he recalls. "Mom also took me to church a lot, so resolutions like the plagal cadence and Picardy third are prominent, too. Listen carefully to anything I've ever done, and it'll jump out at you.

"On this experimental record, I've been trying to explore more jazz harmonies. The thing is—and I'm gonna piss off a lot of people here—the II–V–I hits my barf button like nothing else. It's the most horrible cadence in the known universe, so I've been looking at jazz that takes off in other directions." For bands or musicians that proved formative, "Trevor Horn, New Order, and Depeche Mode were where I went to school," he says. "Depeche in particular are the godfathers of electronic counterpoint, of interweaving a number of synth sounds that create tension against one another. I had their new album pre-ordered on iTunes for, like, two months!"

NEW METHODS

When you spin this new disc, you'll hear BT's signature stutter technique, which fans know goes way beyond Max Headroom, sometimes comprising hundreds of micro-edits to a single syllable or note, each EQed and processed differently, then time-corrected with precision that'd scare Stephen Hawking. Will he give up any more secrets?

"Some of the grids I've made for this go to 2,048th-notes," he grins. "The hi-hat patterns use a new thing I call exponential and logarithmic triplets. It's taking unreal note values [that is, the note values above 64th-notes that don't have symbols in traditional music notation] and putting nonlinear spacing between them. I'll do a 'gesture' of, say, 512th-notes slowing down to 8ths, but up on the fast end, the rests between all the micro-edits get progressively longer according to a mathematical curve. You have to look at it to fully appreciate it. What you hear is like the rhythmic equivalent of portamento. Initially it was all done by hand, but we finished the plug-in midway through the record." The plug-in? More on that in a bit.

You'd think BT would be the last guy on earth to limit his tools on purpose, but he did exactly this on this album, inspired by his Berklee mentor, Richard Boulanger. "Dr. B is like f***ing Yoda!" he says. "He'll assign a book or exercise that seems abstract and weird relative to the musical problem you're having, but if you do it, everything falls into place. It's scary." One exercise he was assigned was to construct a full arrangement from a 15-second audio clip, using as much editing and processing as needed. "It could be a speech by Martin Luther King," he explains. "You'd use the plosives [P's and K's] as drums, then take the word 'how,' time-stretching and pitch-shifting it like crazy to make building blocks for chords, and so on. It forced you to think about the music more than the tools." But back to the new record. "So I came up with three pools," he says, "and allowed one or two things from each pool per song. One was keyboards, soft synths, and stuff I'd find on KVR, as well as the plug-in. The second pool was organic and found sounds: cello, melodica, hammer dulcimer, my daughter Kaia's toy piano. The third was academia-level sound-design stuff like Kyma, Supercollider, and Csound. On each composition, there's no more than half a dozen elements from which I'm building everything."

How does he get around the inevitable creative blocks that come up when staring down a blank arrange window? "Know how you get through 'em?" he asks. "Friggin' write through 'em! You write and it sucks, and you write and it sucks, and every bad chord progression you ever wished you'd forgotten comes up, and your beats are cheesy. Then, maybe accidentally, you get something good, and it breeds, and you're back. If you get to the point where 50 percent of what you complete doesn't make you wanna puke, you're doing better than me!"

NEW SOFTWARE

In our January 2004 interview with BT, he told us how he co-developed a plug-in using Cycling '74's MaxMSP to simulate his stutter edit technique live, strictly for his own use. Since then, "we've dropped the suspension and put 20-inch rims on it," he says. Not to mention starting a software company, Sonic Architects, to develop it for commercial release. "It" being the plug-in he mentioned earlier. It's got to be like having a little piece of BT's soul in a box.

"Thanks to a programmers' library called Wave++, we can reverse-port stuff done in MaxMSP, Csound, or similar sound-design environments into the C++ computer language," explains Professor Transeau, "Which means people can run it on its own, in a DAW, in [Ableton] Live, whatever." We asked for a screen shot, but there's no graphic user interface yet, so instead BT assured us, "When it's out, it'll make it seem like you spent hours squinting at your computer screen like I used to, and I promise, you'll spend those hours remixing your ass off!"

The nice folks at Binary Acoustics are also sticking their toes in the water of scanned synthesis, "an incredibly complicated way of manipulating wavetables. It's been around awhile in Csound and the über-geek programming community I hang out in, but musically, we barely know what to do with it yet. People are learning it by emulating more familiar synthesis models like FM." Imagine samples living on the surface of a hollow 3D object. Now imagine that surface is flexible and can be warped and molded at the same time it's being "scanned" by a phonograph nee-dle–like function, and that you can turn the whole object any way you want, and you begin to get the idea. "Basically, any sample can be used to disturb the overall system, then that can turn around and affect individual samples, and the sound defies description. This blew my mind like the first time I heard granular synthesis."

NEW- (AND OLD-) SCHOOL VALUES

Beginning in 2005, the National Academy of Recording Arts and Sciences recognized a new Grammy category: best electronic/dance album, largely due to the lobbying of BT's good friend, noted producer and remixer Carmen Rizzo. The first winner? The incredible *Kish Kash* by the Basement Jaxx. "It's a long-overdue validation for electronic musicians," approves BT. "But we need to go further."

What he has in mind, and is already up in NARAS's grill about, is a standardized remix format. The idea is "to make it easier for fans to do mash-ups, something I think is a wonderful way for people who might not play an instrument to connect with their music. If an artist is open to having their fans remix their stuff, as they should be, then a standard package of stems gets released with the album: a vocal-down mix, an a capella, drums and bass only, et cetera. Of course, we'd need to make it as cross-platform as possible."

Since BT spends a lot of his performance time in a DJ booth, doing decided-ly non-DJ things, we asked him how he feels about the dance-venue mindset.

BINARY ACOUSTICS: WHERE DIGITS DARE TO DREAM

BT creates nearly all his work at his home studio, Binary Acoustics, on a setup that's "very modest and clean, compared to what I've used in the past," he says. The nerve center is an Apple dual G5 running Logic Pro 7, the 30-inch Cinema Display we all wish we had, and lots of MOTU interfaces. "When I hear 'hard' followed by 'ware,'" he says, "MOTU is what I think of. My Traveler has never crashed at a gig, and I've crashed a ton of interfaces." His main controller is an M-Audio Radium.

"People are surprised I use an unweighted keyboard," he says. "But it feels like all those vintage synths I spent summers mowing lawns to afford."

His newest keyboard is a Dave Smith Poly Evolver. "It's like a little piece of Dave's soul in a box," he says. "He and Bob Moog really imprinted on their instruments." The Roland JP-8000 has a place of honor, and like his workstations in other rooms, M-Audio BX-5 monitors make up 5.1 systems. Shielded behind custom cabinetry, is a rack that is part of BT's main workstation. It contains a Rolls line mixer, Furman PL-8 power conditioner, a racked Neve EQ channel, a Line 6 Bass Pod Pro, an Esoteric Audio Research 660 limiter, two MOTU 2480mkIIs, an HD-192 audio interface, a Digidesign USD sync box, a Digi 1622 audio interface, and a Line 6 foot controller.

There is also a rack containing BT's Capybara 320, the hardware engine that runs Kyma. "It's pimped out with a bunch of cards," he says. "It's still the best thing for esoteric sound design. My Hartmann Neuron [on top of the rack] is almost a Kyma, just laid out like a synth, great for weird pads and textures." Below that are three dual-Opteron PCs (labeled Jupiter, Mars, and Venus) used as sound modules by the Logic/Mac system. "I call this my orchestral render farm. PC Audio Labs did such a great job that they might as well be hardware synths." Strings live on one, brass and winds on another, percussion and miscellaneous sounds on the third, all pre-loaded and ready to go. "I'm using all the East West Symphonic Orchestra stuff, and I have a MIDI track in Logic's arrange window for every articulation of every instrument. I have always wanted something like this!"

A fourth PC is a little less stable due to what's on it. "This one is for all the weird, beta, written-by-a-15-year- old-hacker-from-Norway kinda plug-ins I find on sites like KVR Audio. There are literally thousands of them on there." BT also makes heavy use of Logic's distributed processing. "The Macs around the house are all networked, including a big-ass X-Serve in the basement, and when no one else is here, I'm pinging everything."

"The culture needs to move beyond its emphasis on beat-mixing," he says, "which comes out of its analog purism. Don't get me wrong, good turntablism just amazes me, but I could teach my Boston terrier to beat-mix. That's why I get so excited about what you can do with a laptop and a program like [Ableton] Live. With all the stuff I have going on in a solo club show, there's a precarious factor that's almost like playing with a band: Total groove while teetering on the verge of a train wreck!"

No stranger to technology nor to rigorous training in music theory, BT is well aware that the former can promise the wrong kind of instant gratification, and the latter can lead to academic snobbery. His advice is to shoot for a golden mean. "On one hand, elitist communities drain all the blood from music by making it all about 'Look, I can write a piece that flips between 13/8 and 7/4!'" he says. "Okay, some of my new stuff does that, too, but it came out of wanting to convey an emotion, and being honest about that means being vulnerable, not hiding behind tools or theory. I'd rather listen to a Ramones tune than indulge in complexity for its own sake.

"On the other hand, I'll tell you this. My current project, and Emotional Technology for that matter, would never have happened without the knowledge of harmony, voice leading, and meter I got from Berklee and my studies before that. I don't care how good your ears are, or how hot you are with Reason or Live, there's an empowerment you just don't get any other way.

"Gospel is a notable anomaly, though. It's full of gorgeous complex harmonies that, historically, are communicated outside of formal training."

BT sees the human affinity for music as ultimately physical. "Our bodies are living polyrhythms," he says. "Lungs taking in air as the heart beats to an entirely different meter, as we walk along to a third rhythm, and we don't even have to think about it! The beauty of dance music, of any music, is the auditory driving that brings everyone onto the same wavelength. I don't mean because of drug use, and I don't mean any crystal-toting hippie bulls**t. The connection is physiological, it's primal, and it makes people feel less alone."

> "Our bodies are living polyrhythms. Lungs taking in air as the heart beats to an entirely different meter, as we walk along to a third rhythm, and we don't even have to think about it! The beauty of dance music, of any music, is the auditory driving that brings everyone onto the same wavelength."
>
> —BT

Amon Tobin.

17

Amon Tobin

THE BIG SCORE

By Bill Murphy || *Remix*, April 2007

mon Tobin calls on his cinematic muse to create Foley Room—*a wide-angle beat collage of live and sampled found sound that writhes with signal-processed possibility.*—Keyboard, *2007*

Forget everything you may have heard about the principles of field recording, tape editing, and musique concrète that supposedly went into the making of Amon Tobin's latest album. Although the Montreal-based DJ and producer did spend the better part of a year collecting snippets of environmental sounds and live musical performances—making this the first time he'd even touched a microphone in more than a decade of making records—this was no Matmos or Robin Rimbaud project, where the sound library would become the sole basis of an album. As Tobin describes it, he was going for something completely different. "This was all about transforming sound," he says in earnest. "It was about changing a sound from its origins to try to make it into something new. It's no different, really, from what I've done in the past—it's just that this time, some of the sounds came from places like a Foley room or from field recordings, as well as vinyl. Vinyl still plays a big part in this record. Although I'm interested in a lot of the history of musique concrète, I really just wanted to make good tunes. That was the main objective."

Going back to his debut *Adventures in Foam* (Ninebar, 1996—released under his Cujo alias), Tobin has gradually carved out a niche for himself as an aggressively elastic beatmaker with a keen ear for melody. The musician's sensibility that he brings to DJ culture has not only changed the face of the U.K. drum 'n' bass and experimental hip-hop, but it has also messed with the way people think about sampling and composing in general. As he proved on his breakout opus *Bricolage* (Ninja Tune, 1997) and the forward-leaping *Supermodified* (Ninja Tune, 2000), no genre is off-limits to Tobin's exacting—and yet somehow always seamless and fluid—cut-and-paste production style. It could be batucada or baile funk (from his native Brazil), '70s jazz-fusion or avant-garde neoclassical; chances are it has landed on a Tobin album at one time or another.

These influences are just part of the fuel behind *Foley Room* (Ninja Tune, 2007), which finds Tobin pushing himself toward a more intimate exploration of the essence of sampling—that is, the creation and manipulation of original sound sources—with an emphasis on extreme signal processing and a feel for harmonic structure. The album's title, of course, is a nod to the art of Foley sound effects done for film—and there is definitely a filmic mood to much of the music here—but as Tobin points out, this is first and foremost an album of finished songs, and from the get-go, it plays that way. With guest appearances from the Kronos Quartet, drummer Stefan Schneider (Belle Orchestre), cellist Norsola Johnson (Godspeed You Black Emperor!), sound designer and pianist Patrick Watson, bassist Sage Reynolds, harpist Sarah Page, and more, *Foley Room* undulates with a constantly shifting interplay of rhythms, hummable melodies, and otherworldly tonalities. And sometimes, you can dance to it.

"I definitely wanted the music to stand up on its own as melodically and rhythmically strong," Tobin observes, "without it relying on some kind of 'concept' or school of thinking. It's funny in a way, because I find that my previous stuff is far more conceptually rigid than this record. Throughout five albums, I made things in a really specific way—100 percent from vinyl—where every single sound existed in a previous musical composition of one sort or another but was transformed and made into a new track. That to me is a constant, and I'm still very interested in that."

ROLL TAPE

Ideas for the first stage of recording for *Foley Room* began taking shape in 2005 while Tobin was on tour to support *Chaos Theory* (Ninja Tune, 2005), which he had recorded in collaboration with Ubisoft Entertainment for the company's Splinter Cell 3 video game. "It just sprung out of nerddom, really," Tobin recalls with a laugh. "I'd been talking to my soundman Vid Cousins for a while about getting very tiny sounds and trying to make them into big, epic sounds. We're just into sounds in general, and I wanted to see what musical things could be drawn out of recorded noises."

Tobin soon got his hands on a Nagra IV-S portable reel-to-reel tape deck—the latter-day descendant of the ever-reliable and rugged unit that has been used for decades on remote film shoots to capture ambient sound and dialog while on location. Supplementing that with a pair of high-definition microphones by Earthworks Audio, Tobin and Cousins were ready to dive in, criss-crossing the country on a quest to amass as many animal and machine-made sounds as they could get in roughly a nine-month period.

The journey also included stops at several different studios, including the Kronos Quartet's studio loft in San Francisco. *Foley Room's* opening track (and leadoff single), "Bloodstone," features the string quartet's haunting drones as its central theme (along with Patrick Watson's equally chilling piano figures), but it was the recording experience itself that presented Tobin with a pivotal discovery that added to the song's overall dynamic.

"I sat in the middle of the four of them with headphones and the handheld mics," he explains, citing the near-total lack of handling noise from the Earthworks pair, "and what was delicious about it was that I could hold the mics out, and if I wanted more cello or less viola, I could just move my hands and have the balance I wanted. It was as if I was turning faders on the desk. I'm pretty sure you're not supposed to record that way [*laughs*], but one of the nice things about making this record was that I entered it with no knowledge of how you're meant to record things. I just did what felt right at the time, and I'm sure I made some mistakes that ended up being useful for me in later stages."

DRUMS FOR DAYS

Naturally, percussion and drums constituted an essential ingredient in the making of *Foley Room*, just as they have for the bulk of Tobin's recorded output. Most of the drum elements were tracked with Stefan Schneider at Planet Studio in Montreal—again, primarily using the Earthworks/Nagra setup, along with several overhead mics—and later dumped into Cubase for chopping and sequencing at his home studio. One of the more stripped-down, syncopated, and yet strangely busy examples is the aptly named "Kitchen Sink"—a throwback of sorts to Tobin's more overt drum 'n' bass concoctions, but with a sophisticated organic feel that recalls Photek's classic "Ni Ten Ichi Ryu" at a slower tempo.

"I had this idea of trying to make quite a liquid song by actually taking parts of the drum kit and submerging them to see if we could bend the sounds by hitting them in different areas," Tobin says. "So Stef took his kit apart and put bits of it in these vats of water that we had in the studio. We were just dipping cymbals, and he was striking them at different points of submersion, or he'd float these little metal bowls on the surface of the water, and if you struck them with metal sticks, you'd get that lovely bending sound—like when you're doing the dishes."

Schneider's drums—as sampled and sequenced by Tobin—get another treatment entirely in "Ever Falling." Propelled by a Brian Wilson–esque vocal melody that churns in a murky staccato (an effect created by manually nudging the original taped vocal on the Nagra), the song gets a psychedelic jolt from the layers of shimmery after-effects that seem to chase after the individual drums that make up the main rhythm.

"That was a combination of using noise reduction and EQ," Tobin explains. "Some noise-reduction plug-ins [such as Sonic Foundry's Noise Reduction, which has a Keep Residual feature] allow you to look at the dirt you're taking off a track; I just took that garbled noise from the drum track and ran it through the GRM Tools EQ plug-in, which seems to add a harmonic content when you adjust the different faders. I was left with this really metallic, liquid-y plastic type of sound; I mixed that with the original drum sound and balanced it out so that the drums have this strange sheen to them."

The processing goes even further in "The Killer's Vanilla," which features a long freestyle drum break that was meticulously programmed. "It's a mixture of three different kits," Tobin says. "One of them was recorded with [live drum 'n' bass specialist] Kevin Sawka in Seattle, and then there were parts by Stef and other parts that were just drums that I have. The big crescendo at the end is a programmed mixture of all three—that was all done in Cubase.

"What I wanted to do with that drum pattern was to accentuate the melody," Tobin continues. "There's really a lot of suggested melody in drums that people don't always realize. When you combine that with what's actually going on in the tune, sometimes you can get some really interesting accents to happen."

SOUND COLLISIONS

When it came to crafting melodies from the many snippets of performances—as well as pairing instruments with their environmental "counterparts" (such as the surf guitars and buzzing wasps in "Esther's")—Tobin went all-out with his manipulation regimen. Most of that took place in Cubase, but sometimes it even meant returning to the Nagra to manually flange or pitch-shift the original source material. Since aliasing and unwanted artifacts make digital pitch shifting a tough pill to swallow when a sound is dropping several octaves, the analog flexibility of the Nagra became yet another function to be exploited.

"What's funny is my particular Nagra is a bit of a dodgy unit," Tobin quips, "so sometimes you can even just switch the thing off, and something cool will happen. I used it all the way through 'Big Furry Head'—there's kind of a chuuung! sound there that's just the Nagra being switched on and off. I thought it was a really wicked sci-fi noise, so we kept it."

"Big Furry Head" swivels, of course, on the recorded growls of live tigers that, when layered over the buzzing synths, plucked harp, and eastern-sounding percussive elements of the song, transmit a fittingly Serengeti-ish atmosphere. "They have this quality in their roar that I can only describe as a breaking up in the high end," Tobin says. "I mixed that with synths to try to create a new synth sub sound. It turned out to make quite a colorful picture in the end, but for sure, it's just about trying to make links between these different sounds and seeing what happens when you put them together."

"Straight Psyche" presents another mash-up of seemingly disparate sounds in order to craft a new one, but in this case, the source signals were both from played instruments. By grabbing a Hammond B3 organ and a vibraphone and wrenching them into the same temporal space, Tobin conjures yet another otherworldly mood that seems to emerge from the ether of an alien spaghetti-western set in the distant future.

"There are these really beautiful harmonics from the vibraphone that just seem to get picked up by the Hammond," Tobin observes. "It happened in this really quite magical way, where these intricacies started popping up in the harmonics between the two instruments. And that went through a fair bit of processing, because I didn't want it to sound like something being played—I just wanted it to wash over the backbeat."

Citing his original mission of trusting his instincts by attempting to combine sounds that share similar sonic qualities but might have very different origins, Tobin again points to "Esther's"—part of which was recorded with John Usher (an expert at capturing close-miked insect sounds) at McGill University. The track is yet another of several on *Foley Room* to take advantage of the weird combination of rhythm and angular dissonance that comes from pasting an animal sound onto an instrument; eventually, with enough close listens, one sound seems to enhance the musical qualities of the other until their union seems almost natural.

"I was thinking of the buzzing sound of the surf guitars in that song," Tobin says, "so the obvious sound to try out was a bunch of wasps buzzing in a jar. Then maybe you mix those together with a motorbike revving its engine—so you get the fast strumming of the guitars picked up by the bike, with the wasps suggesting another crazy guitar sound—and suddenly you've got something that really gels."

KEEPING IT IN THE ROOM

Much like a movie editor faced with the task of assembling hundreds of live-action and visual-effects shots and then merging them into a cohesive whole, Tobin has clearly gone the extra creative mile with *Foley Room*. As a testament to the lengths that analog sound sources can be stretched, stitched, and stomped on in a digital world, this is one album that can find as much appreciation among the old-school electronic avant-garde—represented by such august organizations as France's Groupe de Recherches Musicales (GRM), who invited Tobin to perform last year at the prestigious Présences Électronique festival—as it can among the hungry young mavericks still clawing their way up through the club scene, where Tobin still DJs on a regular basis.

"The performance at GRM was showcasing *Foley Room* as a bit of a work in progress at the time," Tobin explains. "It was played over 47 speakers in the performance space at Radio France, which also houses the GRM Institute. It was particularly relevant for me to play there, because the GRM had been home to sampling pioneers like Pierre Schaeffer, as well as Pierre Henri, who played at the same festival."

Tobin is also quick to point out that this album, perhaps more than any other he's done to date, is strictly a studio affair—and thus impossible to present live. "That's been the trouble all the way through since day one," he says somewhat ruefully. "I've been fortunate, though, because I've been received very generously from people with my DJ sets. I mean, I feel like the option is there. I could do the whole thing on Ableton or a couple of laptops, but I think of live shows as something that should be worth seeing, at the very least. As much as I can appreciate the way different people work, for me personally, I don't find much enthusiasm for a laptop set. It just seems really boring to me."

Although his fans may not be seeing him onstage with a live band anytime soon, Tobin is certainly keeping busy in the studio. A new collaboration with the Dutch drum 'n' bass trio Noisia is already in the can, while a down-low project with Doubleclick called *Two Fingers* is expected to jump off at any moment in 2007.

And of course, he still has to make the transition to the mind-blowing expanses of Cubase 4.

"I really didn't want to try anything too new and untested when I was making this record," Tobin confides, "because frankly, I needed things to work. But Cubase 4 sounds pretty wicked, and I can't wait to try it out. If it's anything like what the transition was from VST to SX, then I know it will be inspiring."

Flying Lotus.

18

Flying Lotus

DARKNESS AND LIGHT

By Noah Levine || *Remix*, August 2008

E*DM has extensive connections in its relationship to jazz, but for Steve Ellison (Flying Lotus), the lineage is literal, drawing from Alice and John Coltrane. Coming from different angles,* Remix *and* Keyboard *both unravel how he bridged that world with an electronic one. —PK*

With chopped samples and trippy beats, Flying Lotus creates sounds from the edge. Nothing came together quite the way Flying Lotus (aka Steven Ellison) first envisioned it during the making of his second album, *Los Angeles* (Warp, 2008). Originally, the album was designed to be a "beat version of *Blade Runner*" playing out in his hometown, but the end result found influence in sounds originating far from the title city, and a single bleak perspective couldn't contain FlyLo's musical impulses.

"I wanted to make a really dark record, but I realized that wouldn't have been the best thing to do, because it wasn't all dark in my life," he says. "I had to have fun. I'd rather it's a journey than one constant movement."

Refining and then expanding upon the trip-hop sounds of his debut *1983* (Plug Research, 2006), FlyLo uses the reverberating pads and pointed analog sounds on beatless opener "Brainfeeder" to set the scene for later tracks, showcasing the unsteady breaks and choppy noises that are leading people such as Portishead's Geoff Barrow to mention his name in the same sentence as Public Enemy, EPMD, Marley Marl, and Madlib.

FlyLo is amazed by such high praise, because he's simply making the music he believes in, and every aspect of his life shows up in the beats. The samba groove of "Melt!" and the echoey sitar on "GNG BNG" are influences from his travels.

FlyLo's songs are built from samples lifted from his record collection or recorded from everyday noises, but the source rarely matters, because he likes to repurpose things. He likes to work imperfections on the fringes of his sounds into the rhythm, whether he's working with swaying glitch collections or ground-shaking party breaks.

"I'm not one of these guys who likes to have his samples too clean. That sample's not going to tell me what to do. I'll tell it what to do," he says.

That same sense of control is wielded when arranging the songs, as FlyLo likes to find the narrative connections between his tracks. For *Los Angeles*, he starts in a dark place and heightens the tension and the mood before the amazing third act, where he teams with guest vocalists Dolly on "RobertaFlack" and Gonja Sufi on "Testament" to revise what Portishead and Tricky did so well in the mid-'90s.

Meditative closer "Auntie's Lock/Infinitum," with its samples from FlyLo's great aunt Alice Coltrane (John Coltrane's wife), was a late addition. FlyLo planned an apocalyptic breakcore ending before Laura Darlington's mantra-like vocals came back at the last minute and made a better fit. "I'm really glad, because that track is a favorite of many people; it's a favorite of mine," he says.

While recording, FlyLo sequesters himself with little more than his MacBook Pro laptop. He's tried his hand at programming beats on other gear, but nothing ever felt as comfortable. He's given up the Akai MPC, and his Korg Kaoss Pad and Roland RE-201 Space Echo just gather dust. It's all about finding the right instrument and mastering it, and for him it's the laptop.

"People get caught up in gear, but it gets in the way of making the music," he says. "When I need to find something new, I don't have to update my shit; I just have to update my brain."

Still, he's not too stuck in his ways to miss out on a good thing, and FlyLo gets excited talking about the possibilities he's finding since adding a Monome 40h to his live rig. Currently, he uses the charming box of light-up buttons as a sampler and a step sequencer via the MLR and 64step programs [developed in] Cycling '74's Max/MSP programming environment, but FlyLo thinks there's no limit to the programmable control box's potential. "There's no one way to use it. You have all sorts of programs and you have all these little buttons," he says. "It's supereasy." In addition to the Monome and Cycling '74, FlyLo uses his M-Audio Trigger Finger MIDI drum-control surface, Novation ReMote 25SL MIDI controller, and MacBook Pro in his live rig.

Like the Monome, FlyLo sees that same limitless potential in where music is going these days. With the Internet bringing everything down to one level, FlyLo is ready to find other talented collaborators and keep on making the off-center beats.

"I think people think too much in general when they're working on music," he says. "We should be able to be free and just do our shit."

FLYING LOTUS: ON SPLICING BEBOP AND HIP-HOP DNA
By Drew Hinshaw || *Keyboard*, July 2010

Flying Lotus is best known for the bumper beats that bring Adult Swim viewers back from commercials into the late-night world of Cartoon Network. It's a niche audience, and his freeform beats may keep it always thus. Yet the world knows well his aunt Alice, his uncle John. As in Coltrane. True to 'Trane tradition, FlyLo's atonal, chaotic beats disregard principles of arrangement, songwriting, and engineering. The laptop maestro straddles the line between the bohemias of bebop and beatmaking—Dizzy Gillespie, meet Dizzee Rascal. In fact, "modal hip-hop" might be the term. His synths squeal like Dr. Dre's, his textures crinkle like DJ Premier's, and his rhythms trip on each other like Madlib's, but his improvisational flair is distinctly Coltrane.

When you do a remix, what's your process?
It depends on what's given to me. If I have the vocal stem, all I have to do is build a new song around the vocal. Sometimes, I turn the vocal track into an instrumental. No rules, really. Sometimes people are frustrated, like, "Oh, we didn't want it to be that kind of thing." That's the point, isn't it? Why do the same thing twice? You can build a new universe each time you sit in the chair.

You said you have a "thing." How would you describe it?

Lots of layers and textures. That's my signature. The texture can determine the rhythm. If you sample something, and there's a pop or click in it, you can use that as a percussion thing, and it can inspire the rest of your idea.

> "There was always some kind of music happening. On Sundays we would go to my aunt's ashram. She listened to spiritual Indian music, like Ravi Shankar. That's how I grew up: in that same, searching mentality, always striving to be searching within for the sound, for the ideas."
>
> —FLYING LOTUS

You're related to John and Alice Coltrane. Growing up, what was music like?

It was a very humble thing, but it was always very present, as well. There was always some kind of music happening. On Sundays we would go to my aunt's ashram. She listened to spiritual Indian music, like Ravi Shankar.

One reviewer said that what reminded him about your music of John Coltrane was the meditativeness of it.

That's how I grew up: in that same, searching mentality, always striving to be searching within for the sound, for the ideas.

Is what you do in the studio very improvisational?

Yeah. I try to get the meat of the songs done very fast. If it doesn't come naturally in 20 minutes, I step away. Working on a laptop is not very improvisational for a lot of people.

It *needs* to be. There needs to be an urgency, an energy. I can't produce if I'm feeling sluggish. I have to be kicked up with sugar and green tea.

Any favorite synths or techniques to reveal?

I use a Moog Little Phatty, Wurlitzer, Fender Rhodes, and a bunch of soft synths like [Tweakbench] Triforce. I like to sample with the internal mic on my computer. I'll sample anything, my voice or my keyboard. It doesn't matter—it's all texture. I'm not really a sound snob. I don't like things to be perfect. I also sample my Nintendo, and that becomes a synthesizer, too.

Autechre.

1

Autechre

AUTECHRE: EASY TO BE HARD

By Ken Micallef ‖ *Remix*, April 2008

As part of the innovative '90s Warp Records crew that included such mad boffins as Aphex Twin, Squarepusher, LFO, the Black Dog, and Nightmares on Wax, Autechre holds a rarified position in our collective IDM consciousness. Throughout their 15-year career and nine full-length releases, Autechre's Sean Booth and Rob Brown have ceaselessly stretched their own consciousness years past the sell dates of some fellow electronic-music expanders.

In keeping with Warp's singular sound, Autechre's music has remained unclassifiable, typically existing beyond standard notions of beat programming and synth sequencing, often confounding those enamored with stock rhythms, predictable arrangements, and easy-to-comprehend production methods. Autechre's reputation as a difficult pair who refuse to reveal their working techniques (much less their equipment) is renowned and through the years has only grown more entrenched.

"You guys always expect a barbed response from this corner, don't you?" Brown says with a laugh. "But we're humans, too."

This statement may cause a shudder among those who prefer their electronic music with a humdrum four-to-the-floor groove, but Autechre's latest release, *Quaristice* (Warp, 2008), is more fuzzy and emotional than you might expect. Working on practically identical rigs in separate cities (Booth, Manchester; Brown, London), Autechre pursued conventional recording methods for past efforts like *Confield* (Warp, 2001) and *Untilted* (Warp, 2005), but *Quaristice* is the result of the duo's live improvisations, recorded largely on its touring setup: Apple Mac G4, Elektron Machinedrum and Monomachine, Clavia Nord Modular G2 and Nord Rack, Yamaha FS1R, Akai MPC1000, Alesis QuadraVerb, and Lexicon PCM 80 and 90. Can this old duo learn new tricks? Certainly.

"This album was made from really long live jam sessions," Booth explains. "When I moved to Manchester in 2005, the first thing we did was set up a new studio with the live kit and record these really long jams. It turned out good, so we just kept doing it and writing new stuff with the same setup. Having that ability and so much drive capacity nowadays makes it easy to record everything. We did two hour-long jams a day. It took six months to edit it all down to six- or eight-minute tracks. Then we would reduce them again and again. We had a lot of different versions to choose from. We were also reusing bits of sequences from other tracks. Once we got them in a rough format, we used [MOTU] Digital Performer for all the editing."

A LITTLE BIT CLOSER

Booth and Brown still refuse to delve too deep into the production methods behind Quaristice, but they do reveal more than in the past. Brown is the most upfront and personable, while Booth speaks in riddles that eventually reveal some finer points of Autechre's unusual processes.

Where *Confield* explored algorithms using Cycling '74 Max/MSP, the Quaristice sessions began with the duo recording their live improvisations and ending in Digital Performer. Autechre's fondness for modifying effects and endlessly disguising sounds remained, as did the duo's love of the Akai MPC1000. Algorithms out, Digital Performer in.

"We used all the functions in the Nord Modular and the Nord Rack, but we are not wildly exploring the potential of algorithmic sequence-generation anymore," Booth explains. "When I feel I am not in control of every event, I tend to not like it. So I have to program things that have very fixed variables and run efficiently without a lot of user input. With *Confield*, eventually we were able to think algorithmically in terms of the ways the patterns were being produced, because DP allows you to get really specific about where notes are, but also you can do a lot of manipulation. If we wanted to move something one percent in one part of the track, it was a cinch to do: Just go in there and deal with the data. It was suddenly really liberating to not have to deal with programming the algorithm in a totally different way just for that one bit or incorporating a bunch of modules that are going to knock everything else off.

"There are all sorts of limitations implied with algorithmic music, based on the way the system functions, that we wanted to get around," Booth continues. "That is what the last two albums were about, really. We used almost the same hardware for *Untilted* as *Quaristice*, but in a nonreal-time way, where we programmed all the sequencers to run in quite complex ways, retriggering each other and receiving each other's outputs and inputs. That was press and play and leaving it for a while and adding slight bits of unpredictability. This one being live is a completely opposite path."

ANYONE FOR A GAME?

When Autechre supplied the gear list for *Remix*, it looked like Scrabble playing squares dumped onto a piece paper. Above notations for various hardware and software components, Autechre scribbled "dju76r," "ju5t," "ersh," "654eb," and "4n7m." Taking the veritable British piss out of *Remix*? Responding to our simple demands with a bit of the Mickey? No. Booth and Brown were listing the actual abbreviations used for their gear modifications.

"We don't really have names for them," Booth admits. "We write on bits of tape what they are. We mostly mod old BOSS effects like the RSD-10 and RDD-10; they are two of the finest machines ever made. The BOSS effects have a real gray sound to them. We used to use an RSD-10 as a sampler triggered from a Roland TR-606. The Alesis QuadraVerb is great, as well. It is a sick, sick device. Amazing. I don't think people really understand the intricacies of outboard effects. They think they are all the same 'cause they all offer the same range of functions. But it's all about the weird space in between. The reverbs in those rack effects are beautiful, even though they are digital. They've got a gorgeous tone."

The typical Autechre album features a boatload of multifarious reverbs, including Audioease Altiverb, Waves TrueVerb, MOTU 828mk3 Classic Reverb, Renoise reverb, TC Electronic Native Reverb, and Symbolic Sound Corporation Kyma X Reverb. That the duo goes further in the process—modifying hardware often deemed useless by the electronic community at large—only adds to Autechre's renegade status and the richness of their sounds.

"Most of our mods consist of circuit bending," Booth allows. "These things are so cheap, no one seems to ascribe any value to them. And they are digital, so that makes them somehow not cool. You can do quite a lot with them by crossing over certain points in the circuit on the back. I always come back to those effects because there is a certain magic about them."

But that's not all. When even considering the potential value of mods, Booth's imagination goes into high gear, causing him to wonder: What if? "One thing I did recently," he muses, "was use field-programmable gate arrays. It reminded me of using something like Cycling '74 MSP; it was a really visual way of working. If you could store all the components necessary for most basic synth modules on one board and then use a field-programmable gate array to make it be any module that you wanted, that is a pretty adaptable synthesis system. You could use 30 of them to make the most flexible modular synth ever. That would be quite fun."

SO MANY SECRETS

When it gets down to actual tracks and production details, Booth clams up. The dripping ice sounds and sci-fi tunnel effects of "Tankakern"? "Akai MPC, Elektron Mono and Machinedrum, 606. Nord Lead," Booth peeps. "Fol3" sounds like unwilling farm animals being pulled backward through a death chute. Surely Booth could offer a riddle or two.

"It's all stuff that was recorded with an AKG 1000 mic," he replies, "then processed on a homemade patch, then used as source material and cut up. Just a simple edit job on a bunch of stuff, both physical things and instruments. I can't remember all the sources. The patch itself is running about 50 or 60 samples. Then that got cut up."

As for the animal-accident-barking-crashing sound collisions of "Steels," he only says, "I don't want to talk about how we did that, 'cause there are some secret techniques involved, but most of it is MPC.

"Certain combinations are unusual, and they strike you and have a real dynamism to them," he continues. "We like hard and soft sounds at the same time, like an Oberheim DMX or LinnDrum combined with warm analog sounds. I like the way you can bounce them off each other. There are so many ways to combine sounds."

Brown spills the beans with far greater ease. When asked if Autechre's established ID of using old techniques on new gear—and, conversely, inventive approaches on ancient technology—still rings true, he responds quickly.

"That's true," he says, "if you don't throw your gear away. We have these phases of finding something that has been forgotten about. Sometimes we start a track, and often it just comes from turning on a Kurzweil or SCSI, which we don't use anymore, but let's do a sample dump and see what we can get going. Suddenly, the architecture of a synth will remind you of all those moments you have had with it, if you like. Then all the power that a synth might have in its engines—that has been forgotten in the cheaper, more mass-produced models—becomes apparent. Everything has its value; it's just a matter of investing the time and making sure the gear still works.

"And because the Nord Modular G2 framework is all text based, apparently," he adds, excitedly, "the source materials, the patches, are written in text code. A few programmers can actually use MacPython, a low-level Mac editing terminal, to compare old modular text patches and replace them with new G2 modular text patches. You can actually find patches that were made in 1994 that can be opened up and reused, in theory. It is that way of cheating. You just figure out a few distinct command-line phrases, and you've got all your patches available in the new module."

> "We can have one synth and still not know everything about it after three years. And I don't mean its functions, but how you feel about it and the way that it can sound. It still feels totally endless."
>
> —SEAN BOOTH (AUTECHRE)

Inspired by Marley Marl, Mantronix, and Art of Noise, Autechre today sounds as unique and as radical as their hip-hop heroes did in the mid-'80s. That Booth and Brown still cite those seminal artists as inspirational says as much about their working methods as their music, and that of their musical forefathers.

"All of those people were hugely creative," Booth says, "using equipment in ways that didn't sound like anyone else using the same equipment. They did all sorts of things to make their tracks sound fresh. I really tapped into that as a young teen; it made me think, 'It's not about having all the equipment in the world, it's how you use what you've got.' We can have one synth and still not know everything about it after three years. And I don't mean its functions, but how you feel about it and the way that it can sound. That can take a long time, especially now that one synth can give you such an array of different things. It still feels totally endless."

5 QUESTIONS WITH ROB BROWN OF AUTECHRE

By Greg Rule || *Keyboard*, June 1996

Digging further back in the archives, we find Autechre's Rob Brown at the duo's outset, revealing how they began working and how their unusual flavor of

electronic sound nonetheless managed to land a record deal, years before "Warp"
had fully emerged as tastemaker and brand. —PK

Dubbed the "undisputed kings of the technoid avant-garde" by *Lizard* magazine,
Autechre is another one of those hard-to-categorize electronic outfits. Asked for
a description, bandmember Rob Brown puzzled, "It's a good thing that nobody
seems to have their minds made up as to what genre we are, because we aren't
any genre, really. Our sound is as versatile as possible. We're just whatever we
want to be. Whatever we want to do." Fair enough. We won't attempt to hang a
label on them, but this much can be said about their sound: It's very electronic, it's
very percussive, and it's very good. Gritty loops, spaced-out pads, analog gurgles,
bell-like sweeps, noise bursts—cuts from their third full-length release, *Tri Repeate*,
have been spinning nonstop in our CD tray since arriving a few months ago. How
do they do what they do, and how did they get there in the first place? Rob Brown
lays it down.

1. What roles do you and your partner Sean [Booth] play in the songwriting and recording processes?

Well, quite literally, we both do 50 percent. When we first met, neither of us had
any gear; we started buying gear together. So we sort of developed on the machines simultaneously. At the stage we're at now, we can always fill in for each
other; I might do half the tracks, Sean will finish the other. It's quite freestyle, really,
a very versatile way of working. It may sound a bit weird to people who are used
to playing roles in a band—who might put an ad in the paper for a keyboardist or a
guitarist or a drummer. It's nothing like that at all.

2. Given your non-technical backgrounds, how did you elevate yourselves to the level you're at today?

I don't know. When we first got into making music, it basically was a form of
people's music. We'd get some loops and make mixes. No turntables, no vinyl, no
nothing. We'd record our own sounds and start developing loops from there. When
we were done, we'd just hand it off to our friends; it was entertainment for us and
for our little gang. It really stemmed from that. We eventually got more equipment,
and we learned how to use it.

3. How did you get a record deal?

We started sending tapes out to a lot of labels, as a normal band would. And
most of the time they'd come back. "Nice ideas there, but it needs some sort of
obvious element like a vocal or particular riff or. . . " We just didn't want to know
any of that. We were convinced at the time that all we'd ever be doing is writing
for ourselves and entertaining our mates. But Sean phoned Warp one day, said we
had a tape, and on it was an hour-and-a-half long track—our most self-indulgent.

And when Warp came back and said that was their favorite stuff, we were quite a bit surprised. Not long after that, we started sending them more and more tracks, and after a couple of years they said, "You could probably put an album out with all of this material." So we went ahead and compiled *Incunabula* from a lot of our old tracks. Ninety percent of it was off our 4-track tapes, just mastered straight off a DAT, and through a desk to get a decent EQ.

4. Two-part question: Was the method of writing and recording Tri Repeate much different than on the records before it, and what is your method?

Compared to the previous . . . well, we don't regard an album as a "project." We've never done that, so I couldn't really differentiate this album from the others in anything other than it's just newer. Just new material, really. No radical changes. We've never made any conscious effort to change. It's always been quite instinctive. A bit more of an evolution than a forced progression, I suppose.

As for the process, we mostly get sounds that we've made ourselves. A couple of sounds. And they could be anything. Some of it could be weird samples—sound effects and stuff—and sometimes one-off hits that have little rhythms inside themselves. Like a couple of clicks or whatever. Then we use that, or incorporate it into a rhythm. We start from very small wave sources, anything from a sample or something we've done from a synth, and make that into a loop.

5. What synths do you prefer?

We don't really use anything state of the art. We've got a couple of old Roland analogs—a small setup. We don't follow the latest crazes. I don't want to get into what we've got. It doesn't make any difference, to be honest.

Crystal Method.

2

Crystal Method

CRYSTAL METHOD: UNITED BY SYNTHS, DIVIDED BY NIGHT

By Peter Kirn || *Keyboard*, November 2009

Imagine this scenario: You've made it. You've got a Grammy nomination to your name. Your electronic beats have driven everything from video games to the Thunderbirds fighter drill team to an exercise routine by Nike. The rise of electronic dance music in the U.S. owes a lot to you, and you're celebrating the tenth anniversary of one of your platinum-selling albums. Thanks to all this success, you've been able to build your dream synth studio, and you're powering it up for the first time . . .

That's how Ken Jordan and Scott Kirkland—the Crystal Method—began their latest effort, *Divided by Night*. The first sounds of the album were born as their new studio was finished. What might surprise you is that their biggest challenge was to return to the spirit of the poorly heated converted garage in which their seminal debut, *Vegas*, was crafted. Making the new album was half invention, half archaeology, as the duo rediscovered old working techniques.

Getting a state-of-the-art studio with (nearly) every synth you've ever wanted? A very good thing once your MasterCard can take it. Reclaiming the freedom to make a record for no one but yourselves, to share that effort with your favorite collaborators, and recapture some of the feeling of making your first album? Priceless.

GOING BACK TO VEGAS

The seeds for the new album were planted as the duo deconstructed some of their own work. *Vegas* set the course sonically, technically, and philosophically, for Crystal Method's fourth studio album.

"We were preparing for the ten-year anniversary of *Vegas*, going back and listening to that album," says Scott. "We had it remastered, had remixes done—pulling up some of the parts gave us a chance to reflect a little bit about where we were in the beginning." It wasn't just listening to the album itself, recalls Scott, but recalling some of the scope and ambitions of the duo's first outing that helped fuel *Divided by Night*. "There's a lot of attention to detail on that record, lots of sounds that we crafted from scratch. When you make your first record, you don't think about anything else. You don't think about what this certain person would like, or try to make anybody at the record label happy, because you don't have a record deal. We loved the freedom of that. We loved both *Tweekend* and *Legion of Boom*, our next two studio albums. But we thought, especially on *Legion of Boom*, we left some things on the table. We didn't explore the full potential of a song."

Realizing that potential, Scott explains, meant both fully developing the songs and involving the duo's favorite collaborators to add dimension. "We just had the new studio and had great sounds coming out of it," Scott says. "We warmed up a lot of our old synthesizers and had space to put them out and access them quickly. It was just an opportunity to really expand on where we thought our sound could go. And we reached out to some amazing people, including Jason Lyttle from Grandaddy, Emily Haines from Metric, and Justin Warfield from She Wants Revenge. We wanted to hear more melody and beauty in the music and just really take each song as far as we felt that it could go."

Unraveling *Vegas*'s sonic DNA brought back memories of some of the techniques that made that album tick, as the duo dug deep into archival DATs to find stems for remixing and remastering. "Some of the separate parts were coming back," says

Scott. "A track like 'Busy Child' [from *Vegas*], even—you start to remember exactly how you'd recorded it. We were bringing out some of these old synths that we hadn't used—the Minimoog and the Yamaha CS-40. We've always used the Roland Jupiter-6; it's pretty much a workhorse. It was getting back into that world. We loved the amount of melody that existed on *Vegas*, all the little bits and pieces that put together the song. That's something I think you hear a lot of on this record."

Scott and Ken are both serious about reconstructing the tiny details of how the first record was assembled, even as they replace gear with slicker, new equipment. "As you get more money to invest in the studio, all these little boxes that at the time you thought were great, you look back on as junk," says Scott. "We had this ART DR-X rack-mounted multi-effects pitch thing—it broke. It just wouldn't turn on. And then pulling up [*Vegas* track] 'High Roller,' that delay was from the DR-X."

Ken Jordan, the member of the duo with the dominant engineering background, cuts in, trying to remember the signal flow: "I've got my money on chorus . . . and there was a chain of delays . . . it was like one order, one row of effects . . . I think it was chorus before the delay. . . ."

FROM GARAGE TO CRYSTALWERKS

For a duo whose big-beat sound is defined by meticulous methods with gear, the working environment matters. *Divided by Night* emerges from a new workflow, new software tools, and most importantly, a completely new studio built around the tools that are most significant to the Crystal sound. The result is Crystalwerks, a professionally built North Hollywood studio fusing vintage analog favorites with a Mac-based Pro Tools rig.

It's a big shift from the home-brewed sonic lair in which Crystal Method famously constructed their first albums. "The first three albums, the first piece of music that we put out were recorded in our little studio in a two-car garage north of Glendale, California," says Scott. "It was a studio not well put together, but put together with lots of love and lots of passion for making music. It was really great for us for a long time. We slapped some drywall up and soundproofed this '50s-era garage—and dealt with fluctuations of weather through the years. California doesn't get that hot, but in that studio, it got pretty warm. Eventually we put a window-mounted air conditioner in the room adjacent to the studio."

Ken laughs, "First we just tried to cool the studio that was this big with all the machinery with an air conditioner in a room that was this big right next to it with the door open." It should come as no surprise, then, that the new studio has its own machine room for the hotter gear.

Of course, the duo that began in the garage confesses that switching on your dream studio for the first time can be intimidating. Ken Jordan recalls that first day: "It was

CRYSTAL METHOD'S VIRTUAL REALITY

The new Crystalwerks studio is the perfect fusion of digital and analog, vintage gear feeding into a high-end Pro Tools HD system. Ken and Scott took advantage of non-historical, modern sound-design features on software emulations as they did authentic sounds from the hardware originals. "It was close to 50/50, if you really break it down," says Scott. "Some songs are more geared toward virtual synths; some toward the analog hardware. I think that we found on this record, we found that balance, where we appreciate the sound and the warmth of a Memorymoog or a Yamaha CS-40 or an Andromeda, then we appreciate the convenience of some of the newer Arturia, GForce, Korg, and Native Instruments plug-ins." Here are some of Scott's favorites:

Korg Mono/Poly (from Korg's Legacy Analog Edition 2007)
GForce Virtual String Machine
GForce Oddity
GForce ImpOSCar

overwhelming at the beginning, because it's such a great place—the aesthetic is so good, the natural light. We had pretty much all the gear we wanted—except a hardware Jupiter-8! [*Laughs.*] And it's all hooked up, and it's all ready to go. Everything's beautiful, and everything sounds pretty good. I kind of expected the first day to walk in there and have music just sort of pouring in. And that doesn't happen. There's still a lot of work."

Making the move was an important process, says Scott: "It allowed us to think bigger, to be more comfortable, to record things better. It just gave us new energy and new life. The building we have now is a big jump in professional recording and setup."

In addition to changing the physical surroundings, the move also involved a software switch, from MOTU Digital Performer with TDM support (for Pro Tools plug-ins and hardware) to a full-blown Digidesign Pro Tools HD setup. They also gave up their Mackie Digital 8-Bus Mixer, mixing instead on a Digidesign D-command control surface. That move was ultimately a comfortable one, says Scott. "We were learning Pro Tools, which isn't that far from [the Digital Performer setup]—we already knew the plug-in side of it, the audio side of it. Both being American companies, I think that some of the choices that MOTU and Digidesign made regarding their interfaces and their MIDI are similar. Although for years DP was a lot more advanced on the MIDI side, Pro Tools has made many steps to move to the forefront of MIDI implementation. It did take us a little bit of time to get used to the program itself."

Aside from the software, says Scott, they needed time to adapt to the room: "It's a much different room. We knew what everything sounded like in the old room. We kept the same monitors; we use PMC, a company out of England. But it just took a little while for us to get used to the way the new room sounded."

THE RIGHT TOOLS FOR THE JOB

Writing isn't easy, concedes Scott: "I think it's hard for everyone. You just go in and you try to start with a drumbeat that you like, or a bass line you hear in your head. Or you get a new synth and just have to make a tune with it—on 'High Roller' on Vegas, for example, we really played around with the first Nord Lead when it came out."

"Yeah," laughs Ken. "We were so excited to lock the arpeggiator to MIDI clock!"

Make no mistake about it: Ken and Scott both love plugging in their toys to get inspiration going. "On Vegas," Scott says, "we had distortion pedals and fuzz pedals and tube pedals—you just throw everything in there, so you get excited that way. The same thing happened here." Even surrounded by many of their favorite vintage hardware synths, they got additional creative fuel from virtual emulations of instruments they don't (yet) own. "We got excited going through some of the new virtual instruments—Arturia having a Yamaha CS-80 and an ARP 2600, and GForce having an OSCar and an ARP Odyssey, and we were intrigued by the things they did," says Scott. "It's not ever going to be the same as real analog synths, but the things that were different about it made it fun to jump to those new programs. The sound quality was great, and the updates, as far as locking up LFOs and arpeggiators, were exciting."

"Don't forget having every knob work!" interrupts Ken.

"That was fun," agrees Scott. "Getting in and realizing, wow, now that we can lock these things that we couldn't lock before, let's take this idea that we once had on the CS-80 and expand it here. Every bit, from beats to bass lines to new sounds on synths to things in our heads to amazing songs that we'd hear from different artists that were releasing new music—everything is inspiring to us."

That's not to say there isn't some sense of economy in the Crystal Method's production, as is revealed on the album. "Even if you have all that stuff available," cautions Ken, "if you think you have to use it all on every track, you're really screwed!"

THE CRYSTAL METHOD SOUND

Divided by Night is slicker and more developed than any album since *Vegas.* Oh, and it's faster, too. "Prior, we hadn't had a song as fast as 155 beats per minute," says Ken. Regardless of tempo, moving forward is what keeps the duo creatively energized. "We're more concerned with just moving on," Ken explains. "You can't get trapped in worrying about what people are going to say: 'How come you didn't do what you did last time?' or 'Damn it, you just did the same thing you did last time!' You can't fight that battle. You're never going to win it in your head, so you've got to progress." The result is an album very much in the Crystal Method sound diehard fans crave, but with plenty of fresh ideas—all with the signature, rock-influenced big-beat drums.

"We've always wanted to sound different from our last record, says Scott. "A lot of people were confused when we released *Tweekend*. They wanted us to get in there and have those 16-bar drumrolls and use a lot of the same tricks. "There's a track called 'Black Rainbows' that's more four-on-the-floor, upbeat kinds of sounds, expanding what we're trying to do."

"Black Rainbows" features the delicately floating sounds of Stefanie King Warfield's vocals, but against an animated percussive landscape. "We've got a Roland TR-909 and these great drum machines from the past," Scott continues. "So we brought a lot of those into the mix. Of course, we've always tried to find the big kicks and snares that give us that big-rock, dirty, organic, live drum sound." Add in a "gamut of collaboration," as Ken puts it, and you have *Divided by Night*. Those collaborations "worked out pretty magically," he says.

"When we're making a record," Ken reflects, "we plan on it sounding good forever—we're consciously not trying to say, 'Hey, here's this new sound, so let's put it all over the record.' I think not pigeonholing what we do has always served us well. We are electronic, I guess, but we've never tried to be breakbeat or trip-hop or big-beat or any of those things."

The duo's signature sound, however, is all over this record. "Certainly, you still hear some of the overall grime, you still hear the low-end distortion and the real, you still hear a lot of hard sort of rock and classic sort of rock tones and sounds in everything we do," says Ken. "There's always contrast—the prettiest of things and the dirtiest of things."

Robert Henke.

Robert Henke (Monolake)

THE COMPOSER, ARTIST, AND ABLETON LIVE IMAGINEER LOOKS TO THE FUTURE

By Peter Kirn || June 2011

obert Henke is an appropriate departure point: artist and toolmaker, he has been influential both as a musician/composer and as a co-developer of Ableton Live. His musical work lies at the crossroads of various idioms, from installation to ambient and dance, and what he has done with his tools has helped shape the electronic musical landscape. Amid the fits and starts, crashes and firmware updates, technological cursing and struggles chronicled through this book, he has a compelling vision for the "electronic" in electronic dance music. For all his savvy, in Henke's ideal technological world, the technology falls away. —PK

Can you describe the scene in Berlin as you began working, as you and Gerhard began working together? It seems the ongoing evolution of the computer really opened up experimentation with timbre in the '90s.

The scene in Berlin for Gerhard and me were really two different ones at the same time: The electronic studio of the Technical University, which allowed us to explore the limits of what was possible in terms of synthesis, and the underground clubs, which made it possible to play "strange" music for an open audience. A lot of people really experimented with new concepts, not only musically, but also in a broader context. Groups like Daniel Pflum or Visomat brought video equipment in clubs to experiment with images to music, organizers like Penko Stoitschev and others created permanent nonstop chill-out ambient spaces in huge empty factory buildings, and Gerhard and I were able to play improvised sets of several hours' duration in back yards of abundant inner-city spaces in front of all kinds of people. The driving force behind the development of new musical forces was not so much technology, it was social interaction—seeing Autechre playing live, having beers together and getting inspired, talking with other artists on the Chain Reaction label about how to do that nice deep echo sound, et cetera . . . This was as important as the fact that at some point laptops became affordable and you could leave the heavy keyboards and mixing consoles at home.

Max/MSP of course has taken on new significance in the context of Ableton Live, but going back to some of your earlier work, how did you first approach tools like Max and Reaktor? What drew you to them, and how did that come to influence (or integrate with) your sound and compositional ideas?

Gerhard got to know Max via his studies in computer music, and it immediately became clear to us that we have a tool in hands which allowed to do "machine music" in a new way. So we started building all kinds of sequencers with it, and that shaped the rhythm of the early Monolake releases. Gerhard also wrote the sampling and granular modules for Reaktor 1, and I worked on the patch library. This also had an influence on our music. The *Interstate* album is pretty much a Max + Reaktor album in this regard.

What has granular synthesis, now available to the masses, meant for the development of your music, and subsequently your software? What does it mean for music when you can move so freely between frequency and time domains? Given that music is expressed in relation to time, the ability to change time must be fundamental, yes?

Actually, for us the beauty of granular synthesis lies more in the ability to create spaces, to create timbres that are wide and noisy, just like hot air on a summer day or washes of rain. We found that those timbres worked very well with the harsh, metallic timbres we were able to get with our FM-synthesis-based machines. And there is one remarkable piece where a groove became a timbre; our release *Gobi* is really based on an extremely slowed down drum-and-bass loop. The piece started out as a d&b track in the first place. Parts of that material later made it into a track called "Polaroid," but on *Gobi* it was really transformed into a complete different time scale. It just happened because we typed in a wrong number; instead of milliseconds there were seconds, groove became timbres—and we listened to it and thought: Wow!

> "It just happened because we typed in a wrong number; instead of milli-seconds there were seconds, groove became timbres—and we listened to it and thought: Wow!"
>
> —ROBERT HENKE (MONOLAKE)

You've made music I think can be characterized as dance music, perhaps more so as [artist name] T++, as well as helped create software that has had an almost immeasurable impact on the dance scene. At the same time, your music moves freely into arenas that are very different, from installation to music that draws from concert traditions. How do you see dance music? How has it influenced you; how do you relate to it?

I feel like a satellite that orbits dance music culture from the distance. I never was a classic "raver," but I liked the raw sound, the almost ritualistic energy I took home from parties. I was fascinated by the culture but always felt good in my role as a slightly distant observer—which certainly has to do with the fact that I never was too much into drugs. I was mainly in the scene because I enjoyed the music. Watching Jeff Mills on the turntables, Richie Hawtin with a bunch of drum computers, or listening to a drum-and-bass set by Goldie were just moments of insane happiness.

And then I went home and made something different that shared some of the colors or movements with what I just heard.

How did Ableton Live first come into being? Originally, this was something that emerged as a set of prototypes, correct? At what point did it become an idea for a tool in performance? At what point did it become a conception for a product?

Ableton was founded because Gerhard and his founding partner Bernd Roggendorf wanted to become entrepreneurs. And since at this time all existing commercial music software was tape-style studio tools, it was very clear for us that we want to do something different and that this must have to do with the aspect of performance and play. We basically reviewed what we had developed so far for our own needs, looked at our Max patches, discussed our own usage of hardware and software, and boiled it down to a single concept: the session view in Live. Independently of these decisions about the functionality, fueled by a startup company grant, a bunch of developers led by Bernd and Gerhard had already worked on the foundation of the software side. This parallel process allowed us to come up with a new product after one year of hard work that already was based on a previously unseen concept, and obviously there was a market for it. Since that moment, ten years ago, Live is still under ongoing review by me, simply due to the facts that I am using it all day long and that I talk with a lot of users. This collected feedback then finds its way into the development process.

"There is one aspect that I find remarkable though, and this is the vanishing importance of technology in electronic music. Computers disappear. Software disappears."

—ROBERT HENKE (MONOLAKE)

How do you see the impact of Ableton Live on music making? It seems hard to even conceive or describe, so for that matter, how has it impacted your music making, as both someone who has imagined how it would work and also uses it? Can you get a sense of what it's meant in the larger scene?

It is hard to evaluate this. I would not know how to make music without it anymore. But who knows, if we were not coming up with it, some other company might have been developing a similar product that everyone uses. I have a hard time thinking about the impact of Live on making music; I guess I am too close. But I can look at a different product. Take Pro Tools, and all the other audio editors which came afterwards; of course one can edit tape and do multitrack recordings in a studio. 10cc's "I Am Not in Love" is a mind-blowing example for this—it's all possible since a long, long time. But one would not want to produce a breakbeat album with slices of tape. It would just take too long. The development of genres is certainly connected to technology. And Live makes it really easy to work fast on rhythmical music. Given this, Live accelerated the creation of electronic dance music a lot, probably more than any other single hardware or software tool. If this is a bad thing which floods the marked with generic music, or if this is good because it allows people to quickly check out far-out ideas, is a different discussion. I personally right now enjoy the fact that I can work on transformations of music I made five years ago—I open an old live set and have access to all the details of what I did at that time. Totally impossible for me without this software.

Looking both at your creative circle and the user base of this tool, how do you see the electronic dance scene evolving today? We have in these pages the chance to look back and see, say, what *Keyboard* editors thought in listening to Kraftwerk in 1981 or techno in 1989. Who do you feel has been most significant in recent years? What do you imagine will be most meaningful about their contribution in years to come?

I am a poor visionary. There is one aspect that I find remarkable, though, and this is the vanishing importance of technology in electronic music. Computers disappear. Software disappears. People use services and functions these days. A few years from now, you will not need to care about how many voices a synthesizer has; you will always be able to play the amount of notes you want. You will always be able to add another EQ or compressor, or add a new track to your project. As a result, people will start looking again more at concepts and ideas, instead of tools. The question will become: Can I imagine writing a club track in 5/4? And then I try it out. Or, shouldn't this sound move from the front left to the back right? Composers will not need to think much about the technical side of things—they can focus on the art. And this will certainly separate those with great ideas from those with not-so-great ideas, which is very exciting. I write this text in Apple Mail, running on a MacBook Pro under OS 10.5.something. How much does it matter?